CW00687815

Addresses
To The
Zimbabwean
Nation.

Addresses To The Zimbabwean Nation.

Kudakwashe Kanhutu

Sable Strategy Publications

Harare • Kigali • London

Dedication.

To the people of Zimbabwe, may our peaceful polity long endure.

For Sir Laurie, Bristow
   A scholar!
President Hughes Hall,
   Cambridge University

Find in my Book, the Knowledge
I wish British Policymakers
to familiarise themselves with
in reference to Zimbabwe.

17th Sept. 2024

Sable Strategy Publications
Management Office
Sunny Apt
KG24 Avenue
Kagugu
Kigali
Rwanda
Tel: +250 789 087 418

First published in 2022.

Hard Cover ISBN: 978-1-7392547-2-8
Paperback ISBN: 978-1-7392547-0-4
eBook ISBN: 978-1-7392547-1-1

A catalogue record for this publication can be obtained from the British Library.

Contents

Abbreviations   ix

Preface   xiii

Address I

The Task At Hand   1

Address II

Does God Exist?   15

Address III

Nationalism In Zimbabwe   47

Address IV

Zimbabwe's National Interest   101

Address V

Land Redistribution   133

Address VI

Gukurahundi   171

Address VII
Sanctions   213

Address VIII
Corruption   247

Address IX
The Fourth Industrial Revolution And Us   271

Address X
The Military In Zimbabwe   287

Address XI
Public-Spiritedness   315

Address XII
Concluding Remarks   329

Notes   333
Bibliography   351

Abbreviations:

A2/AD – Anti-Access/Area Denial

4IR – Fourth Industrial Revolution

AFZ – Air Force of Zimbabwe

AI – Artificial Intelligence

ANC – African National Congress

ANC – African National Council

ASEAN – Association of East Asian Nations

AU – African Union.

BMATT – British Military Advisory And Training Team

BNP – British National Party

CCJPZ – Catholic Commission for Justice and Peace in Zimbabwe

CFU – Commercial Farmers Union

CIO – Central Intelligence Organisation

COIN – Counter Insurgency

ComOps – Combined Operations

CYL – City Youth League

DRC – Democratic Republic of Congo

ECOWAS – Economic Community of West African States

EU – European Union

FN – Front National

FRELIMO – *Frente de Libertação de Moçambique* (Front For The Liberation Of Mozambique)

FTLRP – Fast Track Land Reform Programme

G40 – Generation 40

GDP – Gross Domestic Product

ICT – Information and Communications Technology

JOC – Joint Operations Command

MDC – Movement For Democratic Change

MNR – Mozambique National Resistance.

NATO – North Atlantic Treaty Organisation.

NDP – National Democratic Party

NGO – Non Governmental Organisation

NRZ – National Railways of Zimbabwe

OAU – Organisation of African Unity

PCC – People's Caretaker Council

PSMAS – Premier Service Medical Aid Society

RAWU - Railways Workers Union

RBVA – Rhodesian Bantu Voters Association

RENAMO - *Resistencia Nacional Mocambicana*

RICU - Reformed Industrial Council Unions

RMA - Revolution in Military Affairs

RNA – Rhodesian Native Association

RNP – Rwanda National Police

RPF – Rwanda Patriotic Front

RSF – Rhodesian Security Forces

SADC – Southern African Development Community

SRANC - Southern Rhodesian African National Congress

UBI – Universal Basic Income

UDI – Unilateral Declaration of Independence

UN – United Nations

UNGA – United Nations General Assembly

UNSC – United Nations Security Council

ZANLA – Zimbabwe African National Liberation Army

ZANU – Zimbabwe African National Union

ZANU PF – Zimbabwe African National Union – Patriotic Front

ZAPU – Zimbabwe African People's Union

ZCBC – Zimbabwe Catholic Bishops Conference

ZDF – Zimbabwe Defence Forces

ZIDERA – Zimbabwe Democracy and Economic Recovery Act

ZIPRA – Zimbabwe People's Revolutionary Army

ZLC – Zimbabwe Liberation Council

ZNA – Zimbabwe National Army

ZNLWVA – Zimbabwe National Liberation War Veterans Association

ZNP – Zimbabwe National Party

ZRP – Zimbabwe Republic Police

Preface

THE IDEA TO WRITE this book came to me soon after I finished my MSc. in Defence, Development, and Diplomacy at Durham University in the North-East of England. My friends in the military and intelligence services, were encouraging me to do my PhD so that I could return home and teach at the Zimbabwe National Defence University. As someone who really feels indebted to Zimbabwe and wants to contribute to its betterment, I began writing PhD thesis proposals to a few select universities in England with this goal in mind. As I was doing the thesis proposals research, I realised that I was discovering more precise information about Zimbabwe than what the public imagination held. I also found that I wanted this more precise information to be available to other Zimbabweans.

My original plan as I came across this information, was still to do the PhD first, then write a book that would make that same more precise knowledge I was discovering, available to all Zimbabweans. But this soon changed to just writing this book. The shift from PhD thesis proposal to just writing this book, happened when I discovered that, suitable supervisors for exactly what I wanted to cement my Zimbabwe expertise on, were too few and far between. I wanted to research nationalism in Zimbabwe for the purposes of contributing to its continuance. To get a suitable PhD supervisor in England, would have meant me changing my research's true focus, so as to align with the prevailing ideological leanings of the potential supervisors. This is because, most of the work being done in the universities in the West, certainly since our Land Reform programme, has weakening our nationalism as its central goal. Security Sector Reform research clusters in these universities, for example, are essentially working on formulas that can help end the alliance between our military and ZANU PF. This would certainly weaken our nationalism: I want that same alliance strengthened and perpetuated instead.

This situation then, led me, in a rebellious spirit, to find myself thinking that I was deferring to foreigners of very doubtful expertise on Zimbabwe. I was, essentially, asking outsiders to guide me on what to know and think about my own country. I say doubtful expertise because, very few of them have lived in Zimbabwe in an anthropological spirit. They may be brilliant academics, but their knowledge of Zimbabwe is typically from just 3 months of study visits. I had also read their expert advice to the UK government, and their predictions on what was going to happen in Zimbabwe in the past 20 years, much of which did not come to pass. I think their being outsiders, and their ideological biases, militates against them truly understanding Zimbabwe.

Having been born and lived in Zimbabwe continuously for 3 decades before going to university abroad, I felt I could contribute better insights than these so-called experts. There is also an urgent need that more knowledge about the Global South be produced by nationals of the countries in question. In any case, I could write this book before attaining the PhD because, conferment of a master's degree, is generally accepted to mean competence to carry out independent research in the relevant field.

As it had taken me nearly 6 months to write my PhD thesis proposals, the material I amassed during that process, became the main content for this book. I researched this book under the title: *Nationalism In Zimbabwe: Past, Present, and Future.* Nationalism interests me because it is the doctrine which gave us our independence from Colonialism, thereby creating our nation. My research was thus, a survey of our past and present, so as to suggest actions that will ensure the continuance of the Zimbabwe envisaged by the national-ists who fought for its independence.

At the same time, I also wanted the more precise information I now had at hand to become common knowledge among Zimbabwe-ans. But because I know that academic writing is unreadable for most people, I settled on a narrative device that would allow me to write in a non-academic style. The research I did still satisfies academic rigour, it was only in the presentation of my findings that I wanted to remove the rigidity of academic writing and jargon. I want my work to be accessible to the general public.

The narrative device that I thought could help me accomplish this, was one that imagines me standing on a podium, lecturing to other Zimbabweans, who in turn can contribute by asking me ques-tions or offering rebuttals. In this vein, I also hope that other Zimba-bweans will take stock of our nation, then write similar treatises on those topics that are within their specialisations. In fact, in the spirit of disputation that characterised the Enlightenment in Europe, I even hope that someone with a different point of view, writes a book contradicting everything I say in mine.

I wrote my book on 10 topics of importance to Zimbabwe that are within my competence, such as The Military, *Gukurahundi*, and Land Reform. In these chapters, I present the more precise informa-tion about these topics than what is in the public imagination. I also ensured that these chapters are standalone, so though the chapters refer to each other, they need not be read consecutively.

The title of this book, *Addresses To The Zimbabwean Nation*, is in deference to Johann Gottlieb Fichte's *Addresses To The German Nation*. I read Fichte when I was researching the subject of national-ism, and he was one of the handful of thinkers in the world, credited with giving birth to the ideology called nationalism. His book has also been argued to have laid the groundwork for the creation of a unitary Germany. The task Fichte took upon himself, was to state what rationale there was for a German nation to arise. The German nation as we know it now, did not exist at the time. My own task here was much easier because, I was just surveying a unitary nation that already exists – Zimbabwe.

Our own nation came into existence through the nationalists who fought a liberation struggle to end 90 years of white settler Colonialism. It is these nationalists' vision, hopes, and aspirations that I also identify with. Thus, this book discusses Zimbabwe's major issues from a nationalist perspective. What I am calling the nationalist perspective, is that perspective that found Colonialism so egregious that the solution it ultimately settled on, was fighting a liberation war to end it.

I contrast the nationalist perspective with a perspective which I do not quite have a collective name for yet. I can only describe its main proclivity in history – it saw nothing wrong with Colonialism. I have to remind some of my readers that, there were black people who fought on the side of the white settlers in the liberation struggle. These black people fought to perpetuate a system that denied all black people rights, themselves included. This contrary perspective, saw Colonialism as the natural order, and it still subsists in some forms in our country today.

The clearest clash you can find between these two perspectives in our recent history, is on our Land Reform. Zimbabwe's nationalists had to embark on Land Reform, because it was one of the major grievances against Colonialism that had still not been addressed, 20 years after independence. For the nationalist, this had to be done whatever the cost. While the other perspective argued that we should let the status quo persist, supposedly because the white farmers now had all the farming expertise. As if farming was their God given talent, and not just expertise they also just managed to acquire because of the discriminatory policies that favoured them. My own perspective on Land Reform is that, given the same advantages that the white settlers were given, our new black farmers will also have the same proficiency in the 90 years it took the white settlers to become proficient.

Our Land Reform is also the biggest issue in our recent history. Our undertaking of it made us powerful enemies in the West who wanted the white settlers to maintain their unfair privileges. To that end, the West activated its powerful media to create distortions and demonisations of our country. While it is true that our Land Reform was a challenging process, and some of the challenges continue, the Western media has made a point of seeing it as an entirely negative process. This is just not the case, and therefore, an example of one of the deliberate distortions that needs correcting, especially for our posterity.

Some of these distortions have also happened just because of the passage of time. People who were born after independence and did not experience the oppression that was Rhodesia, may just have no frame of reference on issues of that time. This is to be expected because of the generation gap, but what is regrettable is that some have even started to mistakenly claim that Rhodesia was better. I, myself, did not experience Rhodesia, but grew up with people who did, so I got first-hand information of how intolerable Rhodesia was for black people's dignity. My study of the matter also confirmed what I was told while growing up. For this much younger generation then, my book should provide them with facts that contradict the distortions. This will ensure that those who really want to know the truth will, at least, have another source of information besides the distortions now extant.

I have also always felt that, if our progenitors who built Great Zimbabwe had left a written record, we would have had a much better understanding of that early State of ours. But, for their not leaving a written record, a lot of distortions also entered our history, with some even going as far as disputing that the structure was built by black Africans. The oversight of our progenitors not leaving a written record can be forgiven because they were illiterate. I feel it is our obligation now as literate people, to leave a written record of our point of view on all the issues that pertain to us, so that our successors will never have to seek in vain, for the information we currently hold.

Case in point, for reading the book that Nathan Shamuyarira wrote in 1965 – *Crisis In Rhodesia* – I am better informed of the nationalist's point of view of events that were happening at that time. If he had not written that book, the only side of the story I would have, would be that of the colonialist. This is why I also want to encourage even more of our nationalists now, to write their points of view on all the things that affect us. Our points of view are valid, especially on matters that relate to Zimbabwe.

There is, ultimately, also an element of duty to my writing this book. I am too young to have participated in the fight to liberate Zimbabwe from Colonialism. But I benefitted from the free education and free health provided to everyone at Independence in 1980. Thus, I have always felt I owe a debt to the people who liberated Zimbabwe from Colonialism. They allowed me to be judged not by the colour of my skin as was done to them in Rhodesia, but on merit, at least in Zimbabwe. Most of the people who fought to give me this advantage, died in the process and did not enjoy the benefits of an independent Zimbabwe.

I thus feel that I owe them a debt to research their conditions, hopes, and aspirations, and attempt to tell their side of the story. They themselves could not tell their side of the story because, they had been denied access to opportunities in education and economic life that would have given them the expressiveness I now possess. This advantage I now have, should be used in service of the Zimbabwe they hoped for. The people who fought in the liberation struggle played their part; it is now our duty as the people they liberated, to ensure that their vision of our country continues.

Kudakwashe Kanhutu
Kigali, Rwanda, 2022.

Address I.

The Task At Hand.

"Those who receive this privilege, therefore, have a duty to repay the sacrifice which others have made. They are like the man who has been given all the food available in a starving village in order that he might have strength to bring supplies back from a distant place. If he takes this food and does not bring help to his brothers, he is a traitor. Similarly, if any of the young men and women who are given an education by the people of this Republic adopt attitudes of superiority or fail to use their knowledge to help the development of this country, then they are betraying our union" - President Julius Nyerere of Tanzania.

M Y FELLOW COUNTRYMEN and countrywomen, my task here is enviable because I am addressing a nation of literate people. This task would be difficult, nay impossible, if the path had not been made smooth for me by all those who worked tirelessly to educate our nation. Illiteracy is one of those problems that has always got people misled, or outright denied their rights. Case in point, our forebearers suffered that misfortune throughout the period our country was under white settler Colonialism. It was mostly the few literate among our forebearers, who successfully agitated for all black people to finally have their rights. Those few educated of our fore-bearers, initially thought that they could get their rights through negotiations, they were wrong. They, instead, had to prosecute a 14 year armed liberation struggle, before the white settler capitulated to their demands.

At Independence, education was then prioritised because, those who led the armed liberation struggle, understood that education was one of the main tools that could empower us in protecting our hard won rights. Our country nearly bankrupted itself in the 1980s providing free education for all the previously disenfranchised blacks. Every family I know, encouraged their children to make something of themselves through education. It is for this reason that Zimbabwe has been known to have literacy rates of over 90%. This education was an investment aimed at ensuring we would own our country and develop it ourselves. This is exactly why I opened this Address with Julius Nyerere's quote, imploring all those people his nation had edu-cated, to contribute to its development.

The task at hand then, for all of us who benefited from the investment in education that the country made on us, is that we should now contribute to solving our nation's problems. I am one of those many disenfranchised blacks who benefitted from the free education and free health provided to everyone at Independence in 1980. I am also happy that our leaders insisted, from the outset, that both boys and girls get equal access to education. As a result of that policy, I have countrywomen and countrymen who are equally highly literate. Thus, more of us can contribute to solving our country's problems than what would have been the case otherwise. You see, the debt we owe to the country for investing in our education, can only be repaid by our contributing to the country's betterment. This is how I have viewed the matter, ever since I became old enough to reflect on all the sacrifices others have made on my behalf.

For my part, what I have seen fitting as my first contribution to solving our country's problems, is to make a thorough survey of our nation's past and present, so that we can have a more precise knowledge of all our major issues. I have sought to correct the misconceptions there are on all those topics that are within my competence. I think that having that precise knowledge, is a necessary first step in devising the correct solutions for our problems.

Just as an example, some people may think that the solution to our current economic problems, is returning land to white settlers so that their countries of origin will lift the Sanctions they imposed on us. But, this would not be the correct solution, to someone who knows how the white settlers came into possession of the same land. They came to possess that same land by violently evicting black people during the colonisation period. Thus, the solution of returning our land to the white settlers, would be unacceptable to people who know that a lot of black people died in the 14 year armed struggle for independence. This armed struggle's main grievance was the land question.

So, what I want to impress upon you here, is that, for all the technical knowledge we have since acquired, those technical solutions cannot be applied without an understanding of our history. This is why I have made the attempt here, to first ground all our issues in their true historical context. In short, I do not want us, through the prevalent misconceptions on issues, to produce ahistorical solutions to any of our problems.

My main task here then, is to correct all the misconceptions and distortions about our country for anyone who wants to understand Zimbabwe correctly at the present moment. Even more importantly, these distortions have to be corrected for our posterity. Thus, if my Addresses only achieve one thing, I want it to be the providing of more precise information about our nation than what is currently in the public imagination. Restated, the task at hand for me personally here then, is setting the record straight about our nation on all those topics I am competent on.

The Nationalist Perspective:

Our nation was given birth to by the actions of nationalists, so naturally, my Addresses are being made from a nationalist perspective. This is because I identify with the ideas that animated the founding of our nation. I have also studied the ideology called nationalism and understand that it is the one that is most capable in helping us protect our hard won rights. Nationalism is the doctrine that gave us our freedom and its tenets will ensure that we maintain that freedom. These Addresses then, are a restatement of the nationalist conception of our nation.

Contrary to the nationalist perspective, are all those viewpoints that were happy to co-exist with Colonialism. There were black people in our country who had accepted Colonialism as the natural order and even fought on the side of white settler Colonialism. Such mindsets still exist in our nation, and we should not expect them to contribute solutions to the nation of our conception. This is evident from the fact that there were some people among us who called for Western nations to impose Sanctions on us when we embarked on our Land Reform programme. In my view, those mindsets are part of the problems of our nation we have to solve.

I will also not gloss over the fact that there are some problems that need to be solved that have been created by genuine nationalists. There have been mistakes we have made ourselves as nationalists that need to be corrected. I will also point out those mistakes in these Addresses. Further, I will also point out that not all those who claim to be nationalists are nationalists. The true measure of a nationalist, is if the actions they are taking defer to the tenets of "resource nationalism." Against this metric, some people who call themselves nationalists in our country will just not pass the nationalist test. Their actions tend to be as harmful as those of the mindsets that were happy to co-exist with Colonialism.

A Bridge For Our Posterity:

The main reason I want there to be more precise information about our country, is for our posterity. Even now, just over 4 decades after our independence, I have observed that people who were born at the turn of the millennium, do not have the same understanding of our history under Colonialism as older people have. Some have even started to romanticise this crime against humanity that was Colonialism. This has happened because when we carried out our Land Reform, the West advanced a narrative that demonised our legitimate concerns. This narrative has been preponderant and made it look like everything the nationalists do only has negative connotations. By contrast, the white settlers are absolved from their demonstrable crimes against humanity in that same narrative.

I feel then we have to leave a written record of our understanding of our polity as it currently exists. I want us to add to the corpus discussing our nation's history and prospects. Much pain has been suffered by us, for our predecessors not having left a written record about, for example, Great Zimbabwe. We can only make guesses at its method of construction and purposes. We must rectify this error and inform those who will succeed us about affairs in our recent past and present. We have to do this so that our posterity, does not ever have to seek in vain, for information we already hold.

Leaving a written record of things that we know and understand as they happen, is a much needed link between ourselves and our posterity. For reading the book that Nathan Shamuyarira wrote in 1965 – *Crisis In Rhodesia* – and Maurice Nyagumbo's 1979 Book -*With The People* – I am better informed of the nationalists' point of view of events that were happening then. If they had not written these books, the only side of the story I would have received, would have been that of the white settlers. This is why I also want to encourage other nationalists to write their points of view of things that affect us, so that as much of our narrative as possible, also sees the light of day. Our points of view are equally valid on all issues that relate to Zimbabwe.

Our Nation's Major Issues:

I really wish that these Addresses of mine would be dealing with frivolous issues like the ones they have in other countries, like bemoaning obesity and other excesses of wealth. Alas, we have genuine, and urgent issues that warrant serious addressing. At just over 40 years old, we are indeed a very young nation, comparator and competitor countries, like Switzerland for example, have been existent for over 700 years. Our many problems, which make up a large part of these Addresses, are as natural as growth pains in living organisms.

The countries that are now 700 years old, also went through these growth pains to become the strong and stable entities they are today. Now, while it is comforting to think that all we need to do is learn from the mistakes that these entities made in their earlier years, the biology metaphor contends otherwise. As the child today will still lose her teeth as part of growing up, so too are there problems the young nation will experience despite having seen them occur in other nations at their onset. These growth pains are natural, necessary, and ineluctable. We must understand that some bad things are unavoidable in the course of a nation's life.

The only advantage we may have from studying the older nations' growth pains, is that we can sometimes avoid adopting the costly and ineffective solutions the older nations adopted during the trial and error periods of their development. Indeed, it might even be that all we can effectively do at this stage of our nation's development, is discuss the problems we have, investigate how the older nations resolved them, and then create a blueprint for succeeding generations of our nation to draw upon for implementation. For this reason, you will find that I have constantly referenced how issues were resolved in Europe in these Addresses.

The Addresses:

The first topic I decided to tackle is that of Religion in Zimbabwe. My interest in that topic is because of the effects religion has had on our national psyche and economic development potential. I argue that we should make the shift from the religious paradigm to the scientific paradigm.

Thus, the **Second Address** is an appeal to change our mindset from one that expects miracles to one that realises that whatever we want to achieve will not be given to us by God, but by us using scientific principles to achieve the results we want. This occurred to me to be a national problem, when I realised what the preponderance of the number of the people who believe in prophets means for our national psyche. It means we still have a national psyche that believes in God providing solutions where our competitor nations already disputed that belief and have been solving all their problems through science.

This is one of the major lessons we can take from Europe. Our nation has not had the disputation in religion that happened during the Protestant Reformation in Europe. The Protestant Reformation then led to the Enlightenment. As a result of the Enlightenment, God is no longer central to national economic development planning in Europe. With this Address then, I want us to also have the same disputation about God as they did in Europe. Thus, I also pose one of the questions they posed in Europe during the Enlightenment: Does God Exist? My goal is to drive us towards adopting scientific principles to solve our problems, instead of waiting for miracles.

Our competitor countries questioned all their religions and realised that they are just theories of a creator. They thus now rely on science to solve their problems, while we are still holding prayer vigils for rains. The Second Address then, is an appeal for Zimbabweans to understand that the Bible's vision of a beautiful afterlife are just words meant to comfort the suffering, we can create our own heaven here on Earth by just adopting scientific principles for our national economic development. This is my main exhortation here, after having shown that the Bible is just a foundational myth for a Judaic tribe.

The **Third Address** is entitled Nationalism In Zimbabwe. Here, I turn to our conception of the nation, how we came to be, what we have achieved, and what we still need to do to ensure our nation endures the way we want it to into the future. This is the anchor Address for all these Addresses, as it is the one that surveys our past, present, and future. This Address reveals that our nationalism started out very slowly, with even the educated among our forebearers initially only demanding better treatment for the educated only. But with time, this changed to demanding rights for all. It is also here where I suggest what we need to do for our national identity and national character. Nationalism in Zimbabwe itself, is simply the doctrine that insists that we have sovereignty over all our resources. It is not to be confused with right wing nationalisms in Europe.

Having discussed our polity as above, the logical next thing to discuss is our national interest, for this is a pursuit that will ensure our nation's survival. In the **Fourth Address** – Zimbabwe's National Interest – I have laid out all the parameters of the national interest as they are understood in international relations scholarship. I have then introduced these three intervening factors that then determine our true national interest – history, values, and capability. The way those three intervening factors interact with the national interest is what determines our true national interest. I then use three examples from our recent history to determine whether our actions passed what I have called here the "national interest test." The international relations scholarship parameters and the three intervening factors I introduce are timeless, so can be applied to any issue to see whether our proposed actions satisfies national interest considerations.

One of the most important issues in our country was the Land Reform Programme. I talk about it in the **Fifth Address** – Land Redistribution – because I have found out in my discussions everywhere, that a lot of people, even our supporters, do not fully understand the issues involved. The Western Media has been able to dominate the narrative to the extent that the Economist even boldly ran a headline which said: "When Robert Mugabe Stole Land From White Farmers…" This shameless distortion will only stand as long as those of us who know exactly what happened do not correct it. It is in this vein that I have talked about the Land Redistribution Programme in Zimbabwe. Land Redistribution was done because it was the one main issue our independence had not resolved. The Land Reform programme also satisfies national interest considerations as far as our history and values are concerned.

In the **Sixth Address**, I find myself forced to discuss a dark chapter in our history – Gukurahundi. This was a painful subject for me to address, for I feel that no single black life should have been lost because nationalists were fighting amongst themselves. We all had the same ideology and goals; our only difference was over who should assume power at Independence. This was a heart wrenching and very emotional topic for me to address. But I had to address it because, I realised they were also so many misconceptions of what really happened in the public imagination. One of the misconceptions is that Gukurahundi happened because the Shona hated the Ndebele and wanted to drive them out of the country. This is just not true, the primary issue there was political intolerance, not tribal or ethnic hatreds.

The **Seventh Address** tackles the topic of Sanctions that were imposed on Zimbabwe by Western countries. These Sanctions were imposed because we had dared to take our land back from their white kith and kin. The West claimed they were doing this to restore human rights. But I have deliberately put Gukurahundi between the Sanctions and Land Reform Programme to help you see why the Sanctions were really imposed. Gukurahundi happened between 1981 and 1987, where an estimated 5 000 black people were killed by the Security Forces, and yet no Sanctions for human rights abuses were placed on Zimbabwe. Robert Mugabe even received a Knighthood in 1991. In 2000, when 12 white people got killed when we were taking our land back, the West acted swiftly and imposed Sanctions on Zimbabwe for abuses of human rights. They also stripped Robert Mugabe of his Knighthood. I also talk about the impact of Sanctions, their illegality in international law and what we can do to defeat them.

In the **Eighth Address**, I turn my attention to the topic of Corruption and how it has retarded our development potential. While I see a link between Corruption and Sanctions, I also think that some of our corrupt acts have aided and abetted the damage to our country unnecessarily. It is with this in mind that I argue that we have made some unforced errors, and only public-spiritedness can guide us onto the correct path. I discuss the causes of corruption and suggest what needs to be done to stop corruption. My main suggestion is a change of mindset to one where our society finds corruption abhorrent. Once this happens, society will start to self-regulate, which will, in time, assist law enforcement. The laws against corruption already exist in our legal code, it is the public's shunning of corruption that will assist enforcement of those laws.

In the **Ninth Address** – The Fourth Industrial Revolution – I turn to the problematic parts of the scientific paradigm I have insisted we should adopt. The technology and innovations of the Fourth Industrial Revolution are already threatening livelihoods through job losses in our competitor countries. I thus urge us not to adopt the Fourth Industrial Revolution just yet. But I am not making this recommendation because I am against technology and innovation. I am making this recommendation for practical reasons, namely that we have not yet mastered even the first industrial revolution for ourselves.

So, instead, I say we should focus all our efforts on achieving the first three industrial revolutions first. China is a good example to emulate. From being largely a peasant country just 40 years ago, it has achieved all the industrial revolutions to the extent of becoming a leader is some aspects of the Fourth Industrial Revolution. In achieving the first three industrial revolutions, it managed to lift 300 million people out of poverty. Therefore, I think that any adoption of aspects of the Fourth Industrial Revolution, without the foundation of the first three revolutions, just threatens to keep our people impoverished.

In the **Tenth Address**, I talk about the Military in Zimbabwe. Most people are given to criticising our military based on the theories of the military and society, paying scant regard to our context. They are quick to accuse the Zimbabwean Military of being partisan. They accuse it of taking sides with ZANU PF. I instead think that, in the context of our nation, the military is actually fulfilling its constitutional obligations if it does not allow surrogates of outside powers to assume power. The military is actually underwriting our Constitution when it rejects the opposition that is directed by outsiders.

Given our history, the greatest threat to our Constitution, has been the MDC because they made the mistake of being bankrolled and directed by people who were bent on reversing our Land Reform. By being directed by outsiders on policy, the MDC activated the army to come into politics and prevent regime change, as this would have been the equivalent of losing the country to foreign powers. As long as the opposition is reliant on direction from foreign powers, the military remains correct in being "partisan."

As nationalists, we should also remain true to the Constitution, otherwise the military will be within its rights to intervene against us, as happened in the military assisted transition of November 2017. This is one of the examples I use in my discussion of the relationship between our military and society. We should also try to ensure that our vision for our country always accords with national aspirations, because once we are divorced from national aspirations, a disconnect with the Constitution will naturally appear.

The **Eleventh Address** – Public-Spiritedness – is a tentative suggestion for what could be the panacea to most of our problems. I suggest we revert back to our African values of Ubuntu. Our country will do well if all our people ask themselves if any actions they are taking benefits or harms our country. Our problems with Corruption, for example, could be greatly reduced if more people are public-spirited.

Conclusion:

This is the spirit in which all these Addresses have been made: surveying our history to record it accurately, and then discussing our problems so as to offer solutions. This is because, I very much feel that I have a debt to the country, that can only be repaid by me using the faculties the country developed in me, to discuss matters this way. Nationalists who took up arms to fight for our liberation, played their part, it is now up to us, the beneficiaries of that liberation, to chart a course forward for a country that satisfies their vision for us.

Address II.

Does God Exist?

"Religion is regarded by the common people as true, by the wise as false, and by the rulers as useful" – Lucius Annaeus Seneca.

KEEPING IN MIND what I have said in the opening Address, that illiteracy was the main reason why many people were misled in earlier times of the world, I am baffled by how our own nation of demonstrably literate people, continues to be misled by men of religion. The most visible manifestation of this phenomenon are the so-called prophets, and the laughable claims they make to their congregants. These "prophets" are never questioned because, as a rule, we tend not to question anything that has to do with God. In our conception of God, to do so is blasphemy. Anyone who invokes God, becomes immune to criticism. He even finds people who will defend him with words such as, "touch not the anointed," even if the issue at hand is that he has committed crimes.

This example of the "prophets," is just the tip of the iceberg of a much larger problem. I want to call this the "blasphemy" pitfall, where we fear that questioning anything from, or supposedly from the Bible, will earn the interlocutor a place in Hell. This fear then makes us infants all our lives. I call this the problem of religion in our country: the acceptance, without question, of any of the claims made about God in the Bible.

In the "prophets" example, on an individual level, the problem of religion means our impoverished people will be made to fund these conmen's lifestyles. This, on its own, is heart-breaking. But I am even more concerned by what our refusal to question any of religion's claims about God, implies for our national psyche. It implies that, as a nation, we are still in the grip of the age of superstition that our competitor countries left behind a long time ago.

This is where religion becomes inimical to national economic development – which is, ultimately, my main concern in this Address. The depiction of this problem of religion is in all those pictures circulating on the Internet, juxtaposing Chinese and European children in Science Labs, wearing white coats, against African children in various religious garbs. This image is exactly what the problem of religion resolves itself into on a national scale: African nations still putting their trust in prayers, while other nations now only rely on scientific knowledge to solve their pressing problems.

The nations that now rely on science, questioned all their religions, and found out that their conceptions of God, were just theories of a Creator. Below, I will discuss the processes by which our competitor countries came to see that even the God of the Bible is just another superstition. These nations now view the Bible exactly as Betrand Russell viewed it. Russell viewed the Bible as "not divinely inspired, it is just early history legendary, no more exactly true than what is in Homer's epic poems, and its moral teachings sometimes good, but sometimes very bad."

I want us to also come to terms with the fact the Bible is just another book that was written by early people who wanted to organise society for the better. For people to accept the Bible's edicts, these writers made the claim that it was the word of God. This was not true, and with advances in science, most of the Bible's claims, especially on cosmology, have been found wanting. No omniscient God would have inspired the writing of such an erroneous cosmology.

Most of our people here in Zimbabwe, seem to not have come across this information that even the God of the Bible is just a more elegant superstition, but a superstition, nonetheless. The people who introduced the Bible to us are now even less enthusiastic about it than we are. We have now surpassed them in our belief in this God they introduced to us. The issue here, as far as I can see, is that we adopted the God concept as it occurred to these European countries in their Dark Ages, but we did not also critically analyse the concept as these European countries eventually did during the Enlightenment.

This then means that our national psyche is still beholden to what has already been demonstrated to be a superstition. Superstitions impede progress in so many ways. We need to rid ourselves of our excessive belief in the supernatural. Our competitor countries have already done this. They did this by not being afraid to ask this question: does God exist? We need to ask the same question. By doing so, we will also be going to the root of the problem of religion in our country. If we can seriously question God's very existence, we can question everything else. Questioning everything is the prerequisite for abandoning any of our superstitions.

All societies start with many superstitions, with advances in knowledge and ingenuity, they get to shed off these superstitions. They then rely only on science to solve their challenges. Our competitor countries were freed from the shackles of superstition by these three big interlocking processes: the Renaissance, the Reformation, and the Enlightenment. Those processes demanded that they question everything for its validity. This then allowed the shift from blind faith to the Scientific Paradigm to happen there. We, too, need to have this paradigm shift.

You see, blind faith is a total refusal to interrogate cause and effect. A refusal to interrogate cause and effect, in turn, leads a whole nation to hold national prayer vigils for rain. Norway, the Netherlands, and Switzerland do no such thing. Evincing, on Zimbabwe's part, when we hold national prayer days for rain, a national psyche that does not acknowledge the science behind the water cycle. The converse is this; a national psyche freed from the superstition that is blind faith, translates to leaps and bounds in economic development capability. Scientific principles, not favour from God, is what is behind our competitor countries' economic development.

The economic development we can achieve once we fully adopt the Scientific Paradigm is my central concern in this Address. I have conceived every nation's ultimate goal as economic development. Humanity only lives in groups for mutual aid, and that mutual aid can only be best actualized under conditions of economic prosperity. Nations, as we will see in succeeding Addresses, are just human groups instituted for mutual aid.

Defining God:

The famous Atheist of this age, Richard Dawkins, presented the God Hypothesis thus: "there exists a superhuman, supernatural intelligence who deliberately designed and created the universe and everything in it, including us."[1] In this Address, I will also take this as my definition of God: a superhuman, supernatural intelligence who created everything in the universe – a supreme being. I accept this premise *a priori,* because it stands to my reason that intelligent design demands an intelligent designer.

Of course, Dawkins refutes this same premise thus: "any creative intelligence, of sufficient complexity to design anything, comes into existence only as the end product of an extended process of gradual evolution."[2] Here, he is just essentially saying that the logic I am using above, will demand that a Creator also have a Creator, and the Creator of the Creator to also have a Creator. This line of enquiry will lead us to the absurdity called infinite regression. So, I will not press this point that leads to infinite regression further. For the purposes of this Address, I will just assume that the superhuman, supernatural intelligence who created us, does not need a Creator.

Instead, what I will do in my critique of God's existence here, is to concentrate on matters where I can demonstrate that what we think we know about this supernatural being, is merely a conception devised by other human beings, without any input from the supernatural being himself. My focus in this Address is to explain to you, my fellow countrywomen and countrymen, that the Bible we adopted as God's word, is merely a cultural artefact of ancient Jews. A foundational myth of a very small Judaic tribe that became diffuse all over the world.

The refrain was already made, during the Enlightenment, that God made man in his image, but man has since returned the favour. If you are open minded in your interrogation of God's existence, you will see for yourself that, some of the claims being made on God's behalf, are just man's conception of the situation at hand. "I am a jealousy God, so worship no other God but me," these are but typical human conceptions and emotions. But, what really convinced me that the Bible is just men's conception of God, is the limited knowledge of cosmology expounded in it. There is an absence in the cosmology of the Bible, of most of the things we now know due to advances in science. This should tell us that this text was written by brilliant but limited human beings.

What I am also saying to you here is this: all societies throughout history have been known to have a conception of their own supernatural being. The elites of that society, however defined, have taken the lead in articulating the supernatural being's wishes as to how the society should be run. It is my contention on this count, that no one received any secret communication from the supreme being. It is the elites' own ideas of how best to run society. They then just claimed that these ideas were handed to them by a supreme being to obtain obedience from the populace. Moses, if he actually ever lived, did not receive the Ten Commandments from God, he devised them himself.

The claim in all religious texts of having received their ideas from a supreme being, is just a legitimating tool. It does not matter that the ideas will be brilliant and timeless, this alone is not good proof of divine involvement. Do not forget that these elites will be very intelligent and talented people themselves, so their insights will be timeless.

The United States Constitution, which is a secular document, is very inspired and has been relevant 200 years after it was written. What Thucydides predicted about power transitions in international relations while writing about the Peloponnesian War over 2500 years ago, is still relevant today. Plato's description of democracy, tyranny, and a dictator's character still holds true despite being written in the 5th Century B.C.

The only difference between these equally incisive writings and what has been called religious texts, is that the other group of authors, did not claim to have been given these ideas by a supreme being. It takes reading a lot of texts from antiquity to start seeing these patterns. Having read a lot of texts from antiquity, one will start to see that the Bible was written in the same style, and for similar purposes. The purposes were an inquiry into our origins, and how best to organise society going forward. I will make this point clearer below, after we have further discussed the problem of religion in Zimbabwe.

The Problem More Clearly Defined:

The problem of religion, properly conceived, is a world view problem. A world view that refuses to question all the premises of its religion, is a world view that is not able to successfully oversee modern economic life. For it is a world view from a bygone age, an ignorant world view. You see, the problem of religion our comparator countries also had to overcome was, essentially, a problem of ignorance reigning supreme among the great generality of the population.

When Europe was still in the aptly called Dark Ages, every natural occurrence was attributed to some supernatural cause. This happened because, the scientific principles behind natural phenomenon were not yet understood. Earthquakes, storms, floods, eclipses, and droughts were mistaken for an angry God punishing the Earth for some wrong. In this same period again in Europe, witchcraft, magic, ghosts, astrology, and omens very much held sway among the population. In 1431, Joan of Arc was tried and burned at the stake for heresy, witchcraft, and violating divine law by dressing as a man. This was humanity's infancy.

But to be fair to the people of this earlier era, this ignorance was excusable, because then, even the educated did not know better either. This was due to the levels of ingenuity humanity had yet to attain. But, living in the Information Age as we do, and with all the other advances we now have in the world, there is no excuse for anyone to still be beholden to any superstitions. Thus, our refusal to part ways with superstitious beliefs that have already been disproved, is quite baffling to me. It is this wilful ignorance that is inexcusable. The world view that ought to be preponderant among us now, is one that questions everything – the Scientific Paradigm!

Paradigm Shifts:

This observation has often been made in jest, that Africa, with its impossible per capita number of churches, is so poor, while countries like Norway and Switzerland, that hardly have any churches, are so economically advanced. The jesters are onto something here. For, indeed, our comparator countries also had the same problem of religion African countries still have.

To my mind, the "churches and poverty correlation jest," captures the manifestation of two very different world views. Where more churches proliferate than banks and factories, you can be sure that the world view there, is the superstitious one. Conversely, where banks and commercial institutions proliferate, it is the scientific world view that is preponderant there. Our competitor countries adopted this paradigm and started solving their problems through scientific principles.

A paradigm, according to Thomas Kuhn, is nothing but concepts, theories and methods that a society takes for granted at a certain point in time. A paradigm will persist as long as its tenets can explain and solve problems of the time. When new technologies, methods and explanations emerge, the old paradigm will get discarded for the newer, more elegant one. The paradigm that was dominant during the Dark Ages in Europe, was what can be called that of blind faith, or the Religious Paradigm. In that paradigm, the Roman Catholic Church was the final authority on all matters, secular or spiritual. Knowledge was what the Roman Catholic Church said it was, and no disputation was allowed.

This paradigm persisted until the Protestant Reformation, when some thinkers in the Roman Catholic Church itself, successfully challenged the Church's authority. Although this challenge was on matters of theology, it ushered in the tradition of disputation in all fields. Instead of accepting Church authority without question, the new paradigm insisted on disputation and thorough examination of all claims before one accepted them. In short, the Scientific Paradigm.

Some Reservations:

Our society must also not be sensitive to the charge of still being in the Dark Ages. Instead, that charge should be a spur to action. I mention this specifically because, I know that as a nation, we are likely to be sensitive to any accusations of being in the dark over any-thing. For this was the convenient excuse that was used to colonize us. True, the people who used this excuse, never wanted to share with us the insights from their adoption of the Scientific Paradigm. They just wanted to exploit us as they had exploited each other during their own Dark Ages.

Yes, I admit it, the brutality of Colonialism, makes us as a nation, sensitive to any accusation of being in the dark on any subject. Makes us sensitive to any outsider who presumes to talk down to us. But still, I do not like this sensitivity, for it will prevent us from adopting useful courses of action. This sensitivity will make us spiteful towards anyone who accuses us of being in the dark, for not having adopted a certain course. We must not be so sensitive that we will cut off our noses to spite our faces.

In any case, this Address is essentially a discussion amongst co-nationals, with no outsider's input. I must speak forthrightly throughout these Addresses, for it does not serve my purposes to sugar-coat matters. So, if you say I am harsh in saying that we are still in the age of ignorance and superstition where religion is concerned, then you must prove me wrong. You can do this by showing me that, our current understanding of religion, is not exactly like the situation that was overturned in our competitor countries by the Protestant Reformation and the Enlightenment.

The Protestant Reformation:

The adoption of the Scientific Paradigm in Europe was not an event, but a long process ushered in by other processes. These other processes were the Renaissance, the Reformation, and the Enlightenment. The advances in economic development that then followed, led observers to argue that there was a causal link between the Scientific Paradigm adoption, and their economic success. You see, the Scientific Paradigm once fully adopted, translates to rationalization in all fields of endeavour on a national scale.

But what was the Protestant Reformation? For our purposes here, it was the first instance when the Religious Paradigm was successfully challenged. The landmark moment for that was when Martin Luther nailed his 95 Theses on the door of a Church in Wittenberg on 31st October 1517. His 95 Theses were disputations of practices adopted and encouraged by the Catholic Church that he found were not written in the Bible. The Catholic Church had established 7 sacraments, or works, which everyone had to perform to ensure their salvation (only 2 were actually in the Bible).

By claiming to control salvation, the Catholic Church controlled human life from cradle to grave. The control of salvation was a powerful tool in the Pope's armoury. Whole countries feared eternal damnation should the Pope excommunicate their ruler. Salvation was only through the Roman Catholic Church. Of course, this was a deception, only made possible by the prevailing paradigm which did not allow disputation of anything relating to God. With his 95 Theses, Luther challenged the Church to prove him wrong with reference to the Bible. This act of justified defiance did away with Church authority.

The Church could not prove his disputations wrong with reference to Scripture. Not once was the Pope mentioned in the Bible as God's intermediary on Earth. Of the 7 sacraments the Church had instituted, only 2 were mentioned in the Bible. The most problematic of these sacraments was the selling of Indulgences to poor congregants as a way of getting salvation.

The way Indulgences worked, was this: the Church convinced people that, unless they were Saints, there was always going to be a deficit between their good deeds and bad deeds. Thus, they would not make it to Heaven directly when they died, instead they would spend some time in Purgatory – a halfway house between Earth and Heaven, where souls were tormented before being allowed into Heaven. This torment was done as purification before being allowed before the presence of God.

The way to avoid torment in Purgatory was to pay money (Indulgences) to the Pope, who would then, somehow, transfer the excess goodness from the Saints to the ordinary people. It was an elaborate scam, and the Pope even promised to spring dead relatives from Purgatory if their relatives paid Indulgences for them. Unquestioningly, the people paid these Indulgences for years, until Martin Luther questioned the scriptural basis of this practice.

In fact, one of his 95 Theses hit the nail on the head, he asked in Thesis 82: To wit: "Why does not the Pope empty Purgatory, for the sake of holy love and of the dire need of the souls that are there, if he redeems an infinite number of souls for the sake of miserable money with which to build a Church? The former reasons would be most just; the latter is most trivial."

For his 'disobedience,' Martin Luther was put on trial by the Church and asked to recant his statements. He refused to do so, uttering these now famous words; "Unless I am convinced by Scripture and plain reason – I do not accept the authority of the Popes and Councils, for they have contradicted each other – my conscience is captive to the Word of God. I cannot and I will not recant anything, for to go against conscience is neither right nor safe. God help me. Amen." Of course, legend being what it is, this refusal has since been transformed to the more dramatic shorthand: "Here I stand, I can do no other, so help me God. Amen."

Martin Luther's cause was also helped by the fact that the Printing Press had been invented by Johannes Gutenberg at the time, so his ideas were widely disseminated. The Bible was also then printed in local languages, helping the locals to understand the issues for themselves. Just a hundred years earlier, Jan Hus, who had attempted to question Church authority in the same manner, had been burned at the stake, for lack of the facilities Luther now had. What Luther's 'disobedience' then gave to the world was "the priesthood of all believers" and "justification by faith alone," which all amounted to the same thing, that God had no intermediaries on Earth. Everyone could be saved by his or her own faith alone.

In Zimbabwe, we are exactly at the stage of Indulgences with the innumerable "prophets" who have purported to make themselves God's intermediaries on Earth. A practice that was already done away with when the Protestant Reformation proclaimed the Priesthood of all the believers. Martin Luther's 95 Theses effectively overturned the idea of God's intermediaries on Earth. All could confess and pray directly to God as was found in the Gospel by Paul.

The anointing oils and anointing waters being sold to our countrymen and countrywomen are just an unsophisticated attempt to claim to be God's intermediaries on Earth, as the Pope claimed with Indulgences. Something that was already done away with in our competitor countries as far back as 1517. But, let me also be clear, the Reformation did not come about because Luther consciously decided to end the Religious Paradigm. It just so happened that this was the moment of crisis for the prevailing paradigm, and other thought processes had started to emerge.

In this regard, what helped the Reformation to succeed, was its interaction with one of the concurrent processes I mentioned above. The Reformation was facilitated by the ideas contained in the Renaissance. While the Enlightenment was, the logical conclusion of the premises of the Reformation and the Renaissance.

What the Renaissance did was move thinking from a God centred conception of the world to a man centred one.[3] With its insistence that man master all the branches of knowledge in existence for himself, the Renaissance was the greatest accomplice to the Reformation in ending the Religious Paradigm. The Renaissance Man was encouraged to use his ingenuity to unravel the secrets of the universe, and thus improve and control his fate on Earth.[4] The principle engendered in these two processes was essentially that, "nothing can be taken as true unless it can be tried and demonstrated."[5] This very question everything principle, had far reaching consequences for all aspects of life in the world.

Impact of the Protestant Reformation:

The Reformation was truly the mother of the modern world, though its actors did not know what they were about to unleash. In education, it was the origin of mass literacy as the Bible was translated to local European languages, since Luther's main innovation was that people should read the Bible for themselves. Science was eventually allowed to flourish even where its explanations contradicted the Bible.

In politics, the Reformation introduced the concept of national sovereignty. The Peace of Westphalia which ended the Thirty Years' religious war, adjudged that each country was now free to choose its own religion. This developed over time to national self-determination today. But for the purposes of this Address, I am more interested in the impact it made in the economic sphere.

In the field of economic development, Max Weber argued that it was the Protestant "work ethic" that gave birth to Capitalism. He saw a correlation between economic success and adoption of Protestantism, while the nations that remained Catholic generally remained in abject poverty. This division could be seen on a map, with the mostly Northern Protestant nations such as the UK, Norway, the Netherlands, Switzerland, and Germany, looking very advanced, while the Southern Catholic nations, Italy, Spain, and Portugal, were impoverished. There was a clear watershed. This watershed, seemed to Weber, a physical manifestation of the two different world views. The same watershed subsists today, between poor African countries adhering to superstition, and European countries which fully adopted the Scientific Paradigm. This watershed seems to me too, to be a manifestation of the two different world views.

Weber worked out the difference in economic conditions to be down to a change of mindset that occurred owing to the Protestant "work ethic." The Catholic "work ethic" imparted on the majority was that it was okay to live in poverty while awaiting a better life in

Heaven. This was a mindset that believed in miracles. The Protestant "work ethic" inverted this and encouraged people to work hard and manifest the glory of God by excelling in their calling here on Earth.[6]

In the Protestant "work ethic," man could make himself worthy of salvation by leaving the Earth in a better condition than he had found it. This he would do through being industrious and being useful to fellow man. Of course, all these were preliminary developments, over time, the impact of the Protestant Reformation became more pronounced. The Enlightenment was the outcome of what the Reformation sparked in Europe.

Did The Reformation Go Far Enough?

By now, I am sure, you will agree with me that the ideas that are diffuse and impacting our world today, were incubated in Europe. Even Nationalism, the ideology we used to defeat Colonialism, is an idea that comes to us from Germany. It being logical that as the Reformation introduced the concept of national sovereignty in Germany, the ideas undergirding nationalism were discussed there first.

Of course, these Addresses will show that we also very much adapted Nationalism to our own specific conditions. This is how humanity progresses, adopting ideas from a different age or place, improving and adapting them to suit prevailing conditions. One of my complaints in this Address, is that we uncritically adopted religion. I am, therefore, by discussing these developments in Europe, just trying to bring us up to speed with where our competitor countries are, where developments in religion are concerned.

I asked above whether the Protestant Reformation went far enough, and the answer is a resounding no! Martin Luther only set out to correct Roman Catholic Church malpractice. What Luther did is what is called problem-solving theory, merely tweaking the system a little, but not questioning its foundations at all. The converse of problem-solving theory is critical theory, which critiques not just the superstructure, but the foundation as well. Where Luther only questioned the misinterpretation of the Bible by the Roman Catholic Church, critical theory would have questioned if the Bible was even the word of God in the first place.

But, again, to be fair to the early Reformers, perhaps, that is all their level of ingenuity allowed back then. People in our competitor countries have since had another questioning of their religions. The premises of the Enlightenment are what our competitor countries used to question if the Bible was even the word of God to begin with. This is what I want us to also have done by now. As we have not done this for ourselves, I therefore do not redundantly raise this issue in this Address. The whole point is that each polity has to undergo these discussions for itself if it is to accrue their benefits. You cannot outsource this.

So, while the Reformation itself did not go far enough, the Enlightenment did. The Reformation only loosened the potent brew that was faith and power which allowed Christianity to compel men to believe.[7] Before the Reformation, so-called heretics – people who attempted to question the truth of religion – were burned at the stake. When the threat of being killed for what you believe was removed by the Reformation, the Enlightenment was truly launched.

The Enlightenment took over and everything could now be questioned. The Enlightenment asked these question: is the Bible even the word of God? Has God spoken? Is God Trinity? Is there such a thing as Heaven or Hell? Is anything true that cannot fit with my reason? Kant referred to the Enlightenment as the period when "mankind grew out of its self-inflicted immaturity."[8] I want us to also question everything in this manner.

I even wish that our discarding of our Traditional Beliefs, for the God of the Bible, had happened because we had questioned our Traditional Beliefs ourselves and found them to be inadequate. But as it happened, we were forced by Colonialists to discard our religions. We discarded these earlier superstitions of ours because outsiders said they were associated with the Devil. I agree with the discarding of our Traditional Beliefs, but not because they were associated with the Devil. I agree because they were just superstitions whose time was long overdue. But what I am also saying to you here and now, is that the religions we adopted from these outsiders, are also superstitions we can now discard.

Zimbabwe's Religions:

I was raised as a Christian, so the type of religion I can easily dissect and analyse in this Address, is Christianity. We are also considered a Christian Country with 84% of our population confirmed as practicing Christians. The other religions practised here are Islam and Traditional Beliefs. I will, of necessity, have to talk about the Traditional Beliefs, because my argument is that every society in the world, had a conception of God of its own before making contact with other societies. I am thus, very interested in the reasons that led us to discard our conception of God, and to adopt a foreign one.

We adopted Christianity because it was forced upon us by the Colonialist. But besides this force, Christianity must also have proved to be a more sustained and elegant worldview than our Traditional Beliefs. Even when Christianity was introduced by Apostle Paul to the Greeks, in the Sermon at Areopagus Hill, it also proved to be more elegant than the pagan gods they had worshipped there for millennia. Still, it is important to realise that, for all its elegance, Christianity is just a philosophy of life. It is just another alternative theory of a supreme being. Our Traditional Beliefs, Judaism, Islamism, and Hinduism are other such theories of a supreme being.

Our Traditional Beliefs have a Creator called *Mwari Musika-vanhu* (God the Creator), there is no Heaven and Hell, but our ancestors who die become our protectors presumably because they have gone to be with *Mwari*. We did not specify where the Creator resided. Contact with *Mwari* and any of our ancestors was through Spirit Mediums, these were usually *N'anga* (Witchdoctors) who had the 'gift.' They presided over cultural, political and any other religious ceremonies. They also interpreted messages from *Mwari* as well as from our long-departed ancestors.

Here, I am briefly repeating things we all already know, but I am doing this for a reason. I am doing this so that I can point out to you that: there is nothing particularly unique about our Traditional Beliefs, every society has had such a conception of its Creator in its early stages. Before Europe adopted Christianity, they had all these same Traditional Beliefs, multitudes of pagan gods, natural phenomenon as gods, and other kinds of religions that worshipped the Sun, or the dead.

The God Of The Gaps:

The God of the Gaps refers to thinking something is a God until there is a sound explanation, and you have no reason to continue believing this something is a God. The gap will have been filled. If we had been worshipping Earthquakes as a God, and someone explained to us how Tectonic Plates cause Earthquakes, we would cease seeing an Earthquake as a God. The Christian conception of God when it was introduced to us, must have been more unassailable than what our Traditional Beliefs held. So, I suspect that in addition to its being forced upon us, the other reason why we also accepted Christianity, was because it was just a more elegant conception of a supreme being than what we had. The invisible God of the Christian postulation was way more unassailable than the ones we had.

But in our "Enlightenment" exercise, I want to bring it to your attention that, the invisible God of Judaism and the Christian Bible, is no longer that unassailable. Careful study of these texts will yield to you that they are cultural artefacts, as fictitious as the stories contained in the conceptions of God in our Traditional Beliefs. This is why our competitor countries now separate Church and State. They no longer put religion central to their development policy. National prayers for rain just do not feature in their economic planning because of this understanding of affairs.

Our Superficial Understanding Of Christianity:

I said above that we have adopted Christianity more enthusiastically than those who gave us this religion. Additionally, I have noticed that we adopted this religion unreflectingly and superficially. In terms of our superficial adoption of Christianity, we think that the Hebrew Bible (which we call The Old Testament) and the Christian Bible (also called The New Testament) are of one piece. But correctly understood, these are two separate religious texts. The Hebrew Bible is not a prelude to the Christian Bible.[9] The Jewish Religion called Judaism, which gave the world the Hebrew Bible, does not recognize any additional texts outside its 24 Books from Genesis to Chronicles.

By this logic, the relationship between Christianity and the Hebrew Bible is a very contrived one. In this relationship, Christianity tried to fit itself as fulfilment of what was said in the Hebrew Bible. We have conflated the two without realising their distinctiveness from each other. This is where I think we also unreflectingly adopted Christianity.

From a theological perspective, it does not matter that the Christian teachings are an improvement on the caprices of the deity found in the Hebrew Bible. What matters is that the Hebrew Bible is a standalone text, and any religion that claims it as its foundation, is still a different religion from Judaism. We should, therefore, first of all acknowledge that Judaism and Christianity are two different religions. Judaism does not even acknowledge Jesus Christ.

The reasons why Judaism rejects Jesus are also sound. For example, people who have raised issues with Jesus's divinity have pointed out that, if Jesus is the only way, the light, and no one can go to Heaven but through him, how will the millions who died before him, including Abraham, see Heaven? They have also added that God does not play tricks such as incremental revelation on his people. The law and means of salvation were already given in the Hebrew Bible, he cannot then say to them, 4 000 years later; I tricked you, the only way to salvation is to worship my son who I never told you about before.

Jesus not being mentioned once in the Hebrew Bible, doing explicit activity with God in Heaven, is the other reason why Judaism rejects him. Nowhere in the Hebrew Bible do you find Jesus doing any specific activity with God, like being sent to cast out Adam and Eve after they disobeyed God. This lack of specific activity with God in the Hebrew Bible, does not bode well for Christianity's claims that Jesus Christ was there at the beginning of time.

Judaism is quite right to reject Jesus on these grounds. I know that some people have tried to argue that Isaiah prophesied the coming of the Messiah, and that it was Jesus he prophesied. The problem with that claim is that having read Isaiah, Jesus could have styled himself after the described Messiah. The only concrete evidence that would have supported Jesus' claims was if he had been mentioned as being by God's side at the beginning of time in the Hebrew Bible. Instead, Jesus's claims actually contradict what is the unique innovation the Hebrew Bible introduced: Monotheism.

Is God Trinity?

The faith that gave the world the Hebrew Bible did not exist in a vacuum, Judaism interacted with its neighbours in the Middle East who had their own conceptions of God and creation. Invariably, all the other religions worshipped many gods: Polytheism. There was a god of war, a god of love, and even a god of the harvest. In a marked departure from the prevailing practices, the Hebrew Bible introduced the concept of one God. The Christian Bible then reintroduces what could be mistaken for a return to Polytheism. The doctrine of a Trinity contained in Christian teachings, awards Jesus the same status as God. This issue, rejected out of hand by Judaism, has been a bone of contention that has even divided the Christian Church in the past.

If you look to what the Church described as the Arian heresy, or to give its common name, Arianism, you will find Arius of Alexandria refuting Jesus's divinity on these logical grounds: he said that because Jesus was only God's begotten Son, this meant there was a point in time when he did not exist. From this reasoning it followed that he was not co-eternal with God, and therefore subordinate to God. Arius was, of course, condemned by the Council of Nicaea for heresy. But we should never go by such condemnations, because this was at the time when the Church was successfully suppressing knowledge.

Constantine the Great even ordered everyone put to death, who adhered to the Arian doctrine. I only raise these points to remind you that doubtful points of the Christian religion in the past, were enforced by violence. There are so many other examples when the Church suppressed, with violence, the questioning of what did not make sense in its doctrines. It is sad then that, at this point, when the freedom to question everything is granted in the world, most of us still want to pursue blind faith.

For my part, insofar as I have researched the issue, I think Jesus (if he really ever lived) was just one of those genius philosophers, who taught ways to interact with each other which were better for the world than the ones that had gone before him. This follows from my considered position that, the people who wrote the Hebrew Bible itself were truly brilliant people who wanted to organise society for the better. The claim that God had given them this book, is just a legitimating device. Jesus just piggy-backed on the same legitimating device by claiming to have been sent by God to redeem the world.

By piggybacking on the Hebrew Bible, Christianity's claims to being the one true religion also suffers when the deficiencies of Judaism are pointed out. The Hebrew Bible is the foundational document on which the Christian faith is dependent on, and the Hebrew Bible is merely a cultural artefact of the ancient Jews.

The Hebrew Bible As A Cultural Artefact:

As the Zimbabwean nation, we should take issue with the Hebrew Bible's claims that the Israelites are God's favourite nation. For me this is the first sign that the Hebrew Bible is a cultural artefact of the ancient Israelites. It excludes the Zimbabwean nation when it refers to the God of Isaac and the God of Abraham. I cannot establish any logical connection between a Zimbabwean and Abraham, so this would seem to mean that such a God is not the God of Zimbabwe. Everything in the Hebrew Bible also happened within the confines of the ancient Near East. This parochialism convinces me that we adopted other people's foundational myths to the neglect of our own.

Apart from this small gripe, there are other more serious problems with the Bible which makes the claims of its authorship questionable. For brevity's sake, I will only talk about two of those problems in this Address. The first problem is the sources of the Bible: Mesopotamian mythology is the source of the Hebrew Bible's creation stories.[10] The Hebrew Bible borrowed its descriptions of Creation and its immediate aftermath from older Mesopotamian myths. The second problem is the limited knowledge of cosmology in the Hebrew Bible. No omniscient God would have exhibited such limited and erroneous knowledge of the Universe as is found in the Hebrew Bible. On these two counts alone, I contend that the claim that the Hebrew Bible was written, or even inspired by God, is just a legitimating device.

The Sources Of The Hebrew Bible:

On the issue of its sources, the Hebrew Bible's descriptions of creation and its immediate aftermath, are borrowed from older stories that were already known in Persia. These earlier stories were written by people who did not subscribe to the God of the Hebrew Bible. They had their own pagan gods and were also acting on the universal human need to answer questions of our origins. This need is usually satisfied with stories that answer how man and woman were created and given the law by the Creator.

The Creation story in Genesis is borrowed from "Enuma Elish, a Babylonian Epic, which tells how one god, Marduk, attained supremacy over the others and created the world by splitting his aquatic enemies in half."[11] The story of man having been created from clay is also contained in Enuma Elish and the Epic of Atrahasis. The Story of Adam and Eve, and their coming to terms with their humanity in the Hebrew Bible, is borrowed from the Epic of Gilgamesh, an ancient Mesopotamian poem.[12]

The Flood and Noah's Ark Story comes straight from the Epic of Atrahasis, another Mesopotamian story where the gods give one man directions to build an Ark so as to survive the flood they were about to send. The Epic of Gilgamesh also incorporates the Flood Story, but this time the person who saves humanity by building an Ark is Ziusudra. These flood stories were a staple in the ancient Near East, and they all predate the Genesis account. All these myths were known to the writers of the Hebrew Bible because, the stories flourished "beyond the boundaries of any particular language or ethnic group. This was partly because Akkadian was the language of diplomacy throughout the ancient Near East."[13]

All what the writers of the Hebrew Bible did, was borrow known creation myths from other civilisations. They then just retold them with their own God and Israelites as the central characters in the retelling. In this regard then, the Hebrew Bible is just one of the myths of foundation like the pagan myths its writers had contact with. The only difference was that it innovated and introduced some improvements. Monotheism and the concept of a righteous God are two such improvements.

If you read the Hebrew Bible side by side with the Mesopotamian myths it borrowed its content from, you will see the innovation that the writers of the Hebrew Bible introduced. The gods in the Mesopotamian myths bring about the Flood for trivial reasons like population control, or that the humans were too noisy. But in the Genesis Flood story, it is a moral God punishing humans for being wicked. Although, again, Richard Dawkins, disputes this point of a righteous God, because he thinks the punishment for eating some fruit in the Garden of Eden was too heavy handed for such a trivial transgression. I think this was just the limit of human imagination, the writers of the Hebrew Bible could not come up with an original sin, so heinous and egregious, that we would all agree that all humanity deserved to be punished for it in perpetuity.

Again, all these arguments I am making now, were not available to people from an earlier age, The Epic of Enuma Elish for example, was only recovered from the ruins in Nineveh in 1849. People from an earlier age would not have had this evidence against the claim that the Hebrew Bible was the word of God.

The point to take away from all this, is that human beings have been preoccupied with explaining how they came to be. The other preoccupation is organising society for the better. The Hebrew Bible fused these two preoccupations brilliantly in explaining how the ancient Israelites came into existence, and how their Creator wanted them to live. Still, the Hebrew Bible is just another philosophy of life, written by the elites of that society. This is what all religions are.

The reason we abandoned our own conceptions of religion was because they were not as elegant as what the Hebrew Bible proposed. Also missing for us Zimbabweans, was a holy book written in antiquity, because we did not have the ability to read and write until recently. We certainly had the curiosity as to how and who created us. *Mutangakugara*, *Muwanikwa*, and *Chidza Chepo* are all terms that mean the same thing – the first settler. These terms exist in our language because we must have wondered who the first person in our lineage was, and how he came to be – a myth of origin.

Alas, one of the lamentations from those who have written about Africa, is our universal lack of myths of origin. Perhaps we had our own myths of origin that got lost because we did not have written word. Perhaps we never devised any myths of origin. Whatever the case, we do not have systematically written works trying to explain how we were created. Other civilisations have these myths of origin. The Hebrew Bible then, viewed historically, falls in this class of writing.

Cosmology Of The Hebrew Bible:

A leading Irish Clergyman, Archbishop James Ussher of Armagh, reached world renown when he pronounced that the Earth was created by God on 23 October 4004 B.C. He lived in the 17th Century, so by his calculations, the Earth was then 5 650 years old. Isaac Newton, a brilliant scientist of the same century, also placed the date of creation at around 3998 B.C., while Saint Bede, another leading clergyman had placed it in 3952 B.C.. John Lightfoot, an eminent Cambridge Hebrew Scholar, only disputed the time of Creation with James Ussher, he said it was at 0900am, and not the previous day as Ussher posited.

Ussher had arrived at the age of the Earth by counting all the "begats" in the Hebrew Bible from Adam through to when other written records were available to humanity. If you know that Adam was the first person on Earth and how long he lived, then also know the genealogy of his descendants and how long each of them lived, you can calculate the age of the Earth that way. Up until the 19th Century, this way of calculating the age of the Earth was accorded the same respect as the scriptures, because until then, humanity had no other tools to calculate the age of the Earth.

Therefore, going by the Hebrew Bible, scientists and clergymen alike, agreed the Earth to be around 6 000 years old. This age was only accepted owing to the limited knowledge of cosmology of the time. As well, this shows that the people who wrote the Hebrew Bible had limited knowledge of the universe, that is why their chronology of events gave us such a young Earth. Using radioactive techniques, we now know the Earth to be around 4.6 billion years old.

Even if you say, the people who used the "begat" method to calculate the age of the Earth were wrong to do so, there are other obvious examples of limited knowledge of cosmology in the Hebrew Bible. All that this shows is that these were people with limited knowledge, trying to answer difficult questions of their time. Take the explanation in the Hebrew Bible for how different languages came about for example. The writers of the Hebrew Bible settled on the Tower of Babylon story.

In that story, people were building a Tower that would have allowed them to reach Heaven. To scupper their plans, God smote them with different languages and suddenly the builders of the Tower could not cooperate as they could not understand each other. God could not have written, or inspired such a story, as he would have definitely known that building a Tower would not allow people to reach Heaven.

The tallest building on Earth at the moment is Burj Khalifa in the Middle East, it is just under 1 Kilometre high, while the Karman

Line, where the Earth's atmosphere ends and Space begins, is at an altitude of 100 Kilometres. Therefore, to think that people could build a Tower and reach Heaven, is a concept that could only have been written by human beings who had no sound understanding of the cosmos. These were just myths trying to explain away the puzzles of the day, in this case the origin of different languages.

Of course, the people who wrote the Bible had to claim that it was given to them by a Supreme Law giver, this was to ensure obedience without question. For, if a man tells you that he has written a law for how you shall live yourself, your correct reaction is to question all those instances that law will benefit him while disadvantaging you. To have that unquestioned obedience, authorship of the Bible had to be imputed to God.

Again, this does not necessarily mean that God does not exist. It just points us to that fact that the Bible is a cultural artefact, written certainly to order society for the better, but with biases and imperfections that cannot possibly belong to an omniscient and omnipotent God.

Is Religion Good or Bad?

Yuval Harari finds it ironic that witnesses in UK and US Courts have to put their hands on the Bible and "swear to tell the truth on a book brimming with so many fictions, myths and errors."[14] I agree with this sentiment of his. But, having shown in this Address that the God we think we worship was fabricated by people who wanted to organise society for the better, we still have to answer some practical questions.

Can we conclude that religion is good or bad? If we did not have religion, would the world be more chaotic than it is now? Are people only good because they fear punishment in Hell? To these questions, I think the jury will never return a verdict. Religion has some positives and some negatives. The positives of religion are that it has motivated people to do good things; it has inspired great cultural achievements such as the Sistine Chapel frescoes; and it has promoted social cohesion. The negatives are equally powerful; atrocities have been committed in the name of religion; blind faith has been the antidote to progress as it suppressed scientific thinking for a long time; and religion has also promoted prejudice as people seek to enforce what they think is their God's law.

I am also very much opposed to the so-called prophets in Zimbabwe who have been fleecing congregants. Then there are also things like the rape of young boys by Catholic Priests that has been going on for years. It does not seem to me that we can pronounce definitively whether religion is good or bad from deeds. For deeds, I think individual human nature is a better source of explanation: where some people are innately good, and some are innately bad. This is how you get Catholic Priests who rape children, and Atheists who are fighting for the protection of children from such abuses.

But for the case of Zimbabwe, I would say that religion has been bad for us, as we are still stuck in the Religious Paradigm and not the Scientific Paradigm. I would like you, my fellow countrymen and countrywomen, to understand that the religion we have is just a philosophy of life. I want you to understand that the Scientific Paradigm is another philosophy of life, and so far, the Scientific Paradigm is the one that is giving the best results. Cloud seeding (science) is giving more instant results than praying for rain (religion). The Scientific Paradigm will also free us from being taken advantage of by "prophets," as we will ask them to demonstrate cause and effect when they offer us "anointing oils."

I will also admit that religion does satisfy another psychological need despite its falsity: hope and comfort. When we lose a loved one, it is comforting to think that we will meet them in the afterlife, in Heaven. It is also comforting to think there is a reward after a life of goodness. Despair and despondency would set in if we thought our lives and deaths are meaningless. Still, this answering a psychological need, though useful, does not mean what religion is saying is true. For my part, given the question of immortality, I have concluded that the only way we perpetuate ourselves is through having offspring, and I have made my peace with that realisation.

Conclusion: Does God Exist?

I can now directly answer the main question in this particular Address. Clearly our conception of God is that of the Hebrew Bible, who we think is exactly the same God as in the Christian Bible. We are mistaken in that conception, but this is because we adopted our conception of God through having it forced upon us by missionaries under Colonialism.

The missionaries who came, whether they knew it or not, presented Christianity as if it was the same religion as Judaism. In my research for this Address, I have found that these are two distinct religions. The reason that made us discard our own religions for foreign conceptions, is that the foreign one was a more elegant theory of a Creator. For long periods of the Earth, science could not refute this theory. It is only now, with advances in science and other discoveries, that we are able to see that some of the Bible's claims are erroneous, and thus, could not have been written by an omniscient God.

My short answer to the question Does God Exist then, is this; God's existence is probable, but that he is exactly as described by the major religions is simply false. A recurring claim in all the scriptural writings, is that the text was handed to the believers by an authority, usually the supreme being himself. This is just what is called a legitimating device in literally terms. The first law giver of the Roman Civilisation also claimed to have been given the laws by a goddess. It being a human propensity to reject the rules made up a fellow human being.

But there are ways of finding out if something was given by an omniscient being or, by fallible mortals. My look at the Hebrew Bible has yielded to me that it was written by people whose knowledge of cosmology was very limited, an omniscient God would never give such inaccurate information about the age of the earth for example. The fact that the writers of the Hebrew Bible copied myths from older civilisations then claimed this is how God created the Earth, also tells us the Hebrew Bible is merely a foundational myth of the ancient Israelites.

There are many religions in the world, and they all claim to be the one true religion. I have come to realise that different religions are just philosophies of how to live life and theories of a Creator. It will surprise you, my fellow countrymen and countrywomen, as it surprised me too, during my research for this Address, that there are other religions out there, which are equally valid to their adherents, as Christianity is to us. They also believe that their version of religion is the one true religion. It surprised me when I was researching the Address on the Fourth Industrial Revolution, that the "Number of the Beast" (666), so feared by Christians, is meaningless to billions of Chinese and Indian people whose religious scriptures do not once mention this number and the persecution that will accompany it. Thus, a devout Christian is a Heathen to a Muslim, Buddhist, or to a practitioner of Judaism (rejecting as it does, any of Jesus's claims to divinity).

This knowledge then, that all religions are just theories of a Creator, should free us as individuals from the hold that the so-called prophets in our country have over us. It should also free us, as a nation, from believing in divine providence, and instead spur us to adopt the Scientific Paradigm for our development. Science is continually looking for solutions for problems facing humanity, while religion's answer is prayer and waiting for the Second Coming of the Messiah. This is not a good strategy for national economic development. Our nation must understand that Heaven is just a theory of a beautiful afterlife devised to comfort those suffering on Earth. We can make our Heaven here on Earth by achieving national economic prosperity by relying on scientific principles.

Address III.

Nationalism In Zimbabwe.

"The Nationalist does not require that individual members be alike, only that they should feel an intense bond of solidarity and therefore act in unison on all matters of national importance" – Anthony D. Smith.

MY FELLOW COUNTRYWOMEN and countrymen, there can be no discussion amongst ourselves, more important than that which examines, definitively, the main ideas that we take for granted with regards our polity: nation, nationalism, national question, and national identity. We often repeat these terms, but do they apply to us in the way that we think they do? Are we even a nation, or do we just mistake the shadow for the substance when we call ourselves one? In scholarly debates of the matter, most post-colonial African nation-states, are accused of only having juridical, but not empirical existence. This is to say they are a fiction.

A few years ago, Jeffrey Herbst and Greg Mills wrote a very provocative article, in Foreign Policy Magazine, titled: There Is No Congo. Their main premise was that, both the country, and nation we know as the Democratic Republic of Congo (DRC), do not exist. These authors were intervening on the subject of how the size of that country, and the multiplicity of ethnicities therein contained, had resulted in cyclical civil wars. The solution they proposed was, essentially, balkanization. The main problem I found in their thesis and solution, was that it was exactly what people who benefit from the instability in the DRC would propose and promote. I, on the other hand, would suggest capacitating the central authority there to better control its territory. I take the view that, strong unitary nations, are the best ways of protecting African resources from exploitation by outsiders.

Still, the same Herbst and Mills article, set me thinking about our own nation in relation to the very same accusation of not existing. I, thus, traced the history of our polity from antiquity to present day, comparing ourselves to how European nations developed, and what I discovered is the subject of this Address. As far as these main ideas are concerned – nation, nationalism, and national identity – I found out that we are a nation; nationalism created our nation; and it is now in the process of creating our national identity.

How nationalism created our nation, and what it needs to do to sustain the same nation, forms the largest part of this Address. The way our nation was formed, also gave us a very peculiar national question. The most pressing national question, in the first forty years of our existence, was the land question. I will talk about the national question at some length below.

As for type, we are a syncretic nation. The alternative – a homogeneous nation – whereby a single racial or ethnic group is exclusively contained in the same territory, is now very rare on the globe. This fact, of us being a syncretic nation, means I struggled to pinpoint our national identity. Our national identity then, is something that we must strive to create from the multiplicities of influences that are to be found on our territory. Knowing as I do, that national identities are mostly produced by norm entrepreneurs, I also suggest below, the parameters and influences I think will produce an acceptable national identity for us. Nationalists should be the lead norm entrepreneurs on this matter.

Nationalism itself, is the creed of all nations. Once you have proclaimed your nation, you also will have proclaimed your nationalism. There is no nation on the planet that exists without reference to its nationalism. Anyone who thinks otherwise, has just not understood how nations really work. Norway, Sweden, Switzerland, and the United States exist, and continue to do so, because of their nationalism. It is just that some of these same nations, have started to misleadingly claim that nationalism is a vice. It is not.

In the academies, there is also quite an age old debate about which came first, the nation or nationalism. I discovered that in our own particular case, nationalism came first as our nation was created by (African) nationalism. African nationalism itself admits these two distinct stages: Anti-Colonialism and Integration nationalism. These two stages just mean that nationalism created our nation when it fought and defeated Colonialism, and it is now at the stage where it is integrating everyone into the post-colonial nation-state. This last task is still ongoing as, relative to European nations, our nation is still in its infancy.

At this stage, I should also tell you that, the same European nations which are paragons of stability today, experienced the same problems that have made some thinkers proclaim that our nations are fictions. A look into the life of European nations during their infancy, will show us mirror images of some of our current realities. To my mind then, most of our problems so far, are just growth pains – inevitable in the early stages of the nation's life.

Also, despite the contrary desire by Pan-Africanists, the truth of the matter is that, in proclaiming our nation-state in 1980, we were following the lead of the European nation-states. There is, therefore, no escaping comparison with nation-states in Europe in discussing our own nationhood. My approach then in researching our nation and nationalism, was to also survey the development of the nation and nationalism in Europe. This is where the concept of the nation, and the doctrine of nationalism, as we know them today, were developed. So, for comparison's sake, in this Address, I will also talk about some instances in the development of the nation and nationalism in Europe.

Some Pan-Africanists have suggested that we should have, instead, returned to our pre-colonial settings after winning independence. I do not share this sentiment, for two reasons. The first reason is that the whole globe was already divided into nation-states, and the only option we had was to also proclaim a nation-state. The second reason is that, as we were defeated and colonised by European polities organised as nation-states, the nation-state form of organisation had proved itself the strongest form known to humanity. People who want to have sovereignty over their resources, must therefore adopt this form of political organisation and its concomitant doctrine – nationalism.

Indeed, definitionally, in the fewest words, Nationalism in Zimbabwe is the doctrine that demands that we have sovereignty over all our resources. When we did not have this doctrine, foreigners had enslaved us in our own land, and were exploiting our resources for their benefit. If we do not continue to strictly observe the tenets of the same doctrine, foreigners will find ways to exploit our resources again for their own benefit. This Address then, explains how we came to be Zimbabwe, and suggests what we ought to do if our nation is going to exist as we want it 700 years from now.

Vantage Points:

I have deliberately chosen to use lenses and ideas developed in Europe because they impacted us more than others developed elsewhere. In addition to this fact, some of my education was in Western Universities. But I hope that you, my fellow countrywomen and countrymen, who have experiences with other civilisations, such as Persia, China, or Japan, will also make an input to our discussion using insights from your own exposures.

We all know very well the Indian moral tale about the five blind men who each touched an elephant, and then had to describe what it looked like. For my having been exposed to European history and thought, I may be overlooking insights that could be very useful for our polity. I may only be holding the leg of the proverbial elephant, and then telling you that the elephant is like a tree trunk. Thus, your input will also give me a better understanding of the beast. But until you have done so, all I can do for now, is speak from my vantage point.

Definitions Of The Nation And Nationalism:

The consensus among those who have studied nations and nationalisms, is that they are difficult to define. This is also not helped by the ambiguities that arise since we tend to use words like country, nation, and State interchangeably. Still, I think we can achieve some clarity in our terms of reference in this Address. A country is a defined territory presided over by a nation-state. Nation-state is just a helpful shorthand that distinguishes actual nations from aspirational ones.

For our discussion, there are some features an entity just has to have, for it to satisfy empirical nationhood in the international system. These features are set out in the Montevideo Convention of 1933 and accepted in the Charter of the United Nations of 1945. Article 1 of the Montevideo Convention sets out the criteria for nation-states as: (a) a permanent population, (b) a defined territory, (c) government and (d) the ability to enter relations with other States.

For our shorthand – nation-state – the nation is "a community of people whose members are bound together by a sense of solidarity, a common culture, and a national consciousness."[15] While the State is the "legal political organisation, with the power to require obedience and loyalty from its citizens."[16] So, for our terms – nation, State and country - the nation is the group of people who are conscious that they form such a group; the State is their administrative body; and country their defined territory.

The fourth criteria in the Montevideo Convention, the ability to enter relations with other States, is the 'recognition criteria,' whereby claims to be a nation have to be acknowledged by other such constituted units to be valid. Having considered all this, I think the definition of nation given to the world by Josef Stalin in 1913, still suffices: "a nation is a historically constituted, stable community of people, formed on the basis of a common language, territory, economic life, and psychological make-up manifested in a common culture."[17]

As for Nationalism, I agree with Anthony Smith, when he defined it as: "an ideological movement for attaining and maintaining autonomy, unity and identity on behalf of a population deemed by some of its members to constitute an actual or potential 'nation.'"[18] Once this autonomy is attained, nationalism is the doctrine and habit that ensures that the nation is reproduced and maintained.

But, the nation and nationalism defined thus, raises a 'chicken – egg dilemma' that scholars think is irresolvable. The 'chicken – egg dilemma' scholars think arises is that it's impossible to say which came first – the nation or nationalism. This dilemma does hold traction in theoretical discussions of nations and nationalisms, but I think it loses its power when applied to specific African case studies.

It is very possible to identify which came first, the nation or nationalism, in each specific case there. In our case, as will become abundantly clear below, it is very clear that nationalism created our nation. But it didn't do so in a vacuum, the materials were already there: a historical people who had lived permanently on this territory, who then underwent a period of foreign domination, fought and defeated their foreign oppressors, then proclaimed a nation-state: Zimbabwe. In the fewest words, this is how nationalism created our nation. But before we go to talking specifically about ourselves, let us locate ourselves first in the subset we exist in – African Nationalism!

African Nationalism.

The word nationalism invokes, in most people's minds today, notions of exclusion: racism and xenophobia. Adolf Hitler, the British

National Party (BNP), Front National in France, and various other neo-Nazi formations in East Europe, are what typically come to mind when people hear the word nationalism. But this "right-wing" nationalism, is not necessarily the case in Africa. African nationalism, properly considered, has more in common with the formative nationalisms that gave Europe its various nations. Indeed, African nationalism only came into existence as a logical response to European nationalism. What European nationalism proved to us, with Colonialism, was that the model of political organisation we still had – scattered kingdoms – was no longer good enough to resist foreign domination.

Clearly, European nationalism took root earlier than ours, and then became a scourge on Africa. Once constituted into nations, the various European powers competed to capture resources abroad in the advancement of their national causes. The landmark event for this was the 1884 Berlin Conference on the Partition of Africa. At this Conference, European nations agreed to divide Africa among themselves without any input from the Africans.

Africa, having thus been subjected by polities that were formed into nation-states, also had to adopt the nation-state form of organisation. This was the only way we could muster the resources to compete with, or at least, resist subjection by polities organised along the lines of nation-states. As we are continually the target of those who seek to benefit at Africa's expense, African nationalism is necessary for the protection of African resources. African nationalism then, simply implies groups of people, within various defined territories, claiming sovereignty over their resources.

Mindful that the African nation was formed differently from the nation in Europe, African nationalism admits two distinct, and necessary, stages in its development. The first stage was nationalism as Anti-Colonialism, whereby pre-independence movements fought to eject foreign rulers and establish a new nation-state on the same territory as under colonialism.[19] The second stage was Integration nationalism, when the post-independence movements sought to bring the disparate ethnic populations into one new political community.[20] Thus, a justified resistance to foreign domination, was, of necessity, followed by an integration of everyone within the territory into one nation. This latter stage, which is called nation-building, can only be considered successful when 'banal nationalism' takes root in the nation in question.

Banal Nationalism:

'Banal nationalism' is the simple observation that nationalism is the creed of all nations, that when you see a flag flying on a public building, or hear the national anthem of Sweden, what you have before you is 'banal,' or everyday nationalism.[21] Michael Billig expounds on that idea thus: "the term 'banal nationalism' is introduced to cover the ideological habits which enable the established nations of the West to be reproduced... Nationalism, far from being an intermittent mood in established nations, is the endemic condition."[22]

There is a tendency to use the word nationalism derogatorily in the West, by those who do not realise that nationalism is a part of their fabric too. The 'banal nationalism' concept then, corrects the consequent misleading notion that countries like the United States or Norway no longer rely on nationalism for their continued existence. They do. It is just that nationalism now subtly exists there, but in times of crises, it comes to the fore in defence of the territorial nation. What African nationalism is doing, with integration nationalism, is also working towards this same stage, whereby everyone subconsciously identifies with the nation they are in before any other loyalties. A stage when nationalism is subtly promulgated, as it is now most of the time in the West.

This African nation-building has not been without its problems, but the problems are quite congruous with the stage of development of the nation in Africa. After defeating the foreign invader, the different ethnicities now in one territory made the error of thinking that they could go back to their earlier ethnic divisions. This is a mistake that should have never happened. It means the black populations misunderstood the problem that had allowed colonization to occur in the first place. They did not realize that they needed to build strong unitary nations at once. This would have ensured that no foreigners could exploit the same divisions that had been exploited in the original colonization period. But it is also a mistake to think that the Africans flippantly chose ethnic conflict at independence, we should look to the potency of other factors for an explanation.

The Colonial Legacy:

One such factor is the problem that has been termed the colonial legacy. Nation-building was necessary at independence because of the negative effects of the colonial legacy. The colonial legacy most pertinent to a discussion of nation-building, is the arbitrary borders drawn by colonialism. These borders led to what has been termed "Suffocation" and "Dismemberment": "Suffocation" is the amalgamation of multiple ethnic groups within a single State's territory, while "Dismemberment" refers to the partition of a single ethnic group into two or more States's territories.[23]

"Suffocation" then, necessitates nation-building, whereby everyone must be nudged towards identifying with the nation before their allegiance to their ethnic grouping. This entails creating a national consciousness and national identity stronger than any other loyalties citizens may have. But the divide and rule tactics employed by most colonial powers, set the different ethnicities at variance with each other. This, in turn, created hostilities that led them to fear each other after the colonialist had been removed. To an extent, the colonialist may even have calculated this as an insurance, that the different ethnicities may hate and fear each in power so much, that they would have preferred direct colonial rule to continue instead.

What all this means, is that it has been difficult to create a national identity as some people still want to identify with their ethnic group first. So much that the result has been civil wars. However, this is not a reason for us to give up. The African nationalism project is about surmounting these challenges and have everyone finally identify with the nation. This will take as long as it will take. As Africans, we need to understand that the main reason why we were subjugated by foreigners, was that they had organised themselves into nation-states, and that it was partly our disunity which made it possible for them to conquer us. We need to recognise the nation-state for exactly what it is: the optimal ordering principle on a globe populated by many different people.

Strategic Inflection Points:

People of a more emotional disposition would have had us dispose all foreign practices from our polity at independence. Indeed, some of you, my fellow countrymen and countrywomen, may object to the idea that we even adopted ways of doing things from the same enemies we defeated on our territory. I am at pains, in this Address, to demonstrate that the nation-state form of organisation, is the best ordering principle known to mankind to date. I know too, that saying as I am, that our models were no longer fit for purpose, can cause some discomfiture to the more emotional among Pan-Africanists. But as I said in the First Address, I will not pander to such emotions, instead I will discuss matters dispassionately.

What could be more dispassionate than these three concepts: Strategic Inflection Points, Revolution in Military Affairs (RMA) and Paradigm Shifts. The concept of Strategic Inflection Points is borrowed from the business world whereby, at some point, old ways of doing things reach a culminating point, and new ways of doing things must be adopted.[24] The fact that African polities were defeated, and colonised by Europeans, is a very good reason to accept that a better way of organising political communities had come into existence.

Any sensitivities to the African way of organisation being deemed to be inferior, needs to be introduced to yet another dispassionate concept: Revolution in Military Affairs. Simply stated, RMA refers to a discovery in warfighting that makes all previous modes obsolete, the discovery of gunpowder is one such example, all those who do not adapt to these new ways will, invariably, be defeated.[25] Militaries of the world, following Ovid's dictum, that: "you can learn from anyone, even your enemy," have no qualms about copying what works from anyone.

The third concept, that of Paradigm Shifts, which I talked about at length in the Second Address, buttresses the logic behind adopting the model that best serves our needs at a given time. In war, we can capture our enemy's advanced weapon and use it on him. Also, in mathematics, a mathematical truth is a mathematical truth despite that your enemy discovered it first. We cannot refute mathematical truths just because our enemies came across them first. The most optimal form of organisation in the world today is the nation-state model. We should adopt what works even if it is our mortal enemy who devised it. I am confident that restated this way, progressive nationalists and Pan-Africanists will not have any reservations about adopting "foreign ways."

Thus, the argument that the African nation-state should not try to mirror the setup of European nation-states, must be discarded. In this regard, the argument the more emotional Pan-Africanists

59

make, is that the European nation-state model is a superstructure that will never take root in Africa. The argument goes that, there is no fit between the European nation-state model, and the foundation it is being imposed upon in Africa.

The problem I find with this argument is that it runs counter to what is known about bifurcation points in the march of time – once a certain path has been taken, it is not possible to go back in time and change course. For example, uninventing nuclear weapons is no longer possible despite how dangerous they are to humanity. Once the nation-state model and all its advantages had been instituted, it became difficult to discard. I think that the Founders of the Organisation of African Unity (OAU) were well aware of this point when they insisted on keeping the borders drawn by colonialism. Roll back would have also created a new set of problems: South Sudan, which itself fell into a civil war as soon as a new border was drawn in 2011, is just one example.

I agree with Aime Cesaire then, when he argued that, the European nation-state model is not the problem per se, it was the way it came into contact with Africans that is problematic. He said, "... it is an excellent thing to blend different worlds; that whatever its own particular genius may be, a civilization that withdraws into itself atrophies; that for civilizations, exchange is oxygen; that the great good fortune of Europe is to have been a crossroads... ...But then I ask the following question: has colonization really placed civilizations in contact? Or, if you prefer, of all the ways of establishing contact, was it the best?"[26]

Yes, our contact with these outsiders was not ideal, but lessons learnt through suffering have their uses too: we should never allow our conquest to happen again. The best way to ensure our conquest never happens again, is to have functional unitary nation-states. We just must work hard to ensure that the nation-states we proclaimed at independence succeed. On this count, we do not have the luxury of experimenting with pre-colonial models that already proved them-selves weak.

But, in researching the history of nations and nationalism, some-thing else struck me. It struck me that, the Pan-Africanists who oppose African nation-states mirroring European nation-states, per-haps do not realise one thing: that even the nationalism which we used to fight Colonialism, is a doctrine whose roots are European.

European Roots Of Nationalism:

For people like myself, brought up on the gallantry of our resistance to foreign domination that started with *Chimurenga I*, the assump-tion has always been that nationalism is something we organically produced to fight Colonialism. It had never occurred to me that, this doctrine, was developed in the lands that colonised us. This would also surprise anyone who thought that since we fought Colonialism as nationalists, we must have developed the doctrine that freed us.

But, instead, nationalism is a doctrine that has its foundation in European thought in the 18th Century. The concept itself predates its 18th Century discovery and coherent formulation. My contention here is the equivalent of saying that the laws of gravity existed all along before their discovery and explication by Sir Isaac Newton. I think there is something quite natural and inevitable about nations and nationalism. So, I do not say that Europe invented nations and nationalisms, I say they discovered them earlier than us.

There is quite an ongoing scholarly debate on whether nations and nationalisms have always existed, or whether they are mod-ern inventions. In that debate, I fall on the side that sees nations as having always existed, but without the main features modernity then added – the State and Borders. Modernity turned nations into nation-states. This is the innovation that Europe, of necessity, added to a naturally existent mode of political community. This innovation then gave it the force and vitality that allowed it to subdue distant lands. As the units that overcame us were organised as nation-states, it would have been folly for us not to adopt the same organisation after our victory.

In the war metaphor I used above, I have already said that the war fighter can use his enemy's weapon against him. This is what African nationalists did with nationalism: they adopted, and adapted for their own purposes, a doctrine whose intellectual and practical development was in Europe. We learnt the enemy's ways and used them against him.

The people who are thought of as nationalism's founding fathers are Johann Gottfried Herder, Otto Bauer, Giuseppe Mazzini, Jean-Jacques Rousseau, and, importantly, Johann Gottlieb Fichte, whose work inspired the title of this book. In these intellectuals' writings, we find the defence and idealisation of nationalism. This marks them out as the ones who discovered nationalism. But still, let me also insist that, a person who arrives at a river, soon notices that it does not flow uphill. With nations and nationalism, Europeans just 'arrived at the river first.' At our own time of 'arrival at the river,' we also would have observed that the river flows downhill.

The Thirty Years' War:

But what caused Europeans to 'arrive at the river first,' and "discover" nations and nationalisms? It is safe to say that, here, necessity was the mother of "invention." I see the destructive nature of their wars, and limited territorial space, as the chief catalyst for the accommodations they eventually found in sovereign and territorial nation-states. The specific destructive war I have in mind is the Thirty Years' War between 1618 and 1648. This war was caused by the religious intolerance, between Catholics and Protestants, started by the Reformation.

It ended with the signing of the Treaties of Munster and Osnabruck, commonly known as the Peace of Westphalia.

Europe's way of political organisation before the Peace of Westphalia, mirrored what was also in Africa at the same time: an assortment of Empires, Kingdoms and City States. Quarrels and conflicts were also prevalent in Africa. I think it was population density that allowed Africa to retain the scattered Kingdoms model: there was enough space for the defeated Kings to move out of reach of their foes. *Mfecane* in South Africa, in the early 1800s, is a perfect illustration of this idea. But the same could not hold for Europe, its total population was 70 million inhabitants in 1600, compared to Africa's 55 million in the same year. Africa is three times bigger than Europe. Finite space thus may have forced Europe to adopt the concept of a bounded territory for political groups.

This, to my mind, is how Europe 'arrived at the river first,' and so discovered and imposed its innovations to the naturally occurring idea of nations and nationalisms. The convulsion set forth by the Reformation and the limited territorial space in Europe, was one of the main reasons why Europe's political organization changed to that of nation-states. As far as I can see, Europe really only did one thing to innovate the naturally occurring idea of nations: it codified territoriality and sovereignty.

Territoriality And Sovereignty:

The concept of territoriality, or even sovereignty for that matter, is not such an outstanding discovery by Europe. People everywhere, throughout history, have always claimed exclusive usage of the territory they live on. Even some wild animals claim exclusive usage of their territory, so this is a naturally occurring idea. Sovereignty simply means that outsiders cannot interfere in the running of affairs in the territory you claim for yourself, also another naturally occurring idea. The innovation that Europe really gave the world, was the codification of these concepts. Territory was defined and given legally enforceable boundaries. Treaties were then signed that codified the idea that, matters in the domestic jurisdiction of the territory, were not to be interfered with by outsiders – sovereign equality.

Europe's borders are largely uncontroversial, because the concept of bounded territories there arose from agreements reached by the Kingdoms, and in some places, natural borders demarcating the territories actually existed. Also, the forerunners to the nation-state in Europe – Kingdoms – had already largely succeeded in bringing everyone on their territories to identify with the Kingdom. Thus, the nation-state in Europe, just took over a territory where the population was already subservient to a single political authority. This is very close to having a territory which mostly coincided with its occupation by a single racial or ethnic group.

It is different in Africa, where the borders were arbitrarily drawn by Europeans, putting people who belonged to different political authorities on the same territories. This raised the issues of "Dismemberment" and "Suffocation" of different ethnic groups I discussed earlier on in this Address. In most countries, the Colonialist ensured that the different ethnicities hated each other, such that by the time we won our independence, the different people in the same territory were still loyal to their ethnicities first, and not the nation-state. Thus, the African nationalist still has the task of making everyone loyal to the nation-state before any other loyalties.

As nationalists, we already know that sovereign equality is the cardinal principle of international relations. We know that this principle must remain inviolable. Still, it may be useful to rehash how Europe ended up instituting this principle. The reason why it was instituted is still valid in international relations today. When this principle had not yet been instituted, Europe was torn apart by war, killing around 8 million people over an issue only the concept of sovereign equality could resolve.

Whose Realm, His Religion:

The principle of sovereign equality was instituted by the Peace of Westphalia in 1648. This was the peace treaty which ended the Thirty Years' War I mentioned earlier. The Thirty Years' War was fought between Catholic, and Protestant aligned Cities, Kingdoms, and Principalities. Prior to this treaty, people identified with their City State, Kingdom or Principality, but were ultimately subservient to the Holy Roman Empire. The Catholic Church – Catholic means universal – was ultimately where everyone's loyalties lay. Christendom was the main ordering principle at this time. The Germans, the Italians, the Irish, and the English all had to go to war on behalf of Christendom. At this time, this meant that the Pope could tell the Monarch in France, how to run his domestic affairs. This changed when Papal authority was rejected by Martin Luther and the Protestant Reformation he precipitated.

In The Thirty Years' War, the Catholics wanted to restore the authority of the Pope, while the Protestants were fighting to have their own religious denominations in their territory. Around 8 million people died in this war without any victory in sight. The war was then ended by an agreement which essentially stipulated that the Pope could no longer impose his religion on territories that did not want his religion.

The Peace of Westphalia resolved that the warring Kingdoms and Principalities were free to choose the religion they wanted to follow. *Cuius regio, eius religio*, Latin for "Whose realm, his religion," was the principle adopted. Outsiders were no longer allowed to interfere with that choice. This is how Europe gave the world the principle of sovereign equality.

The logical next step, once the principle of sovereign equality was promulgated, was that of "self-determination." For sovereignty to really be meaningful, the people who possess it, will have to have determined themselves, what they don't want outsiders to interfere with. At the time of the Peace of Westphalia, it only meant choice of religion, but it has since evolved to the "non-interference in all domestic affairs" principle enshrined in the United Nations Charter today. Also, at the time of the Peace of Westphalia, sovereignty simply referred to the King's will, but now means the popular will, having evolved with developments in the relationship between Kings and their subjects.

From Kingdoms To Nation-States:

Once the Kingdoms and Principalities in Europe had wrested control of what happened in their domains from the Holy Roman Empire at the Peace of Westphalia, they began to work on ensuring control of their territories and demanding that everyone within the territory they controlled be loyal to the Kingdom. In consolidating power in their territories, the concept of nation-state as we now know it today, was also taking its first steps. These Kings were laying the foundations for the polities that nationalists would take over and proclaim as nation-states.

By establishing institutions to govern their territory and ensuring a monopoly on the use of force within them, the Kings and Queens of Europe set the machinery in place for nations and nationalisms to emerge. Once this was set up, the earlier mentioned idea of self-determination ensured that nations and nationalisms emerged to claim what was rightfully theirs. Where Empires or foreign rule existed, the people agitated against them so as to have true self-determination. An example that comes to mind here is Italy, which had to fight and expel the Austrian Empire to become the Kingdom of Italy in 1861.

Over time, it transformed itself from a Kingdom to the nation-state we recognise today.

The example to follow was that set by the French Revolution of 1789, a logical conclusion to what had started with the Peace of Westphalia. The French people felt that the French Monarch was not a true representation of their popular will. They felt that true self-determination could only come with the removal of the Monarch and establishment of a Republic. Burchill explains this development better while explaining the transformation that happened from Kingdoms to nation-states. He wrote that; "until the French Revolution, the term nation referred to a racial or a linguistic group and, had no political significance. The nation was identified with the person of the Sovereign, so that international relations were essentially relations between royal families."[27] What the French did in 1789 then, was to transfer political significance from the Royal Families to the masses.

This transformation from Kingdom to nation-states in Europe, is what I have said was the infancy of nation-states there. The same upheavals as are happening in the nation-state in Africa now, were also happening in the nation-state in Europe. This is because, this is what typically happens in the infancy stage of all nation-states. The period of power consolidation is invariably violent. Even Switzerland, now a byword for peace and stability, underwent a civil war that decided how power would be distributed there. The French Revolution itself in 1789 involved regicide, civil war, and the Reign of Terror. The Reign of terror alone saw 17 000 death sentences and executions by guillotine carried out to consolidate the new nation-state. The chaos that ensued led to a military strongman – Napoleon Bonaparte – taking over the reins of State to bring order.

This French example also accelerated the adoption of the nation-state model by others. Once France had been successfully set up as a nation-state under Napoleon, with the attendant Napoleonic Code, it began to wage war on its neighbours. These neighbours, in deference to the Revolution in Military Affairs idea I mentioned above, just had to organise themselves as nation-states too, to be able to resist subjugation by France. This is the same logic that informed our own adoption of the nation-state model, and the same logic that should inform our maintenance of it.

Pathways To Nation-States:

A simple way to understand the concept of nations and nationalism is to think of a family homestead in the rural areas. The family homestead will have its perimeter and a boundary, there will also be a head of the household who sets the rules that the household follows. This naturally occurring idea, is just nations and nationalism writ small. The perimeter is the territory, the family is the nation, the head of the household is the sovereign, and the doctrine for running his family is nationalism. From this example of households, there are two ways that a nation-state can arise.

The first way is that these various households, can agree to come to each other's aid if, for example, a wild animal is attacking one homestead. This is a concept called pooling of sovereignty, whereby you forego some freedoms in pursuit of mutual aid. If households in a large enough territory sign on to such a mutual aid pact, a nation-state can arise from such actions. This is how the nation-state we know as Switzerland came into existence. The three forest Cantons of Uri, Schwyz, and Unterwalden, signed a mutual defence pact on 1st August 1291. They agreed to come to each other's defence if outsiders attacked them. A Canton at the time was basically a village. But through continual ascensions to that mutual aid pact, the nation-state called Switzerland was created. The last Canton to join this mutual aid pact, was the Canton of Jura in 1978.

The second way the nation-state can arise from our households example, is if a strongman arises and forces all the households to be subservient to him. He then makes the rules that everyone has to observe. Still, the strongman must provide protection to these households against external aggression. The households must contribute to the protection though, either through taxation or tributes. This is how most European nation-states came into existence. They started off as Kingdoms, essentially when the local strongman forced all households to subserve his will, then later, became nation-states when other people in the Kingdoms made valid rights claims that had to be accommodated by the strongman.

These two ways are largely how nation-states were formed in Europe. Our case in Africa is slightly different. In our case, the strongman travelled from many thousands of kilometres away, and forced all the households in a territory he had marked out on the map to subserve him. When these households made valid claims for rights, the strongman ignored them on the basis of race, because he was white and "of a superior race." He said, "blacks were his inferiors," and so could not be allowed any rights. The households subjected this way, then took up arms to demand their right to self-determination from the unconscionable foreigner. After victory, these households then proclaimed their nation-state and chose one of their own to be the leader. This, invariably, is how the nation-state was formed in Africa. Having made all these relevant preliminary remarks, let us now turn to how nationalism created our own nation-state, and what it needs to do to sustain it.

Locating Zimbabwe: A Permanent Population On A Defined Territory.

Zimbabwe's borders are well defined, and we have not had any border disputes with any of our four neighbours – Botswana, Mozambique, South Africa and Zambia. These borders came about as a result of the claims that were made for Britain by Cecil Rhodes during

Colonialism. Our geography is largely uncontroversial because the major language group on the Zimbabwe Plateau is within the confines of these borders.

The pragmatism of the OAU in keeping these borders, even though they came through Colonialism, is defensible on the basis of Zimbabwe's borders and relations with her neighbours. Even where people were dismembered from their ethnic groups by these imaginary lines on a map, there has not been any agitation for separation here. Thus, the defined territory our nation claims as its own, are not very controversial. The self-government and recognition criterion for our nation, is satisfied by the fact we are a member of the United Nations. It is the permanent population aspect of our nationhood which requires more discussion.

Perhaps, at this stage, it is useful to reiterate, that while we can trace our ancestors as far back as 200 A.D. on the Zimbabwe Plateau, Zimbabwe did not exist as a unitary nation-state that was disrupted by Colonialism. This is the image most people who have not thought about their nation systematically tend to hold. Scholars have called this contradiction; the objective modernity of nations versus the subjective claims by nationalists that their nations have existed since time immemorial.

The idea that one's nation has always existed, is a powerful romantic image which all nationalists in the world tend to propagate, but a fiction, nonetheless. The truth is quite different, we did not even have a collective name for ourselves as the Shona: we did not need one. It is the Ndebele who gave the Shona this name in their interactions as late as the 19th Century. Again, as Shona and Ndebele now occupying the same territorial space, we also did not even have a collective name for our country.

In fact, it was only around the 1960s that the name Zimbabwe entered our consciousness. Gatsheni-Ndlovu records that the first person to introduce the name Zimbabwe to us, is Michael Mawena, when on breaking up from the National Democratic Party (NDP), he named his new political party the Zimbabwe National Party (ZNP).[28] Matopos was one of the names for our country which entered consideration, when black people on the Zimbabwe Plateau became conscious that they wanted to form their own nation-state.[29]

Zimbabwe, derived from *Dzimbabwe* (Houses of Stone), won the day because, the Great Zimbabwe ruins in the South of the country, carried more significance as a proof of a successful black State from antiquity. But none of this disqualifies us from being a nation. We have always had a permanent population on the Zimbabwe Plateau – the Shona. Later arrivals on the Zimbabwe plateau just mean that we are a syncretic nation. Mind you, there are very few homogenous nations on the globe today. Let me also rehash how we all came to be in the same territory here, because this will inform the discussion on our integration nationalism below.

Arrivals On The Zimbabwe Plateau:

There are two theories in contention when we talk about nativism to a piece of land – Autochthony and Migration theories. The Autochthony Theory holds that the natives of a country "sprang from the ground" they occupy, much as the grass and trees did where we find them. The Migration Theory, on the other hand, holds that everyone is a migrant from somewhere. Pursued to its logical conclusion, this second theory holds that all human beings have their origin in Central Africa, from whence they migrated to all the corners of the Planet.

The majority on the Zimbabwe Plateau are Shona speakers, and the Migration Theory that has attempted to explain their arrival is the Bantu Migration Theory. Based on similarities found in Bantu languages, it contends that Bantu speakers originated in an area around present day Nigeria and Cameroon.[30] Another version of it says the place of origin is Katanga in present day Democratic Republic of Congo. This theory has its merits, but as Zimbabweans we should understand that it has been used politically in the past. The Migration Theory was favoured by the colonial oppressors in Zimbabwe because they wanted to use it to claim they had as much right as anyone to be on the Zimbabwe plateau.

But from as far back as 200BC, early hunter gatherer societies were already on the Zimbabwe Plateau, and by between AD200 to AD500, fixed settlements appeared which very well may have been the first Shona presence on the Zimbabwe Plateau.[31] The weakness of the indigenous people on the Zimbabwe Plateau is that we did not have a written history. Still, written accounts of Portuguese Traders show contact with the Shona people as far back 1500AD. This then places the Shona as the original indigenous people among the people still present on the territory that largely became Zimbabwe when Colonialists drew their borders over Africa.

The other written history of the Zulus' interaction with the Boers in what is now South Africa, also tells us that the Ndebele people under King Mzilikazi, fleeing from the wars with King Tshaka, crossed the Limpopo River and settled at KoBulawayo around 1838. The White Settlers under Cecil Rhodes crossed the Limpopo and raised their flag at Masvingo in 1890. These are the three major groupings whose interactions are still relevant to the people who are currently in Zimbabwe today.

The period of the Federation between Northern Rhodesia (Zambia), Southern Rhodesia (Zimbabwe), and Nyasaland (Malawi), from 1st August 1953 to 31st December 1963, also saw free movement of different groups between the three countries. There is a sizable population of Chewa people, originally from Malawi, in Zimbabwe as a result. Except for the time when Robert Mugabe decried "those without Totems," these people are fully integrated Zimbabweans.

The relationship between the Ndebele and the Shona, in the period before the arrival of the white settler in 1890, was adversarial. The Ndebele raided the Shona for livestock, grain, and women. But the claim that King Lobengula was overlord of the whole Zimbabwe Plateau was a patent falsity. There were parts of Zimbabwe that were insulated from Ndebele raids just by distance alone. The British colonialist just found it convenient to claim King Lobengula was the King of the whole territory to ward off rival claims from other European powers.

It is also possible that the Colonialist believed this to be true given what Ranger says, that: Europeans mistook their invented traditions for holding the same import in Africa.[32] One such mistaken assumption could have been that of a King who ruled over a bounded territory. The truth was that, on the Zimbabwe Plateau, in the 40 years of interaction with the recently arrived Ndebeles, there were parts of Zimbabwe, where people did not care in the least what was decided at King Lobengula's capital in KoBulawayo. Having seen how everyone arrived on the Zimbabwe Plateau, we can now discuss the conditions that awakened national consciousness among the black people.

Nationalism In Zimbabwe:

Nationalism in Zimbabwe conforms to everything I said above about African nationalism: it is a sovereignty over the resources in our territory project. Our nationalism is also a textbook example of the two distinct phases that I said above obtained for African nationalism: Anti-Colonialism and Integration nationalism. Zimbabwe's birth on 18th April 1980 – our Independence Day – came about after a 14 year armed struggle against the white settler minority from Britain. *Chimurenga II*, the war which gave us our independence, was waged between 1966 and 1980.

But the demand for the removal of the foreign white minority regime in our country did not start with *Chimurenga II*. It started with the First Matabele War of 1893 – 4, when King Lobengula realised he had been tricked into signing away his Kingdom, and so went to war to try and drive out the white settlers. This war ended with the defeat of the Ndebele Kingdom and King Lobengula fleeing and dying in exile. The black people of Zimbabwe again tried to drive the white settlers out in our First War of Independence of 1896 – 7. This was *Chimurenga I*, an uprising by both the Shona and Ndebele, which also ended in our defeat.

Again, in 1900, Chief Mapondera in Mashonaland, militarily rose up against the white settlers, but again, this ended in his defeat.[33] In these first wars, there was no equivocation about the goal: the goal was to drive the white settlers from our land completely. But what were the conditions in our country that made us demand liberation from the white settler minority?

Servitude On Our Own Territory:

The people we now call the founding fathers of our nationalism – Robert Mugabe and Joshua Nkomo – are people who successfully led the black majority in fighting against racist white settler colonialism. They led the fight to free us from the servitude under which we had been placed in our own homeland.

The most egregious, and unacceptable imposition of white settler colonialism was the exclusion of blacks from owning land in their own country. This was codified by the 1930 Land Apportionment Act. With this Act, around 51% of the most fertile agricultural land was demarcated as European, and blacks were evicted off that land to Tsetse-fly infested areas with sandy soils. The white settler in our country, copied this practice from what other white settlers did when they displaced the indigenous people in what is now the United

States of America. These areas of poor soils in Zimbabwe, were also called "Reserves," which is how we ended up with the word *Ruzevha* in Shona, which now just means the rural areas.

The promulgated logic of this racist practice in Zimbabwe, was that the blacks were sub-human so could live in harsh climates. The true calculation behind it though was economic: black impoverishment ensured abundant supply of cheap labour to the white settlers' farms and mines. Having been so disenfranchised, rights were further denied by such instruments as the 1934 Industrial Conciliation Act which, for example, "excluded Africans in its definition of workers."[34]

All these discriminatory practices were buttressed by a prohibition of black people's participation in the politics of the country. If black people had been allowed to participate and vote, it is reasonable to assume that they would have voted against the laws and practices that discriminated against them. But, in my looking back into these unfair conditions that prevailed in our country, I was surprised to find out that there was a time when we had accepted this as our fate. There was a time when the few educated blacks in our country only asked whites to recognise them as civilised. In so doing, the few educated blacks showed they thought that the uneducated blacks deserved a life without rights in their own country. I was dismayed to learn that the nationalist spirit was this non-existent, at a period in our history, when white settler minority oppression was at its zenith.

Our Nationalism As Anti-Colonialism:

Michael West has helpfully labelled the stuttering way that our nationalism developed, into these three phases; the proto-nationalist period between the two world wars; the national moment between 1945 to 1948; and the nationalist moment from the late 1950s onwards.[35] These three phases accord with what actually happened in our adoption of nationalism to free our country from Colonialism.

Simply put, there was a time when we were not even aware that we were a nation, then came a time when we realised that we had the ingredients to be a nation; and finally, a time when our nationalism demanded that we have this nation for ourselves.

The romanticisation of our struggle for independence has never shown any hiatus between *Chimurenga I* and *Chimurenga II*. It suggests a linear progression between the two armed uprisings. Thus, I had always believed that after our defeat in *Chimurenga I* in 1897, we went away and perfected our war fighting, then returned to the battlefield in 1966. It appeared this way to me because, the rallying cry for *Chimurenga II*, was what one of the leaders of *Chimurenga I* said during her execution for leading that first uprising. The First *Chimurenga* had happened on the instigation of our Spirit Mediums – Mbuya Nehanda and Kaguvi – who were both executed at the end of the uprising. At her execution, Mbuya Nehanda said these words: *Mapfupa angu achamuka* (My bones shall rise again).

When *Chimurenga II* started, indeed, it was the fulfilment of that prediction. Still, this linear representation misses the fact that there was a time when Colonialism had been accepted as the natural order in our territory by black people. This situation threatened to give us the same perpetual disenfranchisement that has happened to the indigenous people of North America and Australia.

Up until the radicalisation of the 1960s, all our founding leaders were operating "within the political system and sought reforms on a constitutional basis."[36] This was a misstep by our forerunners though, because being a minority, any reforms to the Constitution would have meant the white minority legislating itself out of power. The whites just had no motive to reform their Constitution. I admit, this is only blindingly obvious to us now, because we have the benefit of hindsight. Our forerunners did not have this benefit. We had recently been defeated in all our uprisings, which did not stand well for us imagining any other order of things being possible.

International developments at this time also impacted what the black populations under colonialism could even hope for. Naked Imperialism was very much what held sway in international relations. It was only when the two world wars happened, that any other order became conceivable. The Second World War was even more devastating and weakened the main countries that had Colonies – France and Britain – to the point where they could not dispatch armies to quell rebellion. Having been weakened thus, these two countries had to give freedom to their colonies, whilst ensuring they remained tied in a neo-colonial arrangement to the former coloniser. These new developments in the international arena also impacted what we could think as possible in our own country.

Proto-Nationalism:

The road to our nationalism and nation-state then, begins with the proto-nationalist phase, when blacks could not even conceive of any other way of life than under white rule. O'Meara records that the earliest proto-nationalist organisations existed in Rhodesia in the 1920s. One such organisation was the Rhodesia Native Association (RNA). It only sought to get the educated black elite accommodated by whites. For example, it requested to have educated blacks exempted from Native Pass Laws, and for them to have access to European liquor.[37] Then there was the Rhodesia Bantu Voters Association (RBVA) which also had similar aims. The RBVA's motto was: "Honour all men. Love the Brotherhood. Fear God. Honour the King."[38] The King in question was the King of England. So, exactly like the RNA, the RBVA was also just working to have educated blacks accommodated in a white run system.[39]

The African National Congress in Rhodesia that was founded by Aaron Jaca in 1934, and styled after South African nationalist organizations, was equally unambitious.[40] It was so moderate that its

representatives told the Bledisloe Commission that it had no complaints about the Land Apportionment Act.[41] Others such as the
Mandebele Patriotic Society, also known as Loyal Mandebele Society,
had even more limited ambitions. The Mandebele Patriotic Society
only sought to arrest the decay of traditional Ndebele values, but it
did this by reporting transgressors to the Native Commissioner – a
European.[42] At this stage, Van Velsen has correctly summed up that
the new African elite, was only concerned with getting accepted by
whites "as 'advanced natives' in contrast to the 'uneducated masses.'"[43]

The National Moment:

The next stage on the path to our national consciousness was what
Michael West has called the national moment which happened
around 1945 to 1948. This coincided with the ideas that were promulgated in the Atlantic Charter in 1945: national self-determination
was now a recognised principle of international relations. Of course,
the authors of the Charter being Colonialists themselves, initially
excepted Africa by limiting self-determination to "civilised men."
But the seeds were already sown that would allow black Africa to
demand national self-determination in relation to the Atlantic Charter. Consequently, the British African Voice Association was formed
in 1947 and was led by Benjamin Burombo. It got banned in 1952. It
saw itself as Africans' intermediary with the white government and
wanted to do: "all the things that may be necessary or desirable to
advance Africa in civilisation."[44]

In the 1950s, there was an emergency of Labour Movements that
were demanding slightly more. There was the Reformed Industrial
Council Unions (RICU) led by Charles Mzingeli; the Railways Workers Union (RAWU) of which Joshua Nkomo was Secretary General and had Jason Moyo, Michael Mawema and John Chirimbani
as members; and the African Teachers Association which counted

Robert Mugabe, Ndabaningi Sithole and Leopold Takawira among its members. These organisations failed to achieve their aims because the white government refused to bargain with them.[45] I must repeat that, at this stage, all these organisations were only just seeking less discrimination for the educated black Africans.

The Nationalist Moment:

The Rubicon to what Michael West has called the nationalist moment was crossed in 1955, when the City Youth League (CYL) was formed by George Nyandoro, Edson Sithole, Duduza Chisiza, Henry Hamadziripi, and Stanley Parirewa, with James Chikerema as President.[46] On September 12, 1957, the Youth League called a meeting of all black political associations in the country at which the Southern Rhodesian African National Congress (SRANC/ANC) was founded, with Joshua Nkomo as leader.[47] This is what has earned Joshua Nkomo the moniker Father Zimbabwe, he led the first truly political nationalist organisation in Rhodesia.

The SRANC wanted to establish one man – one vote, it was opposed to discriminatory legislation, especially the Native Land Husbandry Act of 1951.[48] It was very successful in mobilising against the Native Land Husbandry Act as it capitalised on the discontent raised by the way the Act clashed with traditional concepts among the blacks.[49] Its successes and potential led to Prime Minister of the time, Edgar Whitehead, to ban the SRANC in February 1959.[50]

On January 1, 1960, Michael Mawema formed the National Democratic Party (NDP), and it aimed to remove all forms of oppression and to establish democracy in Southern Rhodesia.[51] The NDP of Michael Mawema was the first political party to openly demand majority rule, instead of what had gone before: whereby a few educated blacks requested to be treated better by whites, at the expense of the uneducated masses. Membership of the NDP included Stanlake

Samkange, Enock Dumbutshena, Herbert Chitepo, Tichafa Parirenyatwa, Bernard Chidzero, Joshua Nkomo, Robert Mugabe and Leopold Takawira. Mawema was even trying to circumvent the white minority government in Rhodesia and negotiate the NDP's goals directly with Britain. The NDP was banned in August 1961.

It was at this stage that Michael Mawema formed the Zimbabwe National Party (ZNP), thus giving Zimbabwe its name. Joshua Nkomo also formed his Zimbabwe African People's Union (ZAPU). It was ZAPU that then proclaimed a doctrine that approximates to what I was saying above about self-determination. The doctrine implies a removal of foreign rulers so that the native population can chart their own values they want foreigners to respect as sovereign. The objectives were these:

"(1) to fight for the immediate and total liquidation of imperialism and colonialism, direct or indirect, and to cooperate with any international forces as are engaged in this struggle; (2) to establish a democratic state with a government based on one man – one vote and in which democratic liberties thrive; (3) to foster the spirit of Pan-Africanism in Zimbabwe; (4) to maintain peaceful and friendly relations with such nations as are peaceful and friendly; (5) to eliminate economic exploitation and to struggle for economic prosperity in order to achieve the greatest happiness of the greatest number; (6) to foster the best in African culture and thereby develop the basis of desirable social order."[52]

The above objectives, show us a watershed moment when the black nationalists realised that the whites were not willing to give them even the minimal acceptance they wanted. The only way forward would be to mobilise the black population educated and uneducated alike, as their fates were intertwined, and then work together to remove the white oppressor. This is what Michael West's 'nationalist moment' means to me: when the black elites realised that their fates and that of the masses were inextricably linked.

Again, at this stage, the thought of violently removing the whites was not being entertained. The emerging black nationalist only wanted to change the government, but everyone was still welcome to carry on in the country. It was just a change of system and multiracial society that was envisaged. It would take Ian Smith's recalcitrance to tip the black population onto a war footing where the only solution was to drive the white man out of the country. Ian Smith made the Unilateral Declaration of Independence (UDI) from Britain on 11 November 1965, to forestall Britain's plans to give majority rule as was the trend with all its colonies.

This fact, and the banning of all black political parties led to the black people waging an armed liberation struggle – *Chimurenga II* – from 1966 onwards. ZAPU had been banned on September 20, 1962, leading to a split in its ranks as Ndabaningi Sithole formed the Zimbabwe African Nationalist Union (ZANU), while Joshua Nkomo formed the People's Caretaker Council (PCC). ZANU was banned on 26th August 1964, leaving the only route for redress being an armed liberation struggle. The White Settler then capitulated and attended the 1979 Lancaster House Peace talks in Great Britain which ushered in a black majority ruled country on 18th April 1980. This then was how Anti-Colonialism created our nation. At independence, Integration nationalism then took over this task.

Nationalism As Integration:

What the nationalist moment should have revealed to black people in Zimbabwe should have been this: that it did not matter if you were Shona or Ndebele, educated or uneducated, your fate under colonialism was still the same. Just on the basis of skin colour we were denied rights in our own country. When we mobilised for the liberation struggle, we mobilised only based on skin colour. This is the only thing that should matter for our belonging.

But unfortunately, the lived experience of our nation is that even when we were fighting the liberation war, we soon appeared to split into largely tribal based political parties. ZAPU and its military wing – the Zimbabwe People's Revolutionary Army (ZIPRA) – drew its support and cadres from among the Ndebeles, while ZANU and its military wing – the Zimbabwe African National Liberation Army (ZANLA) – drew mainly from the Shona. Tribe or ethnicity though, was not the main fault line, as I will make clear in the Address discussing Gukurahundi. But for our current discussion, in accordance with the public's perception, I am treating it as if tribe and ethnicity was the main fault line.

It is regrettable that we fought among ourselves, both during the armed part of the struggle and even during the mobilisation stage of our politics. One of the reasons why ZANU and ZAPU/ PCC were banned in the 1960s, was the political violence between the black supporters of the two parties. During the war, there were even exchanges of gunfire between ZANLA and ZIPRA. This carried on into independence, resulting in Gukurahundi between 1981 to 1987: the subject of the Sixth Address in this book. Such differences in Africa, have necessitated a phase of Integration nationalism, after independence was attained through Anti-Colonialism nationalism.

Regardless of these differences, we are still emphatically a nation if we look at the definition of nation we settled on above. We do have a defined territory, a historic population, with its own government in place, and our nationhood is confirmed by our membership of the United Nations. It is just that are a syncretic society, but what country apart from Japan, has one ethnicity?

This point of our being a syncretic society, is what necessitates Integration nationalism. At the present moment, one of the complaints from the minority groups is that the country has only ever had a Shona leader. Again, the perception is that people are voting on tribal and ethnic lines, and some people actually do. It should not be like this. Integration nationalism can correct this anomaly. It can do so by urgently defining our national identity and values, and in time, whoever embodies those values, will be voted into office despite which ethnicity they will come from. Our task as nationalists, is to devise ways by which, all other identities other than the national one, lose their potency.

Our story of Integration nationalism so far has tried this, with notable failures and successes on the way. But the missteps are to be expected as long as we understand that the task of running humanity's affairs is never completed. It is a Sisyphean ordeal if you like, in that it lasts an eternity, and setbacks will sometimes occur. Any reverses that will occur, have to be offset by an even more concerted effort towards the goal we want.

Reconciliation:

The first act of our Integration nationalism was with reconciliation with whites. On Independence Day, Robert Mugabe, voted into office as the first Prime Minister of Zimbabwe 1980, appealed for whites to stay on in his "let bygones be bygones" speech. He matched his words with actions by appointing members of all parties into his cabinet. But the white settlers did not take to heart the spirit of reconciliation, for they continued sabotaging the new Zimbabwe. The white settlers remained racist, sabotaged the economy, and some even supported Apartheid South Africa's destabilization of Zimbabwe. Our attempt to reconcile with the white settler minority finally failed in 2000 because of their refusal to have equitable land redistribution.

Reconciliation between the blacks in ZAPU and ZANU did not last that long after independence. Suspicions between ZAPU and

ZANU continued even during the ceasefire, leading to Gukurahundi as early into our independence as 1982. The Unity Accord of 22nd December 1987 was when the reconciliation between ZAPU and ZANU was made in earnest. This was an example of our Integration nationalism trying to resolve the division between the black people. An attempt to erase even the perceived ethnic cleavages. I have reserved a separate chapter to discuss this matter in full in this volume. In this current Address, I am more interested in talking about what can be achieved by our Integration nationalism. Success for me, will be when we will have banal nationalism in Zimbabwe. We still have many steps to take before achieving a time when everyone will be loyal to the nation before ethnicity, guild, or skin colour. But before we look at those steps, let us also look at the nation's most urgent question given to us by our peculiar history.

The National Question:

Anyone who studies the national question, soon realises that it is really a question of belonging and participating in the benefits of the national economy. If we look at Rwanda up until 1994, the national question there was that of a whole section of the population that had been excluded from participating in the economy. The Hutu government in power from the 1960s to 1994, had deliberate policies in place to prevent the Tutsi minority from participating in politics and the economy of the country. Those Tutsis in exile were also banned from returning.

South Africa's national question under Apartheid was also the question of black people being denied their full rights as citizens. From 1893 to 1980, the national question on our own territory was similar to that in South Africa under Apartheid. The black people in Zimbabwe were excluded by the Constitution from enjoying the benefits of citizenship. The only justification for this exclusion was their skin colour. The most grievous way this manifested itself in Zimbabwe was in land alienation. As recent as after the Second World War, blacks were still being evicted from their land, which in turn was given as reward to White British veterans of that war against Adolf Hitler. This is how it happened that the most potent national question at independence was the land question. The land question then, manifested itself in 6000 white farmers owning 70% of all arable land, while 7 million black people were crammed into the remaining 30%. I discuss this matter in full in this volume in the Address titled – Land Redistribution.

Invariably, the national question has an international dimension. The national question in our country was thus tied in with the interests of powerful countries. These powerful countries wanted to protect the rights and privileges given to white settlers by the historic injustice that was Colonialism. They wanted white settlers to continue owning large tracts of Zimbabwe's land while the black majority remained land hungry. The interests of the international community in our national question were fully exposed when we attempted to resolve our national question. When we took our land back from the white settlers in the year 2000, we placed ourselves at loggerheads with international institutional racism. This is how the United States, the United Kingdom and Australia got involved in a matter that the United Nations explicitly stated was purely a domestic affair of a sovereign State.

The racist element of the white countries' intervention in Zimbabwe's domestic affairs is easy to see. Do not forget that when Ian Smith made the Unilateral Declaration of Independence in 1965, Britain said it would not send troops to Rhodesia because that would mean kith fighting kin – read, white people fighting other white people. When we went to war ourselves on our own behalf, Britain still contrived to protect the white settler's unfair privileges. That we could not resolve the land question once and for all at independence as we had hoped to, was due to the fact that, when the white settlers were losing, Britain conspired to protect the rights of the white settlers at the Lancaster House talks. At those negotiations, Britain reserved 20 parliamentary seats for the white minority. Only white candidates could contest and hold those 20 seats in parliament.

The above was done so that the whites could block any legislation that required unanimity before being passed. Britain also ensured that the white settlers would not be dispossessed of the land they stole by using the device of a 10 year moratorium on land redistribution. It was a short-sighted policy, predicated on the thinking that blacks would forget their land grievances if they were given other rights. But this wishful thinking did not pan out. This is also how you can discover the objective national question, no contrivance other than resolving it will work.

The new black majority government tried to follow the prescription of the Lancaster House Agreement to the letter. But the pressures the unresolved national question kept producing, meant the population would not tolerate the unfair precepts of the Lancaster House Agreement. It is for this reason that the government played follow-up to the masses when the demand for land reached its logical conclusion. The Svosve people's 1997 occupation of the land they had been dispossessed of by the white settler was the start of the inevitable. This mass protest reached its apogee with the countrywide land occupations of 2000, which forced the government to embark on the Fast Track Land Reform Programme (FTLRP).

Some Economists have also sought to discuss the international dimension of our national question in terms of the centre – periphery world systems theory. In that theory, the world is set up in a manner that the centre – former colonial power – still exploits the periphery – former colonies. In this conception, the way we addressed our national question, threatened to disrupt that relationship and, as well, have a demonstration effect for other peripheral countries. It is a defensible thesis, seeing as even the mighty United States has gone on to publicly state that Zimbabwe poses an unusual threat to its foreign policy. But for our purposes here, it is enough to just posit that international institutional racism sprang into action in defence of unfair white privilege. The intricate nature of this privilege and how it had continued to benefit our former colonisers, I will leave for the Marxists among our co-nationals to expound.

My fellow countrywomen and countrymen, there are some people who have thought that our national question has always been fixing the economy. People who do not relate the national question from land to the economy have not fully understood the interconnectedness of the two. Study any feudal society anywhere in history, and you will find that the powerful there, were powerful on the basis of land ownership. The landless were the serfs, toiling for hours for pittances, their fate completely dependent on the landowner.

This is the same system the white settler introduced in Zimbabwe. Over a period of nearly 100 years, owning the land here gave whites the power to pass racially discriminatory laws. The result was economic empowerment of whites at the expense of the majority blacks. Educational opportunities were also limited for blacks, meaning they would always remain in a position of poverty. But, even with such handicaps in place, the white settler government still sought to tilt the economic playing field in favour of whites further. It was not enough that whites had access to government loans and infrastructure development grants that blacks did not have. The Maize Control Act of 1934 was a piece of legislation designed to prejudice black growers in favour of white farmers.

These issues, taken in their totality, express the national question in Zimbabwe between 1890 and 2020 when Fast Track Land Reform happened. We were given a feudal society by our peculiar history, solving this feudal society problem was thus the national question. The national question in Zimbabwe restated then, has always been this: how we needed to award economic participation to everyone on the basis of merit. But this could not be done as long as the inequality in land ownership given to us by 100 years of Colonialism was not addressed. The national question to resolve then, has always been the land question. Once that has been resolved we can then look to other questions that are hampering the nation's development. We could have dealt with the other questions sooner, if the white settlers had not lobbied their countries of origin to place Sanctions on Zimbabwe. Thus, addressing the other questions had to be put on hold while we fought this resistance from international institutional racism.

In terms of belonging, the idea of Zimbabwe, even during the armed struggle, has always that Zimbabwe was for everyone who lived in it. To the nationalist in Zimbabwe, the white person has never been the enemy per se, just those who still hold on to the racist attitudes of the settler minority we went to war against. To this effect, the black majority government proclaimed a policy of national reconciliation at independence in 1980. The idea behind this policy was to have a multiracial, multi-ethnic nation where everyone had equality.

But, unfortunately, the hard core racist element of the white settlers did not accept even the letter of this policy. They continued as if nothing had changed, telling blacks on their farms that they were still in Rhodesia and that if the black workers wanted to go to Zimbabwe, all they had to do was leave the perimeter fence of the farm. By the year 2000, when Fast Track Land Reform Programme was instituted, this hard core racist element was to be found in the Commercial Farmers Union (CFU). The CFU was a coterie of 4 000 white farmers who wielded disproportionate economic power in Zimbabwe. This power could not be controlled by legal devices, so had to be disbanded by the redress of the land imbalances we took as nationalists. Outside the CFU, other whites might have been racist, but this could be controlled by legal devices. It also just may have happened that, the dismantling of the privileges of the racist white farmers had a demonstration effect; instances of racist whites are now almost unheard of in Zimbabwe.

It would be remiss if I do not state that the national question is also not static, once you solve one problem, new questions emerge. We should remain alert to this so that our solutions to problems at any given time, reflects the objective reality we are dealing with. After 20 years, the racist white settler has now accepted that land reform is really irreversible. With this question finally settled, we can now focus on the other questions that have arisen since we took action to resolve the land question. I think our task now is to repair the economy and also to articulate the national identity and values we want every citizen to be loyal to.

I am not competent in economics, so I will leave the repairing the economy discussion to the people we, as a country, sent to school to study Economics. I am more competent in discussing how national identity and values advance national causes. We are also in good company in articulating our national identity and values. European countries make new citizens take citizenship tests and swearing in ceremonies where they have to swear that they will uphold the values of the particular European society. These European nations are able to do this because the core values they want people to be loyal to are well known. As nationalists in Zimbabwe, it is thus our task to define the values and the national identity that we want.

Our National Identity

Montserrat Guibernau defines national identity as "a collective sentiment based upon the belief of belonging to the same nation and sharing most of the attributes that make it distinct from other nations."[53] She then says national identity has these five dimensions: psychological, cultural, territorial, historical and political.[54] As far as I can see, these dimensions are just the sources of national identity where, for example, the psychological dimension just refers to national consciousness. The cultural dimension refers to a people's identity emanating from their culture. Thus, the difficulty of articulating a single national identity for us, comes from the fact that we are a syncretic society.

This fact led Mlambo to remark that we cannot talk of a Zimbabwean culture, but Zimbabwean cultures instead.[55] He concedes though, that for the Shona being the dominant tribe, most of the dominant cultural practices are Shona practices. But still, as culture is one of the sources of national identity, where many cultures exist, a single national identity cannot be articulated. Moreover, even where a single national identity exists, it also changes over time. Thus, I also concede to this fact, that it is difficult to have a single national identity in Zimbabwe.

But there is a way out of this difficulty of having a uniform national identity, insofar as national identity implies sameness. Antony D. Smith says that "the nationalist does not require that individual members be alike, only that they should feel an intense bond of solidarity and therefore act in unison on all matters of national importance."[56] Therefore, we should not seek to create an image of a quintessential Zimbabwean – that is impossible. I accept, therefore, that Zimbabwe does not, and cannot, have a single national identity unique to itself. We will always find some similarities between people of different nations just by virtue of us all being members of the human race.

There are just some values all societies hold in common, even before they had contact with each other. The prohibition against stealing is one such value. This is also what makes the Bible such an important book, its 10 Commandments are mostly what all rational beings would agree are excellent societal values. This is also the bottom-line in what our national identity ought to be: it has to be morally defensible. We have to allow all different cultural practices and identities to continue, except where they are a direct threat to national security, are against human decency, or against the spirit of national unity.

Indeed, the dimension of national identity any nation can really control, is the political dimension. The political dimension of national identity does refer to the shared duties citizens have, and the loyalty they owe to their nation-state. Here then, the government is empowered by the Constitution to produce and maintain the symbols of the nation: flags, national anthems, and nationally important days.

An educational curriculum designed to produce good citizens is also another way that national identity is created. We can therefore, as nationalists, produce images that the nation will want to identify with regardless of ethnicity. As the government in power in our country at the moment is the same nationalist one that waged the liberation war, the images it settles on must be informed by the *Chimurenga* Wars. Our drive for unity must be always informed by the result we achieved when we united against white settler colonialism. The positive values from the Liberation Struggle should be given pride of place in our national image.

Challenges To National Identity Formulation:

As nationalists, I think we are all for conservatism and decency in our national identity. But I have to concede another difficulty we will face in our task to articulate conservative values. There are now many more forces that have been arrayed against conservative values everywhere than in previous ages. As far as I can see, the concept of traditional values has been eroded irrevocably. The internet age has reward systems that are far better than what we can offer individuals who espouse those values which we think should accord with our national identity. For example, the sex tape, which just a few years ago was a source of shame, has been shown to propel an individual to fame and financial security. This financial security is more desirable than society's pat on the back. Shame, which used to restrain an individual's behaviour is, therefore, no longer a restraint.

The government's task is not easy either in promoting conservative behaviour. We used to have a National Censorship Board that used to filter indecent content in foreign films, but now, with Netflix, all this content is now being delivered uncensored. The difficulty here then is that the stories that are told by these platforms become what those who watch them aspire to, no matter how decadent they are. These are the forces which the person concerned about national values and decency finds himself arrayed against.

Also, the government alone is not the source of national identity formation, nor should it be. The leading lights in our society can also define and espouse the values that other Zimbabweans will aspire to. Our arts and literature can also furnish what our national identity ought to be. One other source of national identity is a nation's literature. Fiction can create identity if the population identifies with the protagonists and even start behaving as the protagonists did. All these ideas can be introduced by our elites in the arts, sports, and education. We can only hope that such elites in our society produce works that accord with the national identity we want. The government's role will then just be to ensure that the values being promulgated accord with our Constitution and human decency. It is the same in countries that are our competitor countries, whereby multiculturalism and many identities are allowed, but with prohibitions on things such as child marriages.

Despite all the difficulties in articulating a single national identity, I still want to suggest which story we can rely on as the anchor of our national identity. I suggest this story because, as nationalists in power today, it is our duty to produce a national identity that accords with the tenets of the spirit that created our nation. I also say this in the hope that, even if a uniform national identity is impossible, we can still promulgate a national identity that 51% of our population will be proud to proclaim as their own. On this count, I want to suggest that our national identity should be anchored in the values of the armed liberation struggle. It is these values that gave us our nation, and we can depend on them to perpetuate our nation as we imagined it.

Zimbabwe's Foundational Truth:

Literature can be both the repository and manufacturer of national identity. Most nations have relied on their foundational myths and epic poems as sources of their national identity. The Iliad, an epic poem by Homer, was said to be the text that Alexander the Great swore by, while The Aeneid is the foundational epic for the Italian civilisation. These stories though fictitious, furnished valuables lessons and aspirational qualities to these nations.

In the absence of such epic poems and foundational myths for our nation, I must make a tentative proposal that our national identity should ensure from the ethos of *Chimurenga*. Where its ethos were not sound, we as successors of the nationalists who fought in those wars, have the right to correct them. The basic building blocks are there. It is just a matter of using hindsight to correct all the mistakes that were made by the nationalists, and so forge our national identity out of the story of the liberation struggle. The story of *Chimurenga* is suitable because, it is a story of when we put our petty differences aside to defeat a foreign invader. It is a story of heroism and selflessness; values we want our co-nationals to hold.

Ideally, the task of creating a strong national identity starts with a foundational myth. I was at pains in the Second Address to show that the Bible is a foundational myth of the ancient Israelites. This is because all nations have, or ought to have, a foundational story from whence their chief characteristics are drawn. The older nations can rely on fictional accounts such as that of Greece and its 10 year siege of Troy told in Homer's epic poem – The Iliad. The story was manifestly a fiction, seeing as its chief protagonist – Achilles – was born out of a union between a mortal and a goddess. His mother was Thetis – a Sea goddess. Thetis, concerned about Achilles' mortality, had roasted him over a fire as a baby every night, then dunked him in the River Styx to make him immortal. But because the goddess was holding him by his leg when she dunked him in the River Styx, the part she was holding and did not get touched by the waters became his vulnerability. This is how we got the phrase Achilles' Heel, which means a strong entity's weak point.

Further proof that The Iliad is fiction is that the war where Achilles showed his heroic qualities, also happened because a god had decided to reduce the population. So, he instigated the war to that end. The god in question was Zeus, an imaginary character the ancient Greeks believed was the strongest of all their gods.

Still, the story of the siege of Troy, though fictitious, inspired the real ancient Greeks: Alexander the Great was said to keep a copy of The Iliad with him on his conquests. He had been instructed by Aristotle to emulate Achilles. Alexander the Great went on to achieve great things: he ruled an empire that stretched from Africa to Asia. He is a real person the Greeks today definitely want to emulate, though he learnt his chief characteristics from a fictional character – Achilles. This is exactly what I mean when I say a nation's literature can be both the manufacturer and repository of its national identity. People want to identity with excellence, and where none exists, literature tends to furnish that excellence.

The siege of Troy was so popular in antiquity that its derivatives became foundational myths of other nations. Brutus, who founded Britain and built New Troy - now London - after vanquishing the nation of giants who lived there, is presented as another survivor of that fictitious war. The foundational story of Britain which carries this story is Geoffrey of Monmouth's *Historia Regum Britanniae* (The History of the Kings of Britain). The truth is that it is a pseudo-historical tale. In Virgil's epic poem – The Aeneid – Aeneas also survived that fictious war and went on and founded the Latin/Italian civilisation. What I am driving at here is that the older nations' foundational stories were mostly fiction. But the newer nations can only rely on true accounts for what gives them their national characteristics. Modern people have so many tools at their disposal to question fantastic stories such as those told by Homer in The Iliad.

So, for tenable sources of our foundational story, we have to look to the wars of liberation we fought. While most other national identities have been formulated on the basis of their foundational myths, ours will have to be formulated on a foundational truth. As Zimbabwe is only just over 40 years old, I think the main foundational story to rival the Greeks' The Iliad is that of *Chimurenga I* and *II*. Our foundational truth will be the way our Anti-Colonialism united us to fight off an unconscionable foreigner who had enslaved us on our own land. The values that our forebearers held in this regard were admirable. Even without formal education, just three years after the white settler arrived, our forebearers had already taken up arms to resist the outsider. We did lose our way for a while, but the spirit returned when we took up arms again in *Chimurenga II* to liberate our country. This then is a story of how black people from all persuasions, finally realised that their differences did not matter to the colonialist. Only the skin colour mattered.

From the *Chimurenga* story, our creed then is resisting foreign domination and defending our natural resources. This is how we should proceed with our Integration nationalism. Nothing else should matter except that we are united in our sovereignty over our resources, and that we want to remain free from foreign subjugation. These are the values of *Chimurenga*: we are descendants of a proud people who objected to being imprisoned in their own lands. These values of freedom loving, fortitude, courage, and stubbornness against foreign subjugation, should supply the building blocks for our national character. We can have minor quarrels amongst ourselves, what family does not? But as soon as foreigners threaten our resources and sovereignty, we will band together to expel them.

I have said above that Anti-Colonialism gave us our nation and nationalism, so there is no shame then in taking the one thing that united us as the source of our chief characteristics. In 700 years, this story will have the same tinge of religious doctrine that our competitor countries have in their foundational stories. I myself am a product of *Chimurenga* literature, having been too young to know what went on during the Second *Chimurenga*. All my knowledge of our history came from the *Chimurenga* Shona literature that we had to read in primary school.

A lot of academics have criticised this literature as praise songs which did not pay critical attention to the events of *Chimurenga II*. I do not have a problem with that literature: all foundational stories tend to focus on the positives of the people in question. Given the nearly 100 years of distorted history produced by the Colonialist, it was necessary at that stage to present our stories that way. It was by reading this literature that I managed to place myself in the feet of the fighters of *Chimurenga II*. It was from reading these stories that I discovered to which side I belonged. With the passing of time and my maturing, I have since made the effort on my own to critically reflect on the liberation struggle. This Address then, is also a product of my critical reflection on the armed struggle.

My suggestion that *Chimurenga* be the foundational story that anchors our national identity is also an easy suggestion to make. I have made it because we have a government that has been working towards this all along. The First Republic between 1980 and 2017 was aware of the need to use *Chimurenga* as our foundational story. We then got distracted from this task by the exigencies of fighting Sanctions, as well as by infighting to succeed President Robert Mugabe as head of government. Luckily, the War Veterans of *Chimurenga II* succeeded in that fight. The Second Republic led by President Emmerson Mnangagwa came to power on 24th November 2017. This means a continuation of the legacy of the liberation struggle. This will ensure the much needed continuity. I do not think the younger faction that also wanted to replace President Mugabe were as committed to the values of the *Chimurenga* story.

The Second Republic has already achieved many milestones in memorialising the *Chimurenga* story. All the things I would have suggested in shoring up *Chimurenga* as our foundational story are already being done. The most outstanding thing in premising our national identity on the *Chimurenga* story was the removal of foreign names that we had on our buildings and institutions. Changing the country's name from Rhodesia to Zimbabwe in 1980, was part of the reclaiming and creating our national identity. But we did not go far enough as far as removing colonial names was concerned. When the Second Republic took over, all our military bases which had foreign names were changed to those of the heroes of *Chimurenga II*. For example, Defence Forces HQ, which was named KGVI after King George the 6th of England, was renamed Josiah Magama Tongogara Barracks on 6th December 2017. It had been remiss, as far as our national identity is concerned, that our military barracks still had colonial names. This should also be done in schools and suburb names, but you will find pushback among our own people who like foreign names. This is another challenge to national identity I forgot to mention earlier on. Rwanda has managed this well, all the cities and suburbs have Kinyarwanda names. We should find out how Rwanda managed this, given people's propensity to mistakenly think that foreign names are the height of sophistication.

Also, go to every country in the world, and you will find imposing monuments that tell the story of the nation's heroism. This is the image visitors and the people there will hold of that nation. With the installation of the Monument to Mbuya Nehanda in Harare, the Second Republic has also shown that it understands how to create our national identity from the *Chimurenga* story. Monuments to all the heroes of *Chimurenga* are being built and must continue to be built. The only point of difference between myself and the government is that I think the monuments should be on a grander scale.

The Second Republic has also just instituted national awards which recognise individuals impacting society the most. These awards are an excellent thing for national identity in that they reward people exhibiting the positive behaviour we want for our nation. The creation of the national dress under the Second Republic is also important for national identity. The problem of a national dress has been with us for the duration of our existence. Even under the First Republic, attempts were unsuccessfully made to introduce a national dress. I think here we need to get the best designers to create something people will find irresistible. People want to associate with excellence, an excellent design will compel them to adopt it.

On the question of our national unity, the Second Republic has also revisited the disturbances in Matabeleland so as to find a more lasting solution. The First Republic had settled the question of ethnic divisions with the Unity Accord of 22nd December 1987. This was one of the great steps our Integration nationalism took. It had all the leanings of the *Chimurenga* spirit I said should guide us in what our nation ought to be. But new information coming from conflict resolution experts, suggests that there should be compensation and other mechanism in addressing the issue. So, the Second Republic has reinstituted a commission to look into the matter. This can only strengthen our nation.

Conclusion:

My fellow countrywomen and countrymen, in this Address, I have tried to answer all the questions pertaining to our nationalism. I did this exercise as someone who wanted to know these things for himself. An era is now coming to an end as the people who fought in the armed struggle are now passing away. I felt that those of us who will continue their legacy should understand everything around how our nation came into existence. We need to do this so that we can articulate this history better as nationalists.

This Address was primarily aimed at fellow nationalists so that we understand our condition as it precisely is, not as propaganda and other misrepresentations would have it. This is a useful exercise in that, knowing exactly what our problems and prospects are, we can act within that reality. We also have to own our narrative, and the way to do this, is to know our history ourselves exactly as it happened. Secondarily, I also wanted to explain our history to outsiders who may not have heard our story from our point of view.

My starting point was that I know that I am a nationalist because I agree and identify with the aims of the liberation struggle. I also agree with the policies pursued by the armed liberation struggle parties after independence. But beyond this convergence of thoughts, I had no dogmas that would not change if my research showed otherwise. Indeed, had my research discovered that we are not a nation, I would have presented those findings to you.

My research confirmed that we are a nation as we have always stated. In an international system of nation-states, this is also the only way to be masters of our resources. Our nationalism is that habit and doctrine that reproduces our nation and sustains our sovereignty over our resources. We should not be tricked into thinking of our nationalism as a vice, it is a virtue. All nation-states in existence rely on nationalism for their continued existence, but their nationalism has since become banal nationalism over time. This is also the path we are on, and we must stay on it until everyone identifies with the nation before any other loyalties. We do not have to be exactly the same, we should just converge with each other on issues of national importance. There can be nothing more important than sovereignty over our resources and remaining free from foreign subjugation. These are things we can only actualize if we are a united nation.

Address IV.
Zimbabwe's National Interest.

"Nations act on a plan totally selfish. The very essence of patriotism consists in preferring the good of our own country to the good of any other" – William Jenks, Memoir of the Northern Kingdom.

"WHAT THEN IS TIME? If no one asks me, I know what it is. If I wish to explain it to him who asks, I do not know." St. Augustine of Hippo, a very able thinker, said the above words, in utter despair at the difficulties he faced in trying to explain a seemingly straightforward word like time. We all use the same word every day without any difficulty in understanding each other. It is only when someone asks you to explain what time is, that you realise that it is actually a very complicated concept.

It is exactly the same for me with the term national interest: I use the term very comfortably every day. But here, when I find myself having to explain what it is to others, the term causes me some difficulties. Still, explain this term I must, for what follows logically from what I have argued in the Address preceding this one, that we are a nation, is a discussion of our national interest.

To be sure, defining the term itself is not the problem, international relations scholarship has already defined the term. National interest just means the interest of the community in question – nation. It is the question that arises after the definition that is problematic: can 14 million people have the exact same interest? You see, different people conceive the national interest differently. Even in the same government, or business elite circle, individuals will have different ideas on how best to pursue the national interest. These different ideas on how to pursue the national interest, are also testaments to what each person thinks is the true national interest.

Furthermore, even actions agreed upon, and taken in the national interest, can also have detrimental effects on the nation, when the policy environment reacts to them. It is this difficulty of reconciling the millions of stakeholders' viewpoints, and the uncertainty of the policy environment, that makes national interest a difficult concept.

Given these difficulties then, the best I can do in this Address, is to set out all the parameters of the national interest as they are understood in international relations scholarship. Having done that, I will then state what the nationalist perspective conceives Zimbabwe's national interest to be. Given our history, I think the nationalist conception of the national interest approximates to our true national interest.

You see again, all countries' foreign policy pronouncements are similar: they all essentially say that it is their national interest to have physical security, maintain their territorial integrity, and achieve economic development. This is exactly as prescribed by international relations scholarship. But, beyond this similarity in declarations, other factors intervene and dictate what turns out to be each country's true national interest. Sudan in 2011, found out that maintaining its territorial integrity was no longer in its true national interest. While Zimbabwe in 2000, went ahead with the correction of the land ownership injustices inherited from Colonialism, despite the threat of economic ruin.

What all this tells us is that, beyond the generic foreign policy declarations, the national interest is also dictated to countries by other factors, chiefly their history, values, and capabilities. So, while our national interest is to always have physical security, to maintain our territorial integrity and, to develop economically, there are issues from our history that can trump these "givens" of our national interest declarations. Land Reform, for example, was done in deference to a dictate from our history. The same history also dictated to us that it was in our national interest to deploy troops to Mozambique between 1982 and 1992. This was done despite the short-term economic cost to Zimbabwe this deployment was expected to exact. I will expand upon these two examples below, as they are very instructive on how our vital national interest was dictated to us by the "history factor," despite what dry international relations scholarship prescribes.

Relying on the same parameters of the national interest from international relations scholarship, and the above mentioned intervening factors, we can also do another exercise in the discussion of our country's true national interest. We can also talk about the times when we were not forced by national interest considerations into foreign policy actions that ended up being detrimental to the country. The Democratic Republic of Congo (DRC) Troop Deployment of 1998 to 2002, is one such example. I will also expand upon it below, juxtaposed against our Land Reform and The Beira Corridor Deployment. I will do this to show that, unlike the other two examples, the DRC Troop Deployment does not qualify as an action that was taken in our national interest.

For brevity's sake, in this Address, I am relying on just these above three examples to illustrate Zimbabwe's national interest dynamics, but other examples can also apply. Going forward, we should also do this same exercise with any of our major international relations concerns, to determine whether they pass the 'national interest test,' before we take action.

As far as I can see then, our country's national interest, is discoverable by looking at all the prescriptions given by international relations scholarship on the subject. Our true national interest, however, is discoverable by looking at how our country's history, values, and capabilities, currently interact with those same international relations scholarship prescriptions.

Foreign Policy:

The method all nations use to pursue their national interests is their foreign policy. What is foreign policy? Foreign policy is the articulation of national interests and the means chosen to secure those interests, both material and ideational, in the international arena.[57] While foreign policy declarations are a guide to what a nation conceives as its national interest, further scrutiny by others is still required. Even the most well-intentioned practitioners will misconceive their national interest or, pursue policies inimical to the national interest.

The national interest then, stated as end goals of foreign policy, can be used by an engaged citizenry to analyse the adequacy of a nation's foreign policy goals. As Zimbabweans, from whatever political persuasion, it is necessary we also fully understand what is involved in the formulation of our foreign policy goals. This way we can challenge any policies that will be detrimental to the country or, conversely, understand the necessity of the same policies.

The Essence Of The National Interest:

Admiral Mike Mullen, when he was the United States Chairman of the Joint Chiefs of Staff, best summed up the national interest for me. In an Al Jazeera interview, he said that; "in my 40 years of service, the one constant I have observed everywhere, is that people want to raise their children in conditions of peace and prosperity." This is the essence of the national interest; provide peace and prosperity for your people, and you have achieved the national interest. I could even end this Address here, but as with most things, the devil is always in the details. In a world of nations and finite resources, pursuing the national interest is the art of continually navigating competing interests, both domestically and internationally. It is this factor that makes it necessary that I further examine what is our national interest.

Still, the essence of the national interest lies in the provision of economic prosperity and physical security. While these two factors – economic prosperity and physical security – reinforce each other, they can also undermine each other. Economic prosperity allows us to have the wherewithal for our physical security, and physical security allows economic activity to happen – the virtuous cycle. Conversely, where economic prosperity is absent, we also will not have the means to provide for our physical security – the vicious cycle. Thus, leaving aside for now, what I have called the intervening factors of history, values, and capability, the essence of our national interest is achieving that balance which ensures that our economic prosperity and physical security reinforce each other. I believe that, stripped to its bare bones, this is all our national interest amounts to.

But, again, as I clearly stated above, this straightforward view of the national interest gets impacted by other factors which make the pursuit of the national interest quite a Sisyphean endeavour for all countries. This will become more evident once we have defined the national interest and tried to answer the questions antecedent to the definition.

The Meaning Of National Interest:

The conflation of 'national' and 'interest' in this term, signals to us that this is what concerns, what makes a difference to, or is important to a nation.[58] Put another way, the national interest is, to the nation, what everything that sustains life is, to an individual. There is no choice but to pursue it. As an individual breathes, eats, shelters, and works to remain alive, so too does a nation pursue its national interest: all those things that will ensure its continuity. We can actually think of the national interest as each human being's needs writ large: in pursuing its national interest, the nation is just pursuing those ends that cater to its population's collective needs.

Alexander Wendt, essentially agreed with the biological metaphor I have used above, when he stated that the nation has these "four needs: physical survival, autonomy, economic well-being, and collective self-esteem."[59] Human beings have the exact same needs. Physical survival and autonomy just mean that nations pursue policies that ensures their territorial integrity and self-determination. Zimbabwe, having been subjected to Colonialism, will be very sensitive to the issue of territorial integrity and self-determination. Our history is the factor that looms large on this aspect of our national interest.

Economic well-being just refers to running a viable economy. While collective self-esteem refers to every country's desire to be respected by its peers. This particular aspect of the national interest may not be as potent as it was in the earlier iterations of the national interest. When the world was composed of Kingdoms and City States, an insult to the ruler would have been grounds to go to war over. In the modern era, I have yet to hear of a country that went to war purely over mere insults.

Another aspect to also keep in mind in the definition of the national interest, is the foreign – domestic distinction of our interests. Governments do pursue the interest of their nations in both the international and domestic spheres. The foreign aspect of this pursuit is what we call the 'national interest,' while the domestic aspect can be called the 'public interest.' Still, the two are very contiguous, with expenditure on defence, for example, having a bearing on prosperity at home.[60] Also, our Land Reform, a purely domestic 'public interest' matter, quickly became a 'national interest' matter, when countries with vested interests in Zimbabwe intervened with Sanctions.

Lastly, in defining the term, we should also be aware that there is a hierarchy to every country's pursuit of the national interest. Hans Morgenthau presented that hierarchy as consisting largely of vital and non-vital interests. For the purposes of our discussion here, vital interests are all those non-negotiable interests that the nation should be willing to go to war over, while the non-vital ones are that which are open to some compromises. The nation errs, that goes to war over a non-vital issue of its national interest.

Having defined the national interest as I have done here, the next problem to consider is that of different people having different ideas on how to pursue it. In these different ideas on how to pursue the national interest, also lies a testament to what each person believes to be the true national interest. This difference, in thinking that the national interest can be achieved by one method over another, is also reflected by international relations scholarship. Different international relations theoretical traditions also conceive the pursuit of the national interest differently.

Different Theoretical Traditions And The National Interest:

Different theoretical approaches also have different conceptions of the national interest, which, at first glance, seem scarcely reconcilable. On closer inspection though, the views are not that irreconcilable, instead, they just confirm the 'elephant problem.' If we recall the Indian moral tale I mentioned in the Address preceding this one, that of the 5 blind men who had to describe an elephant, having only touched one part, these different views become intelligible. Each theoretical tradition will just be describing the part of the "elephant" it is in contact with. Our task, as Zimbabweans wanting to understand our true national interest, is to act as the fully sighted people, who will take all these different partial descriptions, and use them to understand the "elephant" as it really exists.

The theoretical school called Realism, conceives the pursuit of the national interest as the pursuit of power for security reasons, in an international system characterised by "anarchy." By "anarchy" these theorists mean that there is no overall authority to adjudicate over disputes, so nation-states must rely on "self-help." Self-help, or self-reliance, is the idea that no one will come to your aid, so you have to be sufficiently strong to defend yourself against any aggression.

This idea was illustrated well when Iraq was attacked by the United States in 2003 on a false premise.

So, from a Realist perspective, the national interest is being so militarily strong that no one dares to attack the nation. Russia and North Korea prove this point so far. Realism also says that forming alliances with the strong to avoid being attacked is one of the strategies nation-states use in pursuit of their safety. The North Atlantic Treaty Organisation (NATO) currently proves this point. According to Realist thought then, physical security of the nation-state, is the predominant concern of the national interest. This, they argue, is so, because nothing else will matter if the nation has been destroyed.

Another theoretical perspective – Liberalism – partly refutes this individualistic pursuit of physical security. Liberalism, instead, says that States best pursue their national interest by ceding power to international institutions like the African Union (AU), European Union (EU), and the United Nations (UN). They call this "pooling of sovereignty," and think that it is the best way of pursuing the national interest. They say that as most problems are transnational, they can only be solved if nations act in concert through various international institutions.

For Liberalism then, the national interest is not the naked pursuit of physical security by military means. Instead, it is about pursuing economic prosperity through economic enmeshment, because if economies are intertwined, States will not go to war with each other in the first place, because this will ruin their economic prosperity. They borrow this idea from Kant's postulations about perpetual peace. While this sounds like a valid refutation of the self-help idea advanced by Realism, I think Liberalism's precepts need to be qualified, otherwise they will mislead us.

For "low politics," such as coordinating Air Transport, or Telecommunications rules, Liberalism's precepts are unimpeachable, but it is different when it comes to the "high politics" of national security.

There, Realism's precepts still hold true as very few countries allow even their closest allies inside their defence installations. So, we can pursue all the fruits of Liberal Internationalism, as the theoretical tradition is sometimes called, but we should still be aware that no country ever truly outsources provision for its physical security.

Yet another theoretical approach – Constructivism – thinks that Realism and Liberalism focus too much on the material considerations at the expense of the ideational ones. The great contribution of Constructivist thought is that reality is "socially constructed," and what Realism claims are permanent interests are merely so because people think they are at the time. Reality, for Constructivism, is what people make of it. An individual leader may be able to act in such a way that what the nation thinks are its permanent interests can be changed. Here, the thrust of the argument is that individual leaders can influence the international system more than Realism is prepared to admit.

Where Realism says what happens in the international system is already fixed – all nations seek security in a system characterised by anarchy – Constructivism says individual leaders can achieve different outcomes in the same system. For example, China under Mao was a mortal enemy of the West, but under Deng Xiaoping, it assumed a somewhat different orientation. In our own country, under Robert Mugabe, it seemed we were mortal enemies with the West, under Emmerson Mnangagwa, we have been somewhat oriented to re-engage with the West. This is an example of one of the ways in which individual leaders can redefine relations, and thus the national interest of their countries.

The theoretical tradition called Marxism, weighs in with the idea that the national interest is just a reflection of the economic interest of the political elites, who then use State machinery to pursue those interests. For Marxism, the poor in every nation, essentially do not have an input into the national interest decisions. This view is also what animates the theoretical tradition called Feminism, though it conceives the same matter in terms of gender domination, where male interests are promoted as the national interest. These two theoretical traditions point to the fact that there are power differentials in all societies, so we have to be alert to the possibility what is being called the national interest, is merely the interest of the powerful.

For Zimbabwe, I think the meeting point of all these theories is what approximates to our true national interest. Where Realism emphasizes military strength, it is true that we can only be militarily strong if we are economically strong – an aspect of the national interest emphasized by Liberalism. Constructivism's input is also worth taking on board. While it is true that geography is a permanent fixture of our national interest as Realism contends, what Constructivism also says on the matter is valid. Botswana, a neighbour, was seen as an enemy during the time Ian Khama was President there, and Robert Mugabe was President in Zimbabwe. The same Botswana, under Mokgweetsi Masisi, and the same Zimbabwe, under Emmerson Mnangagwa, currently enjoy friendly relations.

Our takeaway from theory then, when we think about our national interest, should be this: the qualifications different theories introduce to even that which seems set in stone. Having somewhat explained away this difficulty, of people conceiving the national interest differently, I think the last issue we have to resolve is the question I asked at the outset: can 14 million people have the exact same interest?

Is The National Interest Ever National?

This question can also be answered by some resort to theory of government, for that theory tells us who makes foreign policy, and how other branches of government inputs into that same process. Theory of government holds that there are three branches of government:

the Executive Branch – a President or Prime Minister and his Ministerial Cabinet; the Legislative Branch – the Members of Parliament; and the Judiciary Branch – the Judges and the Law Courts.

It is the Executive Branch that decides on foreign policy objectives, but the Executive Branch does not have carte blanche on this matter. The Legislative and Judiciary Branches have an input, even if it is just ratifying or refusing to ratify a Treaty the Executive will have entered into. The Parliament being representatives of the people thus means there is an input from the people. While the Judiciary, being competent in law, as it should be, is an example of how public intellectuals and technocrats have a say on foreign policy. The Judiciary can veto anything that is contrary to the law of the land from being pursued as the national interest.

So, from a purely theoretical understanding of how democracies work, we can see how ordinary people have an input into the national interest. It is through their elected representatives in Parliament. As well, other actors, such as NGOs, Thinktanks, the Media, and public intellectuals, have ways in which they make an input into formulation of the national interest. All this shows us the various ways, in theory, that the millions of people have access to the articulation of the national interest.

Of course, the reality can be different as, sometimes, the exigencies of national security mean that the Executive Branch does not even have to consult the Parliament on some foreign policy actions. Still, there is a remedy to this problem: the population can vote out the government at the next election if its actions turnout to be contrary to the national interest. It is from this position that I think that we can argue that the national interest can be national.

I believe I have now set out all the parameters of the national interest as they are understood in international relations scholarship. In addition to that, I have also introduced the caveats that I have called the intervening factors of history, values, and capability. Of the three intervening factors I introduced, I have not yet illustrated how the capability factor impacts the national interest. I will now say something briefly about the 'capability factor,' before finally talking specifically about Zimbabwe's national interest.

Superpowers, Middle Powers, and Developing States:

While the national interest declarations of all nations will be similar, it is necessary that I talk about what the 'capability factor' means for the true national interest. The gradation in national material capabilities means that, for some nations, most declarations are merely aspirational, rather than actual. Thus, for us to discover our true national interest, we need to discuss our capabilities as they objectively exist. If we do not do that, rhetoric and ego could lead us to misunderstand our true national interest. We need to know Zimbabwe's true place in the international system, where capabilities are concerned.

I say this because I know that our Land Reform programme, made us punch way above our weight class in the public imagination. We ended up crossing swords with some of the most powerful nations on the planet. This was an anomaly and should not suddenly make us think we are in the same rank as these nations in the pursuit of the national interest. It does not matter that the United States felt compelled to proclaim that: "Zimbabwe poses an unusual and extraordinary threat to the United States's foreign policy." This does not mean we can now compete with the United States in global foreign policy objectives. There are very few countries that have truly global reach and global interests. This is because a country's economic power also determines the extent of its foreign policy objectives. The developed countries thus, tend to have more means at their disposal to pursue their national interests.

In this regard, there are three classifications of countries and their corresponding foreign policy capabilities. This classification of countries roughly equates to Superpowers, Middle Powers, and Developing States. There are two or three superpowers that have global reach. These superpowers have interests in every corner of globe, and the capabilities to pursue them, it becomes a matter of choice for them whether they pursue these interests or not. These countries are the United States, China, and Russia. Then there is what Frankel called middle powers: these are such countries as the United Kingdom, France, and Germany. These countries are limited by their capabilities and cannot pursue some objectives even if they wished to. The EU's failure to stay in Afghanistan without US support recently, proves this point of limited capabilities.

The third rank in our classification are the developing States such as we mostly have on the African Continent. While Nigeria and South Africa may be superpowers on the continent, their influence and capabilities are regional, Nigeria in West Africa and South Africa in Southern Africa. Our own rank, properly conceived then, is way below that of South Africa and Nigeria. We are currently a small, land locked, low income country. From this honest classification, we can then decide what our true national interest is, given our capabilities. It is very clear from the above, that we cannot engage in foreign military adventures, except for a neighbour like Mozambique on which we depend on for access to the Sea. We certainly would not have involved ourselves in the DRC War in 1998 had we first held this honest assessment.

The Pursuit Of Our National Interest:

As to how a nation ought to pursue its national interest, Palmerston's pronouncement can be taken as a guide: "we have no eternal allies, and we have no eternal enemies. Our interests are eternal, and those interests it is our duty to follow."[61] According to this formulation, as Zimbabweans, we should be prepared to go to war against nations we call our best friends now, should they ever threaten what we call our vital national interest.

As our most vital national interest is to never find ourselves colonized again, we should be ready to go to war against China, should China ever want to be the new colonizer. Our recent history showed us how brutal foreigners could be towards us once they had overpowered us. We also enjoy friendly relations with Mozambique, but we should also be willing to invade Mozambique, should a new political dispensation there block our shortest distance to the Sea. The bottom line on whether any country is our friend or foe, will be determined by which side of the red line of our vital interests, they stand at a given point in time.

Zimbabwe's National Interest:

As per generic foreign policy declarations, it is in our national interest to have physical security, to maintain our territorial integrity and independence, and to have economic prosperity. However, the intervening factors of our history and values, make issues pertaining to our independence more vital than any others. A country that has never experienced Colonialism, may not be as sensitive to the possibility of being colonised than one that has recently experienced it. We had to fight a liberation war to even be considered to deserve any human rights in our own territory. This dehumanising experience, of being enslaved by foreigners in our own country for nearly 100 years, is what informs the nationalist conception of our national interest.

Maintaining our sovereignty, therefore, is what the nationalist conceives to be Zimbabwe's true national interest. In the Third Address, I said that Nationalism in Zimbabwe, is the doctrine that essentially insists that we have sovereignty over all our resources. Under Colonialism, we were denied any rights, while at the same time, our resources were being exploited for the benefit of our colonizers. As we were only awarded our rights back by the liberation struggle, even the hint of a return to the situation when we were enslaved in our own country, is unacceptable to the nationalist's mind. This is also what our Constitution means when it says that the values of the liberation struggle are sacrosanct. Thus, anything that helps us continue to have full sovereignty over our persons and natural resources, is what nationalists will concede to be in our true national interest.

A strong military, as prescribed by the Realist theoretical tradition, is one way we can ensure we protect our freedom and resources. But, because we now live in a world where resource extraction no longer requires a physical presence of the foreign power, we also have to be aware there are other ways our resource sovereignty can be undermined without use of force. There are now ways to prejudice people of national wealth without conquering them militarily.

It is to this aspect that Zimbabwe always needs to prepare against. While the Liberal Internationalism theoretical tradition proposes economic enmeshment as a way of achieving the national interest, power differentials in the international system can mean this prescription just equating to developing countries losing sovereignty over their resources. This is mostly done by multinationals prejudicing developing countries of revenue by evading taxation and paying very little for raw materials.

Thus, in addition to a strong military, we also need trade policy experts who will always negotiate to Zimbabwe's advantage. Our people who negotiate extraction of resources and trade deals should always ensure that we get the going rate for our resources. Tax evasion practices like transfer-pricing, often happen because the multinationals have an accomplice in government who allows circumvention of rules. We need gatekeepers who will place Zimbabwe's economic interests ahead of their own interests in all these situations. I can only see this task being done well by genuine nationalists. It is, therefore, down to our fellow nationalists the nation educated in the sphere of economics and trade, to take up this task. On this question, I am suggesting that an educated citizenry, that truly believes in resource sovereignty, will also be a great help to the military's task of defending our sovereignty.

It is also in Land Locked Zimbabwe's vital interest to keep good relations with neighbours whose access to the Sea we need. But in the true spirit of the national interest, if our neighbours ever chose to block our access to the Sea, we should be willing to go to war against them to re-establish that Sea access. When Apartheid South Africa was blocking our access to the Sea at Beira in the 1980s, we had to deploy troops to keep that access open. It is fortunate for us now, that the Southern African Development Community (SADC) governments that neighbour us, are all are ex-liberation war movements, so they understand our conception of the national interest.

These friendly relations with our neighbours are also not just for access to the Sea, they also ensure that there is no country that can be used as a base to attack Zimbabwe. The single biggest issue of Zimbabwe's national interest concern in the past 42 years, was Land Reform, and no armed attack came because SADC governments agreed with the nationalist position on that issue. Tony Blair's plans to invade Zimbabwe then, which he wrote about in his book, were thwarted when Thabo Mbeki told him that SADC countries would not countenance such an aggression on a sister country. But while it worked out that SADC was on our side on the issue of Land Reform, it is also now in our vital national interest, that we settle this important national issue, so that even if different government dynamics ever prevail in the SADC region, there will still be no roll back on Land Reform.

Let me now turn to examples that can help illustrate how our history, values, and capabilities have interacted with the national interest prescriptions given to us by international relations scholarship. This exercise's use, is that it can help us determine whether our actions passed, or failed, the 'national interest test.' The 'national interest test,' is that test which ascertains whether any actions we took, were dictated to us by our national interest. Here, I will rely on just our Beira Corridor Troop Deployment, our involvement in the Second DRC War, and our Fast Track Land Reform. But, as I have already mentioned above, we can do the same exercise for every major issue our country will ever face, to determine whether our actions will pass, or fail, the 'national interest test.'

ZDF Beira Corridor Deployment (1982 – 1992):

The first example I will use to illustrate whether our actions passed or failed the 'national interest test,' is our troop deployment to the Beira Corridor in Mozambique. As I want these Addresses to be intelligible, and useful, to people who will succeed us in this country 700 years from now, I must rehash facts about these examples which are common knowledge to us today. Please indulge me on this count.

The Zimbabwe Defence Forces (ZDF), specifically the Zimbabwe National Army (ZNA) deployed to the Beira Corridor in neighbouring Mozambique between 1982 and 1992. 3000 soldiers were first deployed there in November 1982. In a meeting with Julius Nyerere and Samora Machel on 12th June 1985, the then Prime Minister, Robert Mugabe, agreed to raise that number to 10 000 soldiers.

This was done in response to the destabilization activities against the Beira Corridor by Apartheid South African Commandos and their surrogates – the Mozambican National Resistance (MNR), or *Resistencia Nacional Mocambicana* (RENAMO) in Portuguese. The task of the ZNA was to protect the Beira Corridor from attacks by the MNR. This was supposed to free the Mozambican Armed Forces to pursue the MNR. But with mission creep, the ZNA eventually started search and destroy missions against the MNR, notably the attacks on their Gorongosa base. This expansion of mission was also justified because, the MNR had started attacking Zimbabwean border towns in response to the ZNA deployment.

In the discussion of the national interest above, I mentioned that there are what are called vital national interests, and others that can be called non-vital national interests. Vital national interests pertain to the survival of the nation. They usually do not include getting involved in your neighbours' internal affairs, but given our context, it was in our vital national interest that there be peace in Mozambique, hence our intervention there. This is also a case when both our material interests and values, interacted to make the situation in Mozambique one in our vital interest.

As far as our material interests were concerned, Zimbabwe is a landlocked country, so it is always in our vital interest that our access to the Sea remains open. Without that access to supplies, our economy just would not function. The Beira Corridor was our main access to the Sea given that dependence on Apartheid South Africa left us at the mercy of a hostile neighbour. So, we needed the Beira Corridor to remain open so that we could get our fuel supply, and other imports vital for our economy. South Africa then began sabotaging this lifeline of ours. The sabotage of the Beira Corridor was part of South Africa's Total Strategy, aimed at destabilising and making Southern African countries dependent on Apartheid South Africa.

In terms of our values, one of our deepest held values, was to free other people from the oppression of the racism we had just experienced. We had just experienced the dehumanising effects of Rhodesian Apartheid ourselves, and it was the highest of our values that we contribute to the freeing of fellow blacks under the same inhuman system. Having just won our independence from Colonialism with the help of other African countries, we had a duty to also help black South Africans still under Apartheid. Economic dependence on South Africa just helped perpetuate and entrench Apartheid.

Mozambique's problems with the MNR were also partly of our making. Mozambique had helped us by giving us bases to fight the white settler minority in our country. In response to this, the Rhodesian white settler minority's Central Intelligence Organisation (CIO), established the MNR to destabilise Mozambique. When we won our independence in 1980, Apartheid South Africa took over the MNR and continued to destabilise Mozambique.

The issues that came to the fore with regards our national interest in Mozambique are there for everyone to see. The main one was the need for us to delink ourselves from Apartheid South Africa. The Rhodesians we had just defeated had heavily relied on South Africa for the viability of the economy. For this reason, we inherited an economy that was heavily dependent on South Africa. It was this attempt to delink ourselves, and South Africa's desire to demonstrate that a black run country could not be economically viable, that created the situation we had to respond to in Mozambique. Joseph Hanlon's book – Beggar Your Neighbours – has covered all the dynamics that were involved in this episode. I have also talked at some length about the military aspects of this destabilization in the Sixth Address in this volume.

This example also demonstrates the competing interests that I said above naturally exist in the international system. Even if we were not opposed to Apartheid South Africa, Apartheid South Africa just wanted to demonstrate that a black majority run State was unviable. This was necessary as a justification for its minority white rule to continue. To this end, Apartheid South Africa mixed outright Sanctions, embargoes and sabotage against us. As we were initially totally dependent on South Africa for all our supplies just after Independence in April 1980, it was very easy to sabotage us. For example, South Africa created a three week delay on all our cargoes by November 1980.[62] By March 1981, 300 000 tonnes of our goods were stranded in South Africa creating severe shortages that negatively impacted the economy.[63]

In April 1981, in response to Zimbabwe's vote for United Nations Sanctions to be imposed on Apartheid South Africa, South Africa also announced it would withdraw diesel locomotives and technicians loaned to the National Railways of Zimbabwe (NRZ).[64] The result of these disruptions was that Zimbabwe was losing $5 Million dollars per week due to lost exports.[65] This is yet another example of the 'values factor' trumping economic considerations. Given the economic pressure South Africa could exert on us, Zimbabwe could have abstained from a United Nations vote on placing Sanctions on Apartheid South Africa. But having experienced Apartheid ourselves, freedom for Black South Africans was more important than our economic prosperity.

Zimbabwe's response to these attacks on our economy was to reduce our dependence on Apartheid South Africa. This is what made it vital that we deploy troops to the Beira Corridor. The deployment of the troops meant that South Africa never succeeded in cutting this lifeline again, but still the disruption and threat of disruption cost Zimbabwe about US$1.4 billion between 1980 and 1986.[66]

The national interest issues at play here were exactly as reported by the New York Times on 21st February 1988: "Zimbabwe's aim is largely to keep open vital trade routes to the sea. By doing so, it hopes to loosen South Africa's economic stranglehold on the Continent's Southern region."[67] Some Western diplomats and Zimbabwean business elites were of the mindset that the deployment, estimated to be costing $1 Million per day, was untenable without financial support from abroad, and would actually worsen Zimbabwe's shrinking economy.[68] The contrary consideration was that not sending troops there, "meant the almost certain destruction of an alternative, however fragile, to Zimbabwe's overwhelming economic dependence on white ruled South Africa."[69] The choices for then Prime Minister, Robert Mugabe, was one "between short-term economic stability by distancing Zimbabwe from the war, or economic independence over the long haul by getting deeper and deeper into the war."[70]

As an indication of what I said above, that, different people conceive the national interest differently, the newspaper remarked that "senior Zimbabwean Army officers, who view the Mozambican military as ill trained and disorganized, are getting to be increasingly disgruntled over Zimbabwe's involvement in a war that is seen as unwinnable."[71] The same report also said; "many Zimbabweans are becoming more vocal against military participation in the conflict, as a worsening shortage of foreign currency translates into annoying food shortages of basic commodities, from toothpaste to tires and spare car parts."[72]

A Zimbabwean businessman is also quoted in the same publication as saying: "South Africa has a gun pointed at the region and its finger is always on the trigger. But our country has no choice but to support Mozambique for moral and political reasons, as well as economic ones. There is no way we can have peace and prosperity if there is not peace and prosperity in Mozambique."[73] This last example, speaks to what I said above, that an engaged citizenry, will be able to understand the necessity of actions that seem harmful to the country.

Our economic survival, and therefore independence, was threatened by South African actions in Mozambique, and so we used our military to protect our economic lifeline. When a situation in a neighbouring country affects the nation as much as it did Zimbabwe, military action taken in response passes the 'national interest test.' A country is justified in expending human and materiel wealth in fighting such a war.

As a land locked country, it is in our vital interest to have access to the Sea. To this extent, we have to keep friendly relations with our neighbours, but should it ever happen that any of our neighbours decide to block our access to the Sea, we should be ready, and willing, to invade the neighbour to restore our access to the Sea. This is also why countries keep a standing army, to defend their territory, as well as to use armed force against any country whose actions threaten their vital national interest.

The DRC War (1998 – 2002) And The National Interest:

Our involvement in the DRC is also very illuminating for the 'national interest test.' But this time in another direction: we treated a merely important national interest issue as if it was a vital one. I could even go further and say we had absolutely no national interest concerns in the DRC. What we did when we intervened there, was neither supported by any of the international relations scholarship prescriptions, nor dictated to us by the intervening factors of our history, values, and capability. Simply put, the DRC Troop Deployment does not pass the 'national interest test.' But, for the benefit of posterity, I must still rehash facts about the deployment that are already common knowledge to us.

For a better understanding of the issues, the DRC War of 1998 – 2002 has to be seen in its regional context. The regional context that is important for the Second DRC War is the 1994 Rwandan Genocide against the Tutsis and Moderate Hutus. Mobutu Sese Seko who had been in power in the Zaire (renamed DRC in 1997) since the 1960s, had supported the government in Rwanda that committed the Genocide in 1994. When the Rwanda Patriotic Front (RPF) defeated the government in Rwanda, the Hutu genocidaires went into the Zaire (DRC) and were given sanctuary by the Government of Mobutu Sese Seko.

To pay Mobutu Sese Seko in kind, and to also ensure there would be no destabilization in Rwanda coming from the Zaire (DRC), Rwanda supported Laurent Kabila's march into Kinshasa in the First DRC War of 1996 – 1997. Mobutu Sese Seko was defeated and exiled in 1997, and Laurent Kabila took over and renamed Zaire the DRC.

But within the year, there was a fallout between Kabila and Rwanda leading to the Second Congo War of 1998 – 2002. Laurent Kabila must have anticipated this fallout with Rwanda, for he had, somehow, managed to get the DRC, a country with some of its landmass North of the Equator, into the Southern African Development Community. It was on the basis of the DRC being a Member of SADC, that Zimbabwe, Namibia, and Angola got involved in the Second Congo War.

Zimbabwe's intervention was also done in accordance with international law. The DRC requested SADC countries to come to its assistance because it was experiencing an armed attack on its territory. Article 51 of the UN Charter allows actions taken in self-defence, and assistance can be given by countries invited by a sovereign State experiencing such aggression on its territory. Where Zimbabwe erred in the national interest, was giving the assistance without assessing whether its capability allowed it to do so. The SADC Charter is not like the NATO Treaty which contains a collective self-defence clause which compels countries to come to each other's aid. SADC signatories have a choice where self-defence is concerned. This is why Zambia, a neighbour of the DRC, did not get involved, and why we only managed to get Angola and Namibia on our side in the Second Congo War.

The essence of Zimbabwe's troop deployment to the DRC was captured succinctly, by Martin Rupiya, when he wrote that: "the momentous decision by Zimbabwe to deploy a contingent of 600 Zimbabwean forces under Operation Restore Sovereignty was made at the eleventh hour in August 1998. The fast moving events at the time did not allow for prior public consultation or debate regarding the decision to deploy the country's armed forces. When the deployment was done, given the impression that the force threatening Kinshasa was only a rag-tag dissident group, it was widely assumed that this would be a temporary military expedition, lasting no more than three weeks. More than thirty months later, the Zimbabwean force has ballooned to over 16 000, with no end to its role in sight unless the current UN initiative holds."[74]

In the short paragraph above, we can find everything that we need to discuss our involvement in the DRC War. First of all, there was a failure of intelligence, as the Zimbabwe Military should have known that the seemingly rag-tag dissident group, was actually backed by all the countries that became signatories to the ceasefire in 2002. If this factor had been taken into account, the deployment would have anticipated a long costly war. Anticipating a long costly war would have made our planners realise that we did not have the capability to sustain that war. Simba Makoni, the Finance Minister during that war, presented to Parliament that the DRC War was costing US$1 million per day. Thus, from the outset, the 'capability factor' of our national interest calculus, should have prevented us from deploying troops to the DRC. Our experiences in Mozambique should have supplied the basis for calculating how costly the DRC War was going to be.

Yes, the Mozambique deployment was also very costly, but the 'capability factor' was trumped by the fact that it was in our vital interest to keep the Beira Corridor open. Thus, where capability is lacking, a country fighting for its survival is still acting in its national interest. The DRC troop deployment fails the 'national interest test' because our survival was not threatened by what was happening in the DRC. We also have no historical ties, or a border with the DRC. The situation there had no material impact on Zimbabwe's economy. Our national interest concerns there were negligible. When there is an absence of national interest considerations to that extent, a country is said to have fought a war of choice.

Some people have gone on to conclude that this was just a case of individuals in Zimbabwe using State resources to enrich themselves with the DRC's minerals. While it seems so, the truth is that this was not the initial reason for our deployment. The deployment was done in deference to international law as I have already pointed out above. Martin Rupiya also agrees on this point, as he said, "whatever economic interests Zimbabwe subsequently acquired in Congo were not part of the initial calculus of intervention."[75]

The DRC Troop Deployment example is also a very good illustration of what I said earlier about the relationship between the domestic facing "public interest," and the international facing "national interest." I said above that expenditure on defence abroad, can impact prosperity at home. This is exactly what happened to us with the DRC deployment, as within two years, we had opened another war front back home when we started our Land Reform programme.

Thus, the expenditure of national wealth in the DRC, for something that was not in our vital national interest, turned out to be folly on our part. Whatever wealth we expended in the DRC could have, instead, been used to capacitate the new farmers we put on the land we took back from the white settlers. This would have helped us circumvent some of the difficulties we faced due to the Sanctions our Land Reform invited from the white settlers' countries of origin.

Land Reform And The National Interest:

The two examples I have tackled above are what corresponds to the "national interest" proper, in the distinction I made above between the "national interest" and "public interest." The example below of our Land Reform is what corresponds to the "public interest," but exhibiting the contiguity I mentioned earlier, our Land Reform turned into a national interest issue when foreigners intervened in our domestic affairs.

I made the distinction above between the national interest and public interest, merely for conceptual clarity, in reality, they are inseparable. Our Land Reform programme is an example of how issues we think are the domestic facing 'public interest' can traverse the divide into the 'national interest.' The importance of this knowledge is that it makes us aware that there are some issues which we know are purely our domestic affairs, but which outsiders also consider to be in their national interest. For example, it is in the national interest of all countries to protect its citizens abroad. This knowledge should have helped us anticipate how Britain would react to our Land Reform. Rightly or wrongly, Britain would have needed to react to our taking our land back from its citizens who were masquerading as Zimbabweans.

With this knowledge at hand, we would have also known that though ours was a purely domestic issue, there was going to be intervention from outsiders. With such an anticipation, we then would have had contingencies in place against those reactions to our Land Reform by foreign powers. For example, we would have known that Western powers would have been willing to use military force to stop our Land Reform. If we had put that into our calculus, we would not have sent 16 000 soldiers to the DRC, who certainly would have been needed to defend the country if an invasion of the country had come. This is not idle speculation either, Tony Blair actually asked his Chief of Defence Staff to draw plans to invade Zimbabwe. This was only thwarted because SADC did not support the idea. Also, the 11th September 2001 attacks with civilian aircraft on the United States, somewhat drew attention away from our Land Reform.

Let me assure you though, that our contingency planning would not have involved stopping, postponing, or reversing our Land Reform. This is one of those issues that was so in our vital interest as dictated to us by our history and values. It just had to be done at all costs. I will talk about the actual dynamics of the Fast Track Land Reform Programme (FTLRP) in full in the next Address. For the purposes of the current Address, I will just mention that the way the situation stood, where just 4 000 white farmers, owned 70% of all our arable land, was just not conducive to the 'public interest.' It was also a case whereby our territory that was annexed by the Colonialists, was still in the hands of the beneficiaries of Colonialism. I have also said in the Fifth Address that, the continued disenfranchisement of blacks from their land, was the equivalent of having 51% of our territory annexed by foreign agents. It was in this way, that our national interest declaration of maintaining our territorial integrity, was compromised as long as these land ownership injustices persisted. This situation also meant that the white settlers were practicing feudalism in Zimbabwe. The blacks would remain impoverished serfs, while whites controlled the economy by virtue of their land ownership given to them by 90 years of discriminatory colonial rule. Land Reform had to be done whatever the cost.

The other factor people forget, where Land Reform is concerned, is that the primary motive was the need to correct the historical injustice, production and efficiency were secondary issues. So, any criticism of our Land Reform which says production suffered as a result, will have misunderstood the issues completely. All those attacks that say Zimbabwe lost its "breadbasket" status because of Land Reform, are just propaganda serving the goals of those opposed to our taking back our land. Our Land Reform still passes the 'national interest test' in that our history and values dictated that it had to be done.

The only real mistake we need to correct, for the sake of our future national interest actions, was our not anticipating the extent to which foreign powers would oppose our Land Reform. If we had done this anticipation accurately, we would not have taken some of the actions we took prior to our Land Reform. Some of these actions turned out to be unforced errors, because they aided the foreign powers in their attack on our economy. I have already stated above that the DRC Troop Deployment of 1998 – 2002, was one such mistake, as it drained national wealth at the same time when we were about to undertake Land Reform. In war parlance, we ended up fighting a war on two fronts.

The other serious mistake we made was when we gave war veterans an unbudgeted for lump sum of ZW$50 000 and monthly payments of ZW$2 000. This was done on 14th November 1997, a day which economists have come to know by the label Black Friday. What happened thereafter was that the Zimbabwe Stock Exchange crashed by 46% as a result of the Zimbabwean currency losing 72% of its value against the US Dollar. There was a sudden shortage of foreign currency as people tried to exchange their Zimbabwean dollars for the stable US currency. Therefore, this awarding of compensation to war veterans, was done in an unreflecting manner.

At the time, having not studied affairs, my instinct still told me that it was not necessary to pay war veterans a cash lump sum. I thought the freeing of the country from Colonialism was enough payment for the genuine freedom fighter. I still stand by my first reaction. As it turned out, Black Friday eroded the value of the lump sums to nothing within months. So, just by outcomes, this particular action was, ultimately, not in the national or public interest. It also gave opportunity for looting, because these funds were abused. Going forward, we should always appraise the public interest value of any policy and the likely long term effects, if it is deleterious to the public interest, we should not pursue such an action.

The taking back of our land which incurred Sanctions from those who supported the racist privileges of the white settlers, does not fall into that category. It had to be done at all costs. I have estimated that if we persevere, in 50 to 100 years' time, the injustices of land imbalances will never be an issue again. Having gone to war and lost so many lives, it was an affront to the nationalists that our land remained in the hands of a few whites who had gotten that land by violently evicting blacks from the same land. Thus, Land Reform was in our objective national interest despite the economic damage done to the country by international reaction.

Conclusion:

My fellow countrywomen and countrymen, in this Address, I was particularly keen to discuss the nature of the national interest. I did this so that we can all begin to discern our true national interest. What I was driving at the most, in this Address, is that there exist some unimpeachable prescriptions of the national interest from international relations scholarship. But I also wanted us to understand that these prescriptions are tempered by the intervening factors of a nation's history, values, and capabilities. The national interest then, is whatever international relations scholarship says it is, but the true national interest, is what a nation's history, values, and capabilities dictate.

Our declared national interest, in deference to international relations scholarship prescriptions, is to have physical security, maintain our territorial integrity, and to achieve economic development. Our history, values, and capabilities, then dictate what we will actually be able to pursue.

The three examples I have used here were for the purposes of illustrating where we acted as dictated to us by our values, history, and capabilities. The instability in Mozambique threatened our very existence, as it was our lifeline to the Sea, so we had to get involved. Our troop deployment to Mozambique passes the 'national interest test' because, it was what international relations scholarship would have prescribed. Our history and values also dictated that deployment. The DRC Troop Deployment, on the other hand, was a war of choice which we should have never involved ourselves in, the situation there did not threaten our existence in any way. Our Land Reform had to be done at all costs because, it was addressing the economic imbalances we were given by the annexation of our land and 90 years of racial segregationist policies.

Other issues pertaining to our national interest will arise in the future, I believe we can use the same principles I have outlined in this Address, to assess whether the actions we will want to take to address them, will pass the 'national interest test.'

Address V.

Land Redistribution

"I could go into the whole theories of discrimination in legislation, in residency, in economic opportunities, I could go into that, but I shall restrict myself to the question of land because I think this is very basic. To us, the essence of white domination is domination over land. That is the real issue" – Herbert Wiltshire Pfumaindini Chitepo, ZANU Chairman, 1973.

THE RESOLUTION OF THE land question in Zimbabwe, once and for all, will be a resolution of the main question all other questions in our country rest on. The land question is the pivot on which all our fortunes have turned since 1890. As that remarkable fellow nationalist, Nathan Shamuyarira, noted in 1965; "No issue is of greater dimension, and of deeper emotional appeal, to Africans in Southern Africa than land shortage, in a motherland that has thousands of acres, abounds with fish, fruit, and honey, but is occupied by foreign landlords."[76] 42 years after independence, the question still has the same vitality.

I, for one, am pleased that this issue is still this emotive. I am glad that we have not been lulled by the false promise of city lights, to forget what must remain of non-negotiable value to us – our land. Nowhere do we owe more, to all those who sacrificed their lives in Zimbabwe's liberation struggle, than in ensuring that their vision of us reclaiming our land back succeeds. Given that our liberation struggle was about land, this is the one issue we should be willing to go back to war over. Thus, the death of all nationalists, should be the only condition under which the resolution of the land question in Zimbabwe, can be allowed to fail.

Zimbabwe has a total landmass of 39 million hectares, of which 33.3 million hectares are reserved for agriculture, while the remaining 6 million hectares are reserved for national parks and urban settlements. The land question arises because, Europeans arrived here in 1890, and declared that around 51% of Zimbabwe's best land belonged to whites only, and this, on no other qualification than just the colour of their skin. Whenever conditions allowed, black Zimbabweans took up arms against this injustice: as in the Anglo – Matabele War of 1893 – 4, in the First Chimurenga War of 1896 – 7, and then again, in the Second Chimurenga War of 1966 - 1980.

Still, at Independence on 18th April 1980, 6 000 white farmers held 15.5 million hectares of the most arable farmland, and 8 500 black commercial farmers held only 1.4 million hectares, while 700 000 black families were crammed onto about 16.9 million hectares of the most unproductive land in the communal areas. Zimbabwe's total landmass is divided into five natural regions, with regions I and II having the richest soils and best rainfall patterns, region III can also support agriculture, while regions IV to V are on a spectrum of erratic rainfall to outright inhospitable for human habitation. All the best land in regions I, II, and III, was reserved exclusively for European occupation by racist legislation enacted between 1894 and 1979. This way, in 1980, 70 percent of the most arable land was in the hands of less than 1 percent of the population. A totally unacceptable state of affairs, given the origins of the European occupation of our land.

Thus, the land question as it stood in Zimbabwe at Independence in 1980, challenged one of the four criterion I said in the Third Address, is definitive of nationhood: the territory criterion. The definition of nation rests on these four criteria – historic territory, permanent population, self-government and recognition by other states. Take away one criterion, and suddenly the definition is not satisfied. In 1980, European farmers still occupied around 40 percent of Zimbabwe's total landmass. Even in 2000, two decades after Independence, the needle had barely moved on the percentage of Zimbabwe's landmass still under foreign occupation. This is the aspect I see as an assault on the very definition of nation. It was quite the sleight of hand by the United Nations, when it admitted Zimbabwe as a Member in 1980, when the territorial criterion of the definition of nation was this compromised.

Some will say I am being unkind, in describing white farmers in Zimbabwe as European and foreign occupiers. But saying that the white farmers are Europeans and foreign occupiers, is just a matter of accurate historical record. All the discriminatory legislation the whites passed between 1890 and 1979, demarcated the land they had stolen as European. It was with this fact in mind, that President Robert Mugabe once questioned the validity of their "Citizenship by Colonialism." As recent as 11 years before our Independence in 1980, white settlers were still officially proclaiming their Europeanness. The Land Tenure Act of 1969 was one such official proclamation. This Act, in further entrenching separation, describes the European as someone who is not African, while the native is "any member of the aboriginal tribes or races of Africa and the islands adjacent thereto including Madagascar and Zanzibar: or any person with the blood of such races and who lives as a member of an aboriginal native community."

What further does not help the white farmers' claim to Zimbabwean nationality, is that they still refused to submit to equitable land redistribution with blacks. They even went further by inviting foreign powers to come to their aid. They were willing to see the country destroyed than have true equality with blacks. Remembering that when they took the same land, they designated it European, our conclusion must be that they were still agents of the initial annexation of our land.

Indeed, honest assessment will yield to us that, what the white colonial settler did, by coming into our lands, and declaring them "European," was annexation of our territory. While Independence in 1980 granted us back the self-determination criterion of our nationhood, the territory criterion remained outstanding. As long as that original annexation was not reversed, this was an assault on our declared national interest.

In the Fourth Address, I insisted that maintaining territorial integrity is one of our vital national interests. This is a cornerstone principle of our Constitution and Foreign Policy, but the reality of the matter mocked us. As long as up to 40 percent of our best land was in the possession of people who obtained it by annexation, it was quite ridiculous on our part, to claim to stand in defence of our territory. It was a true case, if ever there was one, of closing the Stable door when the Horse had already bolted.

Nationalists, however, are not to blame for Zimbabwe's liberation war failing to end the white occupation: circumstances have their share of the blame. When our war of liberation was about to succeed, international institutional racism sprang into action and created those circumstances. Britain, ever protective of the white minority, and well aware that a military victory by nationalist forces would end in a massacre of the whites, sued for peace by calling for the Lancaster House talks. At these talks, Britain conspired to ensure that the white settlers would benefit in perpetuity from their annexation. But, in doing so, Britain was either myopic, or completely misinformed about what land meant for black people. All what her conniving at Lancaster House achieved, was a temporary extension of the 1890 occupation.

The attempt to tie blacks into a situation of continued land disenfranchisement, was also folly on the part of Britain and the white settlers. A more public-spirited attitude with regards land would have ultimately given them a better deal. I know black Zimbabweans, we are not mean spirited, in fact, we are very accommodating – and there is a litany of proofs to this fact. It is only when we must react to callous injustice that we become implacable. The patience with which we conducted ourselves, until the Fast Track Land Reform Programme (FTLRP) in 2000, is testimony to black Zimbabweans' accommodating nature.

Black Zimbabweans even tried to correct this injustice through legal channels between 1980 and 2000, despite that the legal channels were rigged against us. The Government of Zimbabwe initially paid to get back land that had been taken from us without payment by the white settlers. In following the dictates of the Lancaster House Agreement, the Government of Zimbabwe paid 50 percent towards any land it acquired to resettle the landless blacks. Britain was supposed to pay the other 50% according to the dictates of the same agreement. To complicate things for us, Britain asked the Zimbabwe government to pay 100% then ask for a 50% reimbursement from Britain afterwards.

For land justice, the government's target was to resettle 162 000 families on 9 million hectares by 1985. This was going to be done on land acquired back from the white settlers. Still, in 1998, after two decades of pursuing these legal channels, Zimbabwe had only resettled 70 000 families on 3.1 million hectares of land. 4 000 European farmers still held 11.2 million hectares of our best farmland.

Clearly, following the dictates of the Lancaster House Agreement, was designed to make it impossible for us to get our land back. Zimbabwe then came to be in the international headlines in 2000, but the way the headlines were made, you would never know that black Zimbabweans were in the right on the land question. This is because international institutional racism came into play again and decided to fight on the side of injustice. If you really think about it, the way the land question exploded in anger in 2000, was actually the powerless responding to land hunger through the only avenue that was left open to them.

The disregard for economic imperatives that ensured is also very instructive for what I mostly discussed in theory in the previous Address: the tensions in the national interest. This is a concrete example of how ideational values interact with material considerations in people's conception of their national interest. The people of Zimbabwe valued land justice more than the supposed economic stability of the status quo.

To be sure, the land cannot be separated from the economy, but Zimbabwe's detractors had hoped that the fear of economic ruin would ensure that the disparity in land ownership would be maintained. Instead, black Zimbabweans decided that it was better to correct the historic injustice of their land that was stolen from them, then deal with whatever economic consequences that would come. It was not a completely irrational decision either, because land ownership as it stood, was explicitly devised to keep blacks in poverty, and thus to keep producing cheap labour for the whites. Only the change of the ownership pattern, would alter the trajectory of perpetual poverty for blacks that the land alienation was guaranteed to produce and reproduce.

International Institutional Racism:

The land question in Zimbabwe is also pertinent to an international audience, given the question of protests against slavery, racism, and colonialism that exploded in America and Europe in the year 2020. Black people who have been the subject of institutional racism in white countries, have now become more aware of seemingly unconnected issues. This latest awareness should make them see the connections between their condition abroad, and the conditions of white oppression subsisting for blacks in their supposed countries in Africa. The case of the Western countries defending racist land ownership in Zimbabwe, should now make them see parallels with the institutional racism they face in the white countries. It was the exact same process as a white police officer kneeling on the neck of a black person until he died, when Western countries placed Sanctions on Zimbabwe so as to reverse land reform. There are parallels there in processes and outcomes. Sanctions cut vital supplies to the Zimbabwean economy and also led to deaths of blacks in Zimbabwe.

Perhaps, it has been a misunderstanding of the land question in Zimbabwe that has caused fellow blacks abroad to fail to be outraged by the plight of their black counterparts there. I do not think many have made the explicit connection between their being discriminated against in Europe, and the same way the European countries tried to protect white privilege in Zimbabwe. This point occurs to me because of the realisation that black people abroad, did not mobilise against the Sanctions and the demonization that happened when Zimbabwe took back its land. Whites have always mobilised in defence of whites even when they are in the wrong. You will recall that when Rhodesia was placed under United Nations Sanctions, whites in Britain and America lobbied their governments in support of the racist minority in Rhodesia. Western countries only paid lip service to the UN sanctions. Whites, with the tacit support of their governments in the West, also volunteered to come and fight against black people to prevent attainment of independence.

This kind of international mobilisation has been missing on the part of black people in relation to the land question in Zimbabwe. It is also true that the international mainstream media controlled the narrative at the time we took our land back. Their distortions of what was happening in Zimbabwe may have been the only narrative that was widely disseminated. It is necessary then, for me to give an explanation of the true nature of the events in Zimbabwe. Our posterity will not know all these dynamics as we know them, so we have to make these facts accessible to them.

As well, not all the supporters of our cause beyond our borders may be fully conversant with Zimbabwe's land question. Their only knowledge of what took place in Zimbabwe may only be the distortions that have been communicated by the mainstream media. The mainstream media had a vested interest in demonizing land redistribution. Of course, all these people will know, from experience, that mainstream media distorts facts. But they may also not have the side of the story of black Zimbabweans who were aggrieved by the dispossession of their land. It is with these people in mind that this Address rehashes facts that are common knowledge to you all my fellow countrymen and countrywomen. The land question is also topical for countries like South Africa and Namibia. Thus, I must elaborate our experiences as they will be beneficial to them as well. So, please indulge me on this count.

European Land Grab 1890 – 1979:

The land question begins with the arrival of the Pioneer Column on the Zimbabwe Plateau in 1890. On failing to find the mineral wealth Cecil Rhodes expected to find, the decision was taken to make Zimbabwe a settler colony producing agricultural products for Britain. In 1889, Cecil Rhodes had been granted a Royal Charter by the British Government which essentially meant he would administer the colony on behalf of the British. All land that was called Crown land thus referred to land that belonged to Britain. Every theft was backed by legislation and supported by Britain which agreed that blacks were too uncivilised to own arable land. As I have already pointed out above, 51 percent of the best land was thus annexed as European.

The fiction has been advanced, certainly by Ian Smith in his book, Bitter Harvest, that the reason why the blacks are in areas with poor soils, is that they did not have the tools to cultivate the heavy soils of region I, II and III. But this fiction is refuted by the facts: that the settlers evicted hundreds of thousands of black people from the land they had annexed and declared "European," is a matter of historical record. Even as recent as after World War II, Europeans were still dispossessing blacks of their land to settle British veterans of the War against Adolf Hitler. The black people's prior settlement is also proven by the graves of the African people in the areas claimed they could not cultivate.

But even if this was the case, that Africans preferred to live in sandy and tsetse fly infested lands with poor rainfall, it is still problematic that the "government" instituted by whites, still had to promulgate laws prohibiting Africans from occupying land they did not want. Why these laws for people who had no use for the land in question? Why the need to exclude with laws, from free market participation, people who do not want to participate anyway?

Herbert Chitepo, whom I quoted at the beginning of this Address, expounded the land question to its logical conclusion. He explained that land was the cornerstone of white domination of blacks in Zimbabwe: by annexing 50 percent of the best land for exclusive use by whites for all time, they controlled the black man's destiny in perpetuity.[77] As of 1973, 230 000 whites, controlled 50 percent of the land, at 200 hectares per person, while 6 000 000 blacks had to share the remainder, working out to just 8 hectares per person.[78] Every 20 years, the black population was expected to double, which meant that this would become 4 hectares per person by 1993, and then 2 hectares per person in another 20 years.[79] Without land you cannot cultivate, if you cannot cultivate, then you have to sell your labour.[80] If there are too many of you selling your labour to white farms and mines, labour becomes very cheap for the whites.[81] This situation, pursued to its logical conclusion, meant perpetual poverty for the black people.[82]

One thing that is often not highlighted, is how the white settler government also deliberately made sure that black farmers would fail while white farmers succeeded. Road and railway connections were made to serve white farms. Loans and subsidies were made available to whites and, additionally, policies that protected market share for whites were constantly getting promulgated. The 1934 Maize Control Act was one such policy designed to favour white maize growers over black growers. Thus, the claims that blacks were lazy and unproductive, are false given how all these impediments to success were deliberately placed in their way. The claim that whites were naturally good farmers is also a falsity on this count. White commercial farming success by 1980, was just a product of 90 years of discriminatory laws giving every advantage to white settlers.

Land Theft And Racist Legislation:

The detractors of our land repossession have claimed that their opposition to our programme is based on the observance of the "rule of law." In reference to the land question in Zimbabwe, the rule of law argument is just not valid. This is because it is clearly a case of thieves who enacted laws to protect what they had stolen. When Western countries said Zimbabwe is not respecting property rights, they wanted us to respect laws put in place to shore up the theft of our land. The fact of the matter is that when whites confiscated our land, they did so through violent eviction of the original owners of the land. They did not purchase any of the land they claimed for their own. So, for Zimbabweans, there was just no way the "rule of law" could be observed before the initial injustice had been corrected.

I also want you to always remember that these injustices were openly racist. This 1895 Rhodesian newspaper openly proclaimed that: "For the Rhodesian, it was absurd to take the untutored savage, accustomed as he is from time immemorial to superstitious and primitive ideas of law and justice, and suddenly try to govern him by the same code of laws that govern a people with many centuries of experience and enlightenment."[83] While a 1935 Journal of the Royal African Society explained that Europeans should not live in low-lying tsetse fly infested areas, but saw no reason why the natives should not live in those areas.[84]

So, on the basis of this racism, the European settler stole our land then codified the theft in laws which we were now supposed to observe. It is a morally bankrupt section of the international community that saw nothing wrong with our continued land disenfranchisement. The so-called rule of law errs in upholding land laws passed under Colonialism. This is a disregarding of the original crime and a rewarding of brazen theft. This is the truth of the matter as things stood in Zimbabwe just before the Fast Track Land Reform Programme in 2000.

But, to further understand international institutional racism, we can also reframe what the Western countries were saying to us when they said we should uphold the "rule of law." They were saying we should not challenge their right of conquest. The reason why these same people were able to impose their will in perpetuity in the United States and Australia, was that they thoroughly decimated the indigenous populations there. The indigenous population in Zimbabwe was resilient and still maintained population preponderance. International institutional racism was now trying to circumvent the fact of our population preponderance by referring to the rule of law. We should not be fooled by any of these false arguments.

In any case, the rule of law has never been a true measure of justice. Properly conceived, the rule of law is whatever the laws of the country in question say it is. Lovemore Madhuku has correctly pointed out that; "a State which passes unjust laws and complies with them, is acting according to the rule of law."[85] This was in reference to the fact that white settlers were really observing the rule of law when they annexed our land and passed laws to legalise the annexation. The white settlers passed many unjust laws to consolidate their theft of our land. These laws, taken in their totality, would have given black Zimbabweans perpetual land disenfranchisement had we observed them. As we will see below, despite its pretence, the Lancaster House Agreement was the crowning achievement of all the racist laws ever passed to disenfranchise blacks in Zimbabwe. What was worse about the Lancaster House Agreement, was that it also forestalled our imminent battlefield victory.

The first law that codified white colonial land seizures was the Land Apportionment Act of 1930, where "51 percent of Rhodesia's territory was set aside for less than 3000 White European Farmers. Black Farmers were prohibited from owning or occupying land in the European areas, and much of the white-held continued to be underutilised."[86] White politicians affectionately proclaimed it the Magna Carta of the European in Central Africa.[87] Shamuyarira also records that, through several alterations to the Act, "the absoluteness of the segregation was made most precise in the 1945 Amendment where it states:

No owner or occupier of land in the European area, or his agent shall

1. Dispose or attempt to dispose of any such land to a native.
2. Lease any such land to a native.
3. Permit, suffer or allow any native to occupy such land."[88]

Black people became illegal squatters on land they had possessed for generations before the Europeans came to our country.[89] And this is not ancient history either, or a product of a time when the whites did not know better. Even after fighting Adolf Hitler's Fascism, the whites saw no reason to self-correct their similar attitude towards blacks. British Servicemen who fought in World War II were rewarded with land in Zimbabwe in 1948, and 300 000 blacks were evicted from that land.[90] The Chief Rekayi Tangwena case, as proof of violent expropriation, is also very instructive for how recent this took place.

All these actions kept creating land shortage pressures for blacks in the already poor soils they were limited to. The Native Husbandry Act of 1951 is instructive of the attitude of the whites towards blacks. It was a response to the overcrowding and resultant environmental degradation. Freeing up a lot of the land that was lying unused in the European areas to blacks would have been a more just solution. Instead, the whites settled on culling blacks' livestock and further reducing the land possession the blacks had.

The Land Tenure Act of 1969 further entrenched white settler land ownership. Those who think Zimbabwe should have followed the "legal route" do not understand that the laws were rigged against us. They also mistake the Lancaster House Agreement for an equitable peace agreement. Properly conceived, the Lancaster House Agreement was the crowning achievement of all the racist legislation ever passed by the white minority in Zimbabwe. What it did, was consolidate and make unassailable, all the racist land ownership legislation ever passed by the white settlers.

The Gordian Knot:

The legend of the Gordian Knot has come down to us through its retelling by the Roman historian – Quintus Curtius. He describes an ancient oxcart that Alexander the Great encountered on entering the city of Gordium on his campaigns. The oxcart itself was unremarkable except for the yoke, "which was strapped down with several knots all so tightly entangled that it was impossible to see how they were fastened."[91] This knot then, was the Gordian Knot, named after Gordius, the father of King Midas. Gordius himself had become king when he arrived in the same place as a lowly person driving an ox drawn cart. The place had had no king, but an oracle had prophesied that the first person who would arrive on an ox drawn cart would become king. When that happened, he dedicated his oxcart to the townspeople by tying it in the centre of the town in an elaborate knot.

The next prophesy the townsfolk held, was that whoever could successfully untangle the Gordian Knot, would go on to conquer Asia and rule over many nations. Many people had tried and failed to untie that knot. Alexander decided to make his own attempt, at which point our Roman historian feels compelled to reiterate that; "the series of knots was pulled so tight that it was impossible to work out, or see, where the tangled mass began or ended."[92] "For some time," Curtius continues, "Alexander wrestled unsuccessfully with the hidden knots. Then he said: 'It makes no difference how they're untied' and cut through all the thongs with his sword."[93]

The endurance of this legend then, has given us the concept of the Gordian Knot: a shorthand for a very complex or intractable problem. The way Alexander the Great solved the problem, is also one of the earliest instances of thinking outside the box. Solving an insurmountable problem has since been referred to as cutting the Gordian Knot as a result. Shakespeare, in Henry V, also knew about the Gordian Knot, but mistakenly thought it could be untied any other way; "turn him to any cause of policy, the Gordian Knot of it he will unloose familiar as his garter." It is my contention that, the Lancaster House Agreement we were forced to accept by circumstances, was designed in deference to the principles of the Gordian Knot. To solve that problem, we also had to resort to the same method Alexander the Great used to untie the Gordian Knot.

The Lancaster House Agreement:

The Lancaster House Agreement was the document that was signed at the end of the peace conference between Zimbabwe's guerrilla armies and the white settler minority. The talks took place at Lancaster House in London from 10th September to 21st December 1979. This agreement gave Zimbabwe its first Constitution and the terms of the transfer of power. One of its notable stipulations was the 10 year sunset clause – which prohibited compulsory acquisition of land in the white settler's hands. The same agreement reserved 20 Parliamentary exclusively to the white settlers for 7 years. This ensured they could block any legislation that required unanimous votes to pass. We can better understand the difficulties of taking our land back any other way than how we eventually did it, if we look at all the difficulties that were put in our way, especially by the Lancaster House Agreement.

I have often heard fellow Zimbabweans opine that land reform needed to be done, but the way we did it was wrong. Here they will be referring to our method of retaking our land, as well as to the beneficiaries we allocated the land. When I ask them how we should have allocated the land, they invariably say we should only have allocated it to Agriculture graduates. This, they say would have ensured that food security would not be compromised. This assertion misses the point that land reform was primarily about reversing one legacy of colonialism: the overcrowding of black people on unproductive land.

These people who say that land should have been given to Agriculture graduates, also do not realise that the whites were not Agriculture graduates when they were given land here – only their skin colour mattered. Over a period of nearly 100 years, they became proficient in Agriculture. I give our new black farmers the same allowance in timeframe to also become proficient in Agriculture. But where I find that most people have misunderstood matters, is when I ask them about what method we should have used to retake our land. They say since we were the government in power, we should have changed the law first, then negotiated with the whites to amicably hand back the land. You see, all that was done, but to no avail.

One of the patent falsities that has been advanced around Zimbabwe's land redistribution programme, is that we only embarked on it as a political exercise. The accusation is that President Robert Mugabe's government only cared about land reform as a political survival tool. The claim is that it was only when the Zimbabwe African National Union – Patriotic Front (ZANU – PF) was politically threatened, that it decided to use land reform in a populist way. This is a claim that can only be entertained by people who know absolutely nothing about Zimbabwe's history.

The same people who accuse ZANU PF of using land reform because it was politically threatened, also accuse it of rigging elections since 1980. Why threaten the economy with ruin by taking back land from the white settlers, when you can just rig the elections? The opposition was also funded by white farmers who wanted to maintain the land imbalances. This begs the question: to which political threat then, did ZANU PF respond with land reform? The accusation further says that only ZANU PF cronies benefited from land reform. How then was this an exercise to get votes if the land was not transferred to the population? For these reasons, the claim that ZANU PF only embarked on land reform because it had now become unpopular with the electorate, has an internal inconsistency.

The reality of the matter is different. There were legal, financial, administrative, political, and geopolitical factors that interacted to cause the delays in land redistribution. All of these factors were mostly due to the way the Lancaster House Agreement was crafted. It had been crafted to make sure it was difficult to proceed with land reform. The Zimbabwe government was restricted by the Constitution from embarking on land reform for the first 10 years after independence in 1980. During those first 10 years, the Zimbabwean government could only acquire land on the basis of the "willing buyer, willing seller" principle. This principle favoured the seller every time – the white farmer. When the 10 year land reform moratorium elapsed in 1990, geopolitics intervened. The negotiations to end Apartheid in South Africa also delayed any drastic action we could have taken to address land reform in Zimbabwe.

Chief Emeka Anyaoku, the Secretary General of the Commonwealth, appealed to President Robert Mugabe to delay land reform action to allow for smooth negotiations between blacks and whites in South Africa. There was still a need to persuade South Africa's white settlers that they would also keep the land they had expropriated. Zimbabwe was supplying the example of unequal but harmonious co-existence between blacks and whites. Even the willing buyer, willing seller principle of the Lancaster House Agreement, was also used in the negotiations to end Apartheid in South Africa. As South Africa got its Freedom Day on 27th April 1994, their negotiations alone, delayed our land reform by at least four years. Thus, those who claim that ZANU PF did not care about land reform until it became a tool to win elections, do not know the true recent history of Zimbabwe.

There was just no time when the land question ever stopped being an issue. In 1985, observing that the white settlers had remained avowedly racist, President Robert Mugabe reminded them that: "We will not live with that indignity and insult very much longer. That dirty piece of paper [Lancaster House Agreement] will be cleansed."[94] Even when we were waiting for Apartheid to end in South Africa, the legal route was already being pursued to correct the land possession imbalances in Zimbabwe. After the 10-year sunset clause had lapsed, the 1992 redraft of the Land Acquisition Act was made to allow government to compulsorily acquire any land. This faced resistance from the white farmers, who in their myopia, allowed their selfishness to lead to a situation where they would eventually lose all the land.

The Zimbabwe government still hoped that the white farmers would avail the land of their own accord. Still, this did not happen. It took Britain shirking her responsibilities under the Lancaster House Agreement, for Zimbabwe to finally resort to a radical approach. It was only then that the black population began occupying the land they had been dispossessed of by whites earlier. This started with the people of Svosve in May 1997 and became countrywide by May 2000. It was also then that the government passed The Land Acquisition Act of 2000. This Act codified the Fast Track Land Reform Programme where 10 million hectares were to be redistributed from the white settlers back to black farmers.

Given the lobby power that the white farmers had in Britain and the United States, I would not be surprised if they had an input into Britain's decision to essentially abandon the terms of the Lancaster House Agreement. The calculation would have been that once Britain had stopped funding the acquisition of farms, land reform would also stop. Britain announced the decision to shirk her responsibility under the Lancaster House Agreement on 24th May 1997.

In a letter to Kumbirai Kangai, Zimbabwe's then Minister of Lands and Agriculture, Clare Short, the then British International Development Secretary, made it clear that Britain was no longer bound by the Lancaster House Agreement. She wrote that: "I should make it clear that we do not accept that Britain has a special responsibility to meet the costs of land purchase in Zimbabwe. We are a new government from diverse backgrounds without links to former colonial interests. My own origins are Irish and as you know we were colonised and not colonisers."[95] It was at this point that the civility of the Lancaster House Agreement also ceased to bind our government.

But why have I called the Lancaster House Agreement the crowning achievement of all racist laws ever passed by the white settlers? I have called it so, simply because it conspired to make it impossible to dispossess white settlers of the land they had stolen. What made the Lancaster House Agreement formidable, where land reform was concerned, was Section 16, Article 5 of this document. It had been crafted to make it impossible for Zimbabwe to repossess its land. Article 5, in its four paragraphs, is exactly the Gordian Knot I described above. These four paragraphs anticipated all our claims for land redistribution and conspired against them. With this knot, the British had protected the white settlers' theft. They succeeded, until black Zimbabweans remembered that cutting the Gordian Knot was also another acceptable way of untying it.

Article 5, the Freedom from Deprivation of Property article states in the first Paragraph that; "Every person will be protected from having his property compulsorily acquired except when the acquisition is in the interests of defence, public safety, public order, public morality, public health, town and country planning, the development or utilisation of that or other property in such a manner as to promote the public benefit or, in the case of under-utilised land, settlement of land for agricultural purposes. When property is wanted for one of these purposes, its acquisition will be lawful only on condition that the law provides for the prompt payment of adequate compensation and, where the acquisition is contested, that a court order is obtained. A person whose property is so acquired will be guaranteed the right of access to the High Court to determine the amount of compensation."

But paragraph 3 of the same Article 5, made it high cost to acquire such land by stipulating that: "Compensation paid in respect of loss of land to anyone who is a citizen of or ordinarily resident in Zimbabwe (or to a company the majority of whose shareholders are such persons) will, within a reasonable time, be remittable to any country outside Zimbabwe, free from any deduction, tax or charge in respect of its remission." Article 5 was also one of the articles that was amendable only by unanimous vote. This would have meant that, in theory, even after the 10 year sunset clause had elapsed, the 20 parliamentary seats reserved for whites could block amendment of this article.

White settlers who worked in the civil service were also provisioned for by the Lancaster House Agreement even when they chose to leave the country. The new Zimbabwean government was going to pay their pensions. Zimbabwe was obligated under the Lancaster House Agreement, "to allow the repatriation of pension funds: with the consequence that capital outflows jumped from $14 million in 1979 to $206 million in 1982, adding to problems with the balance of payments."[96] Having given the new government this financial headache, the agreement further complicated the Gordian Knot by forcing the government to purchase land in the currency chosen by the settler.[97] This prevented the government from using domestic mechanisms to raise the money for land purchase such as issuing sovereign bonds. Mkandawire has observed that this also placed "the government's land purchasing scheme on a treadmill. Any announcement that the government would receive foreign exchange for the purchase of land simply raised the price of the land in foreign exchange terms."[98] So, this foreign currency stipulation, ensured that the government could rarely afford the land on the market. This then kept forcing the government to declare that it had no interest in buying the land that was made available on the "free market."

No Present Interest Certificates:

Eddie Cross, while an MP of the opposition Movement for Democratic Change (MDC), explained what No Present Interest Certificates were. He said that while most resettlement land in the 1980s came from under-utilised farms that the government could compulsorily acquire, the government also had first refusal if a white farmer wanted to sell their utilised farm.[99] If the government declined to buy such land, it then issued a No Present Interest Certificate which allowed the farmer in question to sell on the open market.[100] He concluded, from tracing all No Present Interest Certificates ever issued, that 80% of land seized after 2000 had been purchased after independence, "indicating a vibrant property market."[101]

This is another situation that has often been misconstrued by people who are not really conversant with Zimbabwe's history. I have often heard it claimed that 80% of the land reclaimed during the Fast Track Land Reform Programme, had been purchased by white farmers from the government after independence. This did not happen: the government just did not have the land to sell to anyone. What resulted then was that; there was an exclusive free market where only whites could participate. This is how we ended up with multiple farm ownership by white settlers, with one white farmer having as many as 35 farms. This was because of the inequalities in economic power that had been created by 90 years of discriminatory laws.

I also have some more reservations about the No Present Interest Certificate narrative, it pretends that the government willingly approved those sales. The fact of the matter was that the government had been priced out of the market by the tenets of the Lancaster House Agreement. As well, it was also morally wrong to buy land that had been taken from us free of charge. I would also implore my fellow countrymen and countrywomen who have the time, to investigate whether these No Present Interest Certificates actually meant sales happened as claimed. I would not put it past the white settler to just have transferred the land to other whites at much lower prices. This would have been done to make sure that land was continually owned by whites only.

Do not forget that these same people celebrated a Rhodes's Day, and a Founders Day, until 1980 when we abolished those holidays. These two consecutive days were holidays that celebrated Colonialism. I would not put it past them to have wanted to keep land in whites hands in deference to their warped ideology, and as homage to their hero – Cecil Rhodes. Whatever the case, No Present Interest Certificates are not a measure of justice in land transfer. Furthermore, whoever buys a stolen thing, makes himself an accomplice in the theft. The people who bought the land thus became beneficiaries of the initial theft. The white farmers who bought stolen land in Zimbabwe, should have been smart enough to understand the context and the coming storm.

Some will also ask why the nationalists ever agreed to the manifestly unfair Lancaster House Agreement. Clearly, the agreement stood in the way of us immediately achieving the main aim of the liberation struggle – getting our land back. I have always said that I agree with Herodotus's observation that; "circumstances rule men, men do not rule circumstances." This is exactly what happened here, circumstances worked against us at that point in time. Let me rehash the circumstances that led to our agreeing to this unfair peace deal. The first major circumstance here is what I lamented in the Third Address: our disunity. We were colonised because we were disunited.

Even when we were fighting the colonialist, some of our black people were fighting on the side of the colonialist. If you look at pictures of our First Liberation War Heroine – Mbuya Nehanda – just before her execution, you will notice that the foot soldiers guarding her are black people.

Similarly, there were black soldiers in the Rhodesian Army fighting against the guerrilla armies. These black soldiers were fighting to protect white privilege. We currently have the same problem with the puppets of the West that are the MDC. In February 2000, when we held a referendum on land reclamation, these same people were activated to help defeat that referendum. They are still doing the bidding for the white settler at the behest of the West. I can also tell you about this problem in its other iteration during Africa's darkest period: Slavery. Then, it was also fellow black people who captured other blacks and sold them to Slave traders. So, throughout our history, we have people who will always take sides with foreigners. I leave it to the psychologists to diagnose this complex.

When Ian Smith started to see the impossibility of winning against the ZANLA and ZIPRA forces, to forestall outright defeat, he concocted a plan that was called the "Internal Settlement." In this plan, he co-opted black people who were willing to be his puppets and signed an agreement with them. They would become the black faces of the white occupation of our country. This was signed off on 3rd March 1978. The people who stepped up to be his puppets were Bishop Abel Muzorewa and Ndabaningi Sithole. In that agreement, universal suffrage was given, but Joshua Nkomo and Robert Mugabe were banned from participating as candidates. Bishop Abel Muzorewa won the ensuring election, but it was such a sham that no country recognised the short lived Zimbabwe – Rhodesia that the "Internal Settlement" had produced. Abel Muzorewa had become the black face of Colonialism, with Ian Smith holding the real power in the background. No one was fooled.

But still, this circumstance gave Britain and the white settlers wiggle room and an ace to connive with at the Lancaster House Conference. The ace was that Britain could now threaten the guerrilla forces with recognising the "Internal Settlement." This fact alone of our disunity as black people forced us to have to accept the Lancaster House Agreement. If there had been no blacks who wanted to be the face of the white settler, the only condition for stopping Chimurenga II would have been the immediate return of our land. I can take a guess at Ndabaningi Sithole's motivation for siding with the white settler, he may have been bitter about his ouster from leading ZANU. I will leave the explanation of Muzorewa's motivations to those who have followed his fortunes more closely. I feel he was the archetypal sell-out and puppet.

The other circumstance that worked against us at Lancaster House, was war weariness in the countries that housed our bases: Mozambique and Zambia. These allies encouraged the guerrilla armies to accept the unfair deal. To give the Devil his due: Lord Carrington smartly manipulated all these divisions and got the whites a great deal. These were the circumstances that forced us to accept such an unfair deal. The thing with circumstances though, is that they change and become favourable at some point. All we had to do then was wait until circumstances allowed us to take our land back. This is exactly what happened.

Negotiating For Kith And Kin Again:

The British Foreign Secretary at the time of the Lancaster House Agreement – Lord Carrington – records in his Memoirs that he constantly used the threat of recognising the Muzorewa – Smith government. He used this threat to force the guerrilla armies to accept whatever proposals he made at Lancaster House. It is clear that the constituency he negotiated on behalf of was the white settler, and he says as much. He wrote that; "The war had strained Rhodesia's economy and society to the limits, and in spite of a good many local successes for Government forces and some skilful military operations it was not being won. It was exhausting Rhodesia, and in this context that meant it was particularly exhausting the white Rhodesians."[102]

He then exposes his trump card at the negotiations, when he further writes that: "In that case – If Nkomo and Mugabe were to withdraw cooperation – everybody, including Smith and Muzorewa, would at least be seen to have tried, really tried. Their 'internal settlement' might lack enough domestic support and their war would drag on, wretchedly, but we, and with luck, the rest of the world might be able to do more for them with a clear conscience."[103] His strategy to force the guerrilla armies to accept the unacceptable, was to cast them as spoilers and then try to get Rhodesia recognised by the United Nations again. Britain was ready to recognise Rhodesia; "Nkomo and Mugabe, of course, knew that if they went home, we would recognize the 'internal settlement' come what may."[104] This then was the trump card that forced the nationalists to accept an unfair deal at Lancaster House.

That Britain took sides with her white kith and kin should not come as a surprise to anyone. Britain had done this openly when she did not send troops to put down the rebellion that was the Unilateral Declaration of Independence by Ian Smith in 1965. In suing for peace in 1979, this was another variant of protecting kith and kin again. In a just world, Britain should not have overseen the peace talks that ended the war against the white settlers. Joshua Nkomo, speaking on behalf of the two nationalist formations at Lancaster House, stated affairs as they really stood in his opening remarks there:

"Clearly it is not our purpose in coming to London to betray or abandon any of these victories of the people of Zimbabwe who have partly liberated themselves and are continuing the task precisely because Britain failed to carry out her responsibilities. This

Conference is not only unique in British colonial history because it must achieve peace as well as a future Constitution: it is unique because this is the first time that two decolonising forces have to co-operate in this task. The Patriotic Front representing the people of Zimbabwe are here as the effective decolonising factor, while Britain is here asserting her diminished legal authority. In this connection it must be pointed out that Britain, despite its claimed experience in decolonisation has had no success in Zimbabwe or did not give any determined effort. The task has had to be undertaken by the people themselves. Through their sweat and blood, the process is well on its way. The most positive proof of this is the admission of Britain's agent in the form of the declaration of martial law in over nearly 90 per cent of the total area of the country."[105]

Our leaders had correctly figured out how objective conditions stood, Britain had no moral ground to officiate in the talks to bring peace to Zimbabwe. But unfortunately, the Commonwealth had agreed in Lusaka on the peace talks. Tanzania and Zambia, our most important allies in the Commonwealth, had also blessed the talks based on a framework that had been agreed in Lusaka. The fact of our disunity was then manipulated against us by Britain at Lancaster House. If we had been united, and spoke with one voice, the white settlers would never have had a foothold as long as they did in our country. Given these unfavourable circumstances then, nationalists had to compromise at Lancaster House and wait for favourable circumstances. What happened was that we allowed the white settler to disarm, and as soon as we had the monopoly on the use of force in our territory, we went back to address the land issue.

Land Repossession. Untying The Gordian Knot:

I have heard it said that; Possession is nine points of the law, there are but ten. This is a concept that is also well known to military strategists, that if you control the facts on the ground, the law can be made to conform to those facts. This is why for all our being right about land, as long as the white settlers were in possession of the land, our laws and pleading meant nothing to them. The material facts had to change first, or else the laws would remain divorced from the reality. Land reform was very also urgent and had to happen at the point it happened. There was a danger that if the generation that had fought in the liberation struggle had not forced the change in land ownership patterns, the younger generation would just accept the status quo.

Here I am speaking from personal experience. My own rural home is in Mzarabani in the Zambezi Valley. This is the tsetse-fly infested, low lying area we now call home because it was one of the reserves for black people. When I was growing up there in the 1980s, we occasionally took the bus to Harare. I remember noticing the whole 260 Kilometre length of the journey after the Mavhuradonha Mountain was all fully fenced with signposts that read: "Private Property, Trespassers Will Be Prosecuted." I used to look at that expense of land and silently admire how much land these people owned. It never occurred to me that this was my birth-right that I had been dispossessed of, and also that I was very much entitled to it. If the older generation who experienced Colonialism first-hand had not acted on this, the land issue may never have been resolved to our satisfaction. The Social Media generation we have now would not have had the impetus on their own, to address the land ownership injustice.

I said above that some people think that we could have taken our land back peacefully. They are wrong about this; time and the Lancaster House Agreement had entrenched the white settler firmly. It was just not possible to go through the legal, or the negotiation route, because no one is willingly going to give away thousands of hectares of land to live in a small semi-detached house in the city. It was for this reason that untying the Gordian Knot the way Alexander the Great did became the only option available to us.

The untying of the Gordian Knot that ensured then, was the people of Zimbabwe, led by the War Veterans, taking back the land without reference to law. The law now had to follow and fit the facts on the ground once we had created those facts. Trying to change the laws in Parliament had been frustrated by a legal system that was created and rigged to support the claims of the original thieves. The referendum on land reform in February 2000 had also been defeated because the white settlers mobilised against it. This also speaks to our disunity as blacks on matters of national importance. The only way that legal system could be defeated was if new factual realities were created, and then the law forced to follow them. Legal is whatever the Constitution of Zimbabwe says is legal, a lesson we learnt well from how we were dispossessed of our land by Europeans.

Chimurenga III:

So, the only way we could get our land back was by continuing where Chimurenga II had left off. It is in this vein that the period of land repossession has been called Chimurenga III. In 1980 we observed a ceasefire period, but as long as the enemy was not willing to abide by the rules of the ceasefire, it became necessary to restart the war. Much credit for the land reclamation must go to the Zimbabwe Liberation War Veterans Association (ZLWVA), they brought coherence and leadership to an issue that was exceptionally important. The War Veterans brought steel and resolve to this issue and made sure with their 'propaganda of the deed,' the issue succeeded. They led from the front. The land reclamation was titled *Jambanja*, or Chimurenga III, and it corrected all the conniving that had occurred at Lancaster House. *Jambanja* is a Shona word which means resort to force, and thus, by the same means the white settler had taken our land, the blacks were also going to do the same. Thus, the Gordian Knot that was the Lancaster House Agreement was untied.

The timing was also inspired because Apartheid South Africa had been dismantled. We also now had the monopoly on the use of force on our territory. No longer would our army be serving foreign interests. But people also tend to forget that President Robert Mugabe was very much the spearhead of land reclamation. Lesser academics have tried to suggest that President Robert Mugabe was railroaded by the War Veterans into taking back the land. This is a misrepresentation of reality. President Robert Mugabe had already stated the direction land reform was going to take in 1997. In response to Clare Short's letter, he had already said: "We are going to take the land and we are not going to pay for the soil. This is our set policy. Our land was never bought and there is no way we could buy back the land. However, if Britain wants compensation, they should give us money and we will pass it on to their children."[106] If you care to notice, this was exactly the path our land reform took shortly afterwards.

Some Cabinet Ministers even wavered and ordered land occupations to stop while the President was away on a foreign trip to Cuba. I was there at Harare International Airport when President Robert Mugabe returned from Cuba. Before his arrival, a British Airways Boeing 747 plane had arrived and was rushed by demonstrators carrying placards that said; "Britain Go Home!" This is the same crowd that President Mugabe arrived and addressed. He told them to continue occupying the land they had taken back. A lesser person, concerned only with the whites' approval, would have ordered the eviction of the people occupying the farms. Thus, President Robert Mugabe's enduring contribution to land reform, was his refusal to set the army and police on their kith and kin in defence of white settler privilege.

Despite the conniving at Lancaster House, there was still a chance for a fair multiracial society. But the whites squandered this possibility because of their greed. If you recall what I said in the

Second Address, the proto nationalist in our country initially only wanted to be included in the system, they did not want to overthrow it. Their attitude only hardened when whites did not allow them inclusion. Also, if the white settlers had paid heed to Britain and allowed independence and majority rule to go ahead in the 1960s, they might have kept their position of prominence as benevolent dictators. Instead, they made us go to war first, where many black deaths occurred. This then made black people's attitudes harden towards them.

But even after the war, there was a still a path of reconciliation and advantage to the white farmers. The black people had even forgiven them and accepted them as co-nationals despite the violence and oppression they had unleashed on the blacks for nearly 100 years. Still, they were obdurate and keen to maintain racist privilege at the expense of millions of black people. All these missteps by the white settlers, from arrogance and callousness, led to the violent takeover of land in 2000. It was this arrogance and selfishness that made "cutting the Gordian Knot" the only viable solution. It became necessary to take with force, what also had been taken away from us by force.

Agrarian Reform In Zimbabwe:

What we did in Zimbabwe when we took our land back, was to accomplish just the first stage of agrarian reform. This was necessary for the purposes of land justice. The white settlers just wielded too much power that prevented the needed legal transfer of land for agrarian reform to be kickstarted. Agrarian reform itself is a broader term which encompasses land reform, the capacitation of the new farmers, and recalibrating the value chain infrastructure to support the new farmers. This then secures livelihoods and ultimately achieves food security for the country.

What we have achieved in this respect as of 2022, is a move from large scale commercial farms owned by a few elites. We now have small to medium sized farms owned by many. Given our projected population growth, and concomitant land hunger, this is a model more suitable for us. It is now necessary to ensure that these new farmers match the production of large-scale white settler farms of a previous age. This is not impossible to achieve; rural farmers, on even smaller farms, have always produced a substantial amount of the grain required for our food security.

I should also restate that land reform was never about taking all the land in the white settlers' possession. Our government has always been amenable to letting them keep some land as they were contributing to the economy. The government only wanted to take back 5 – 6 Million hectares, but for the white farmers' greed and myopia, that target was surpassed by 4 million hectares under the Fast Track Land Reform Programme. The government had only wanted to acquire under-utilised farms, land from whites with multiple farms, and land held for speculative purposes by absentee landlords who were in Britain, Australia and the United States. We have been very successful in this first stage. Our first stage of agrarian reform has since changed the pattern of land ownership in Zimbabwe.

Despite the false claims that land reform only benefited cronies of President Robert Mugabe, different researchers have shown that, in fact, it was hundreds of thousands of landless families who benefitted. Sam Moyo records that: "The FTLRP phase of the land reform officially benefited 168 671 families, comprising mainly the rural poor and their urban counterparts across 9.2 million hectares. These families acquired an average 20 hectares of land and hold 70 percent of the transferred land through the A1 Schemes."[107] He adds that by 2010, a further 22 000 black farmers benefitted in the A2 Scheme which averaged 100 hectares per farmer.[108] He also points out that not every white farmer was dispossessed, some stayed and are also still equitably represented in the country as a percentage of the population.[109]

While Ian Scoones, a professor from Britain estimated that land reform benefitted around 220 000 black families. It is a dishonest definition of crony then that sees President Robert Mugabe having nearly 1 Million cronies. But despite what was achieved in land transfer, as of 2009, there were still 100 000 people on the waiting list for land, indicating that there is still very high demand for land despite the redistribution.[110] This tells us that any mistakes we may have made in land reform need to be corrected as this is an issue that will not go away.

Our Mistakes:

Our first mistake as nationalists, leading up to land reform, was when War Veterans pressured the government to give them gratuities to the tune of ZW$50 000, and ZW$2 000 monthly payments. This was an unbudgeted for amount, and it resulted in "Black Friday" when our currency crashed. On 14th November 1997, the Zimbabwean dollar lost 75% of its value against the United States dollar. The economic problems that cascaded from this action meant that we ended up doing something no strategist has ever recommended ever: fighting a war on multiple fronts.

For our war veterans, freeing the country from bondage should have been payment enough. Most of the people who went on to claim the compensation were already in other government jobs. Freeing the country and getting equality of opportunity should have been enough payment. With the war veterans' gratuities, we put ourselves at a disadvantage just before we took the important task of resuming Chimurenga II/III.

This mistake of gratuities properly conceived, is not a mistake by war veterans, it was a case of corruption by government. The War

Victims Compensation Fund had existed since 1980, and high rank-ing politicians had long benefitted from it, whether deservedly or not. It only came to the attention of everyone else when a local news-paper published about it in 1996. This is when the war veterans who had had no access to it also demanded their compensation. The mis-take here then was the initial corruption in the operation of the fund.

On the same topic of fighting too many wars at the same time, I have also lamented our involvement in the DRC war in the Fourth Address when I was discussing the national interest. We were fight-ing too many wars on too many fronts. This is a recipe for disaster. The DRC was costing the economy US$1 million a day, money which could have been better deployed in capacitating our new black farm-ers, These were the preliminary economic problems and the mistakes we made in that regard. All what these means is that we ended up fighting on too many fronts at the same time.

The second mistake we made concerns when fellow black people replaced the white settlers in being multiple farm owners, as well as being absentee landlords. This would have happened inevitably as a result of some corruption that will have happened during the land takeover. If European farmers had not chosen the path of confronta-tion and sabotage, after the Fast Track Land Reform Programme, we should have been immediately seized with the issues of that corrup-tion. The issue of multiple, and absentee, farm ownership by some blacks in authority could have been resolved by now. Instead, we had to leave that fight alone, because you do not win by fighting too many enemies at once. So, some of the delays in fighting the corruption in land allocation were due to our deference to this principle.

On a social responsibility note, it was unfortunate that most black farmers workers ended up in a situation of insecurity. We had not calculated how they factored in the land reform programme. Indeed, some farm workers fought to defend the white settlers. I think this is a problem that has been aptly called the "man in the middle problem"

– they are in the thick of it, and do not know whether to support the new dispensation or stick with the comfortable old boss. There is quite an element of Stockholm Syndrome in that some people saw their fates interlinked with the whites. Still, I do not like it whenever black people are pitted against each other, so I will call this our mistake. We did not cater for these people who had been victims of the same system of disenfranchisement.

This has been a recurrent theme of this volume, that we should not be pitted against each other by outsiders, this is what our integration nationalism should always be driving at: unity and mutual aid. There are some farm workers who saw the light early and got awarded land, but some did not. It is our task to correct this wrong. Sam Moyo has recorded this disturbing statistic that as of 2011, around 45 000 former farm workers were physically displaced and are now living as squatters.[111] This is unacceptable to me, and it should also be unacceptable to you all my countrymen and countrywomen.

People like Professor Sam Moyo have also said that access to land opened up mineral resources that were once hidden to us on white settler farms. I would say it was a mistake that we started digging for mineral instead of farming. A concern for the environment would have had us stick to food production and leave mining only to designated areas.

The last mistake I want to point out is the occupation of Agriculture Research Stations and Estates that were protected by BIP-PAs. This happened because the only method left to us was violent occupation. For this reason, there was no time to vet farms before occupation. You have seen in wars, when armies sometimes inflict casualties on their own during friendly fire incidents. The situation we were in during land reclamation was a similar to a wartime situation. Now that sufficient time that allows reflection and self-correction has passed, we can revisit our programme and correct the mistakes we made.

What Ought To Be Done?

Our population is growing, and so the land question will arise again. What we ought to do now, because we corrected the historical injustice, is now to focus on the upstream and downstream sectors of our agricultural economy. As long as land is now in black hands, let us now make the agriculture value chain the mainstay of other black owned businesses. To the extent that not everyone will own a farm, but they will still benefit from owning related businesses. The way to do this is to learn how a small country like the Netherlands manages its agriculture value chain and copy those methods. I said in the Second Address that we are not opposed to foreign ways. It is only when there are demonstrably impeding our economy that we need not adopt them. This is the theme of this volume as well, taking what works from wherever we find it and applying it in our advancement. After the reacquisition of our land, our task now is efficient production.

Some have said that we should give title deeds to our new farmers. I do not think so. I say it is the fiduciary duty of government to not give title deeds, as land reform could be reversed by the simple mechanism of buy out. Britain, which explored the option of invading Zimbabwe to restore white settler privilege, will have found a cost free way of reversing land reform. A war against Zimbabwe would have cost them billions of pounds in addition to the white settlers who would be massacred in retaliation once invasion occurred. It would be far cheaper to just buy out the poor blacks farmers who have been further impoverished by Sanctions. The Sanctions' calculation was that black farmers would think it difficult to be farmers and instead settle for any money they could get. This does not mean land is not important to us, it only means our people will be forced to abandon what is truly in their interest, by extraneous circumstances.

The Second Republic under President Emmerson Mnangagwa, since 2017, has been revisiting the land issue with a view to correct all our unforced errors. The actions President Mnangagwa has authorised so far are acceptable to the nationalist. You will find they also accord with the new Constitution which was written with the input of the white settler's surrogates – the MDC. The concessions we are making now are the minimum we can make.

Even the President of the Second Republic understands that he cannot reverse land reform. This is also what General Vitalis Zvinavashe (Sheba Gava) meant when he said the Presidency is a straitjacket, whereby the man wearing it cannot go against the values of the liberation struggle. I am personally opposed to the money for the improvements on the land that the white settlers have demanded. First of all, the amount is exorbitant, and thus just shows that some of these white settlers are crooks, and even worse, still irreconcilable to our nation. Also, by paying the money for the infrastructure these white settlers erected on the stolen land, it has been argued that we are paying twice for the same thing. The same infrastructure they are demanding compensation for, was built by loans and debt our black government then inherited from the white settler regime in 1980. But having studied warfare, I accept that, sometimes, you have to concede some ground to the enemy, for you to be able to advance forward.

In terms of capacitation, we have introduced the *Pfumvudza*, Command Agriculture, and now the Presidential Inputs Scheme. If we apply ourselves in a public-spirited manner, these initiatives will bear fruit. But we have to eschew Corruption to achieve our goals. I have spared a whole chapter in this volume, to talk about Corruption and how it thwarts national goals.

Conclusion:

My fellow countrymen and fellow countrywomen, excuse my tone in this Address, the land issue is that emotive for me. I, who did not experience the violent expropriation that happened when the whites took our land, feel the injustice and cruelty so vividly. There was just no way we were not going to take our land back. The Lancaster House Agreement had contrived to make it impossible to reclaim our birth right. But as difficult as the Gordian Knot was to untie, Alexander the Great found a shortcut to it. This is also what we were forced to do by circumstances. And we should have no regrets, it was a solution whose moment had come. What was taken from us by force, when the time was right, we also took back by force. We should not only jealously guard our possession, but now move on to a productive footing to ensure our land supports livelihoods.

Address VI.

Gukurahundi.

"When brothers fight to death, a stranger inherits their Father's Estate" - Chinua Achebe.

"Make us enemies of every people on Earth, but save us from civil war" – Lucan, The Civil War.

THE SITUATION WE FACED, between 1981 and 1987, of co-nationals killing each other, is one I hope we never face again in our country. Gukurahundi is a concrete example of what I said in the Third Address, was our mistake as Africans at Independence: attempting to return to whatever earlier divisions we had after defeating Colonialism. We failed to turn our unity of purpose in fighting the Colonialist, into the new foundation of our nation. This was a grave mistake, and it is reflected in lots of places in Africa. It is one of the problems I said falls under the rubric of Colonial Legacy. The Rwandan Genocide of 1994 shows how dangerous not resolving these differences can become. There were cyclical pogroms in Rwanda starting in the 1960s, and these culminated in the 1994 Genocide. I want to suggest to you that, large scale killings, on the proportions of the Rwandan Genocide, are still possible in our own country, if we do not close the Gukurahundi Chapter and its antecedents in our own history. As long as there are parties who remain aggrieved and waiting for an opportunity to take their revenge, cyclical pogroms will be our fate going forward.

The way to arrive at closure for the victims of Gukurahundi is to honestly interrogate what went wrong, so as to ensure that it does not happen again. For our nation-building project, I am satisfied with the 22nd of December 1987 Unity Accord reached between Robert Mugabe and Joshua Nkomo. The Unity Accord signed by these two leaders, saw unification of the Zimbabwe African National Union (ZANU) and the Zimbabwe African People's Union (ZAPU), to become the Zimbabwe African National Union – Patriotic Front

(ZANU – PF). There was an amnesty for both dissidents and army personnel who had committed human rights abuses. In addition to that, there was consociationalism which saw a Ndebele person occupying one of the two Vice President positions in government. Further, Ndebele people moved to various public services positions in Harare, while Shona people replaced them in Bulawayo so as to foster a deeper integration.

To my mind, the 1987 Unity Accord was the best solution to Gukurahundi, but I am also now persuaded by the victims of Gukurahundi, and other conflict resolution experts, that there is still a need to revisit that period. They have argued that properly acknowledging what happened, compensating, and apologising to the victims, is the best way of arriving at true catharsis. In terms of apologies, Mkandawire records that no official apology was ever issued, except for when Minister of Defence, Moven Mahachi, said in the *Sunday Mail* of 6 September 1992 that: "...events during that period are regretted and should not be repeated by anybody, any group of people or any institution in this country."[112] It is also my fervent hope, in addressing Gukurahundi, that it should never be repeated in our country.

As for why Gukurahundi happened, I think the public imagination is slightly misinformed when it holds that it was purely because of tribal hatred between the Shona and the Ndebele. It was not tribal hatreds; it was political intolerance. The distrust between ZAPU and ZANU of the other political party in power is what laid the ground for the insecurity. This then led to a situation that conflict theorists call the Security Dilemma.

I do not think that Gukurahundi was an attempt to wipe out a hated Ndebele tribe from the country. Instead, it was a National Security response to insecurity, where crimes against humanity then got committed by the security services. The National Security response was informed by the violent history between ZAPU and ZANU. Both political parties had been trying to reunite since the

1963 split, and neither wanted to be the junior partner. If you really think about it, the Unity Accord of 1987, was the reunification of nationalists who had split 24 years earlier. The proximate cause of Gukurahundi then, was the rivalry for control of the State between ZAPU and ZANU, embodied by Joshua Nkomo and Robert Mugabe.

ZAPU drew its members largely from the Ndebele in the South-west of the country. This is also where the insecurity occurred and, logically, the target of security operations. Once the security operations started, the security services also targeted the civilians there who they thought were harbouring the Dissidents. This was based on a now outdated Counter-Insurgency (COIN) doctrine. This doctrine harks back to the scorched earth policy and extermination of civilians employed by the British in the Malayan campaigns between 1948 and 1960. The British also used torture, put civilians in concentration camps, and executed Mau-Mau guerrillas in the rebellion in Kenya between 1952 and 1960. This must have been the same COIN template the North Koreans who trained the 5th Brigade of the Zimbabwe National Army (ZNA), in 1981, were still using.

The idea that you can deliberately target civilians and crush them into submission was once a normal part of Counter-Insurgency operations. The reality though, was often that these actions actually awarded the insurgency more recruits to their cause. Ian Smith tried the same approach against black civilians with the Selous Scouts in our liberation struggle. The establishment of the protected villages, the torture and killing of civilians, were all Counter-Insurgency tactics designed to stop the civilians from supporting the guerrillas in the fight for Zimbabwe. Still, this did not win him the hearts and minds of the civilians. Only the addressing of the underlying cause of the insurgency can resolve the matter.

What convinces me even further that Gukurahundi was a Counter-Insurgency operation based on a flawed doctrine, is how Gukurahundi ended. Gukurahundi was stopped by an agreement to share power between Joshua Nkomo and Robert Mugabe. If it was purely about tribal and ethnic hatreds, only the total annihilation of the hated ethnicity, or a military victory by the persecuted, would have ended the killings. This is what the 1994 Rwanda Genocide example shows us.

The Colonial Legacy?

In the Third Address, I mentioned how the arbitrarily drawn colonial boundaries in Africa resulted in "Suffocation" and "Dismemberment." "Suffocation" was the putting of different tribes and ethnicities in one country. While "Dismemberment" was the splitting of people who belonged to one political authority between two countries or more. Putting people who had never belonged to the same political authority under one central political authority, was a potential source of conflict on its own. For his lack of legitimacy to rule, the Colonialist had relied on naked force to establish and maintain his rule. The Colonialist had also used divide and rule tactics to shore up his non-existent legitimacy. The new governments that took over after the Colonialist was defeated, would also face the same problem of political control the Colonialist had faced.

In some places in Africa, "Suffocation" exists as a source of conflict as hatreds created, or just exploited, by the Colonialist as he favoured one tribe or ethnicity over the other. This was usually the case in Colonies where there was indirect rule. In Rwanda, the Germans and the Belgians turned people who had benign differences – Hutus and Tutsis – into mortal enemies. They did this by introducing ethnicity identity cards, based on quite arbitrary features such as height. They then favoured the people that they had classed as Tutsis for higher education and positions of power. We have already seen the consequences of these manufactured divisions in the cyclical pogroms that ended with the Rwandan Genocide of 1994.

This was not our type of Colonial Legacy in Zimbabwe: the white settler in our country discriminated equally against all black people. For example, education for all black people was equally deliberately underfunded. The only thing that the white settler did here was to co-opt the traditional chiefs to make rural administration easy. Where it mattered, at the national government level, the white Rhodesian excluded all black people. What then happened in our country was that when the blacks were fighting to dislodge the white settler, they were aware of the potential of "Suffocation" to be a source of conflict later. Whoever inherited the central authority would have to also rely on force if the other party did not want to yield to his authority. This is how I think the Colonial Legacy manifested itself in our country.

This is also the reason why there were clashes between ZAPU and ZANU during the liberation struggle. Though the two formations were fighting for the same cause, they were already jostling to be the government after the white settler was defeated. The way to achieve this was to be seen as the most competent fighting force that had defeated the white settler. This could be seen in the language of denigrating the other, which, because of the tribal constitutions of ZAPU and ZANU, would end up just looking like tribal hatreds. Still, I am insistent that tribal and ethnic hatred was just a background factor. I say this because, I know exactly what happens when tribal and ethnic hatreds are the foreground factors in a conflict.

What Happened?

Gukurahundi is a Shona word which means "the early rains that wash away the chaff." It is a term that comes from agriculture, and it refers to the chaff that will be left on the threshing spots after the harvested crop has been threshed. The first rain that falls and washes away this chaff, is what is called Gukurahundi. After it washes away this chaff, the threshing spots will be ready for the next planting season and harvest. The term thus implies the washing away of the unwanted husks.

One of the earliest mentions of the concept with regards to ZANU, was in the 1979 strategic document announcing a liberation war strategy that would force the white settlers out of Zimbabwe. 1979 was proclaimed the Year of the People's Storm – the Year of Gukurahundi. In this context, the people's force was to be the early rain that would sweep away the white settlers from Zimbabwe. But, just in time, the white settlers managed to negotiate an end to the war – the Lancaster House Agreement – which protected them. After this happened, it has been said that the Gukurahundi strategy was then redirected towards the Ndebele people who supported ZAPU. This happened during the period of insecurity in Matabeleland.

The disturbances in Matabeleland started as early as 1980. These were armed activities of mostly former ZAPU fighters who had deserted from the Army with their weapons, and some who had never availed themselves for demobilisation. They were robbing, raping and killing civilians and tourists in the Southwest of the country. The government labelled these former ZAPU fighters, "Dissidents," and described their intention as overthrowing the State on behalf of ZAPU.

The picture was further complicated by Apartheid South Africa's destabilization activities, as well as by acts of sabotage by the remaining white Rhodesians who did not want the new black government to succeed. The Zimbabwe Republic Police (ZRP) Police Support Unit, the Central Intelligence Organisation (CIO), and some Zimbabwe National Army (ZNA) units, were initially deployed to combat this dissident activity. These units, while highly efficient, still did not succeed in ending the insecurity there.

The 5th Brigade of the Zimbabwe National Army was then raised, trained, and deployed to Matabeleland, specifically in response to these disturbances. Gukurahundi then, was the Operation that was carried out by the 5th Brigade of the ZNA, in Matabeleland and the Midlands, between 1983 and 1984. The total number of people killed during this operation is contested, with the government saying it was 5 000, while others say it was 13 000, and others have said it was as high as 20 000. It may never be possible to say which one is the accurate figure, but for our purposes here, one death due to ingroup - outgroup intolerance in the same nation, is one death too many. This simply should not have happened.

The events leading to Gukurahundi are a matter of recorded fact, but recorded fact is usually disputed when different parties put different spins to the same event. The protagonists do so to ensure that their side comes across as being in the right. It is quite possible for the government of the day, to have recorded incidents that did not happen, so as to justify its heavy handedness. While ZAPU, the target of government action, could easily refuse to acknowledge any acts of violence it carried out, so as not to appear culpable for the government response. What I will have to do in this Address, is to take what an arguably neutral party has reported to be the events as they happened. Taking the record of events from a neutral party, will allow us to have a clearer picture of what really happened. This will then allow us to use our own faculties to decide who was right, and who was wrong, despite their protestations and justifications.

A judicial commission of enquiry report is usually a good source of such unbiased information. Two judicial commissions were raised by the then Prime Minister, Robert Mugabe: the Dumbutshena and Chihambakwe Commissions. The Dumbutshena Commission was raised to look into the underlying reasons for dissident activity in 1981, while the Chihambakwe Commission was tasked, in 1983, with investigating the actual claims of human rights abuses in Matabeleland. Unfortunately, both Commissions' findings are lost to us; the resultant reports were filed away as Top Secret. Instead, the Catholic Commission for Justice and Peace in Zimbabwe's *Report on the 1980s*

Disturbances in Matabeleland and the Midlands, has been widely acknowledged as a document that was written by a group that had no ulterior motives. So, it is to the Catholic Commission for Peace and Justice in Zimbabwe (CCJPZ), we must turn to, for the timeline of events.

Some Continuities:

But, before we even go to the post-independence timeline, it is useful to recall what we already know about the pre-independence relation-ship between the main liberation struggle formations – ZANU and ZAPU. Continuities in that relationship, post-independence, will help shed light on the events we are addressing here. One of the main factors was the tribal and ethnic make-ups of both the leadership and support base of each formation. While there were Shona people who supported ZAPU, and Ndebele people who supported ZANU, these were just exceptions that proved the rule that: ZAPU was a Ndebele party, and ZANU was a Shona party. This truth is borne out in voting patterns in the first majority elections of 1980, and then again in 1985.

ZAPU was the earlier umbrella party that was established to agitate against white Rhodesian oppression, after the banning of the African National Congress (ANC) and the National Democratic Party (NDP). The ANC and the NDP were the first black nationalist organisations in Rhodesia. At the onset, just as the ANC and NDP had done, ZAPU did encompass all African tribes and ethnicities, but then it split in 1963. The initial reason that caused ZAPU to split, and the formation of ZANU, was a dissatisfaction with Joshua Nkomo's leadership. He was seen to be prevaricating on strategy and goals. When this disagreement in strategy and goals occurred, the fracture eventually turned on tribal lines, with most Ndebeles remaining loyal to Joshua Nkomo, while most Shonas decamped to

ZANU. At this point, ZAPU which had been banned in 1962, was existing as the People's Caretaker Council (PCC). The relationship between ZAPU and ZANU was adversarial from this split onwards.

Indeed, the platform on which the events of 1981 to 1987 stand, is the relationship between the two main formations that prosecuted Zimbabwe's liberation struggle – ZANU and ZAPU and their respective military wings – the Zimbabwe African National Liberation Army (ZANLA), and the Zimbabwe People's Revolutionary Army (ZIPRA). One of the reasons given by the Rhodesian government for banning ZANU and ZAPU (PCC), was the violence between their black supporters in the townships which was said to resemble a civil war.[113] This, because, shortly after the split in 1963, the relationship between ZANU and ZAPU was adversarial to the extent of violence between the supporters in the townships.

When the two formations finally turned to armed struggle as a strategy against white oppression, there were, sometimes, gun battles between ZANLA and ZIPRA in the field. This carried on into the independence era, with both sides trying to outmanoeuvre the other to be the government of the day. Thus, the relationship between the two political formations, has always been that of deep distrust and hostility. From these preliminary remarks, we can now turn to the events that happened leading up to the deployment of the 5th Brigade in Matabeleland and the Midlands provinces.

The CCJPZ Timeline Of Events:

Under the terms of the Lancaster House Agreement, which we dwelled upon at length in the Fifth Address, ZANU and ZAPU's fighting men were to be confined to Assembly Points, awaiting integration into the Zimbabwe National Army. The ZNA would comprise all the belligerents in the Liberation War. It was in the context of being in these Assembly Points that the disturbances began. Developments in the political arena, and the staffing of the post-independence State institutions, especially the ZNA, also had their bearing on the events of 1981 to 1987. The most significant incidents among those recorded by the CCJPZ here follows:

Among the incidents of insecurity recorded by the CCJPZ, the attempts on Robert Mugabe's life would have influenced government response the most. These assassination attempts would have made the government think that there was an attempt at overthrowing the new State. Instead of responding with just the criminal justice system, the government would have had to respond with armed force. During the campaign for the first post-independence elections, held in February 1980, there was an assassination attempt on Robert Mugabe near Masvingo. Another plot to assassinate him during the actual independence celebrations on 18th April 1980 was also thwarted.

In December 1981, South African operatives attempted to assassinate Robert Mugabe in a bomb attack that destroyed ZANU headquarters, killing 7 people and injuring 124. The attempt only failed because the Executive Committee of ZANU cancelled their scheduled meeting in the room where the bomb exploded at the last minute. In June 1982, there was another attempted assassination of Robert Mugabe, this time by ex-ZIPRA fighters who made an armed attack at the Prime Minister's residence. From a National Security perspective, all the attempts on the Prime Minister's life, could only have been seen as takeover of government attempts, by whoever was responsible. The government imputed all this to ZAPU.

The other incidences that were occurring at the same time were the armed clashes between guerrillas in the Assembly Points. In November 1980, there was a gun battle between ZIPRA and ZANLA Guerrillas at Entumbane Assembly Point. Then again, 3 months later, in February 1981, there was a major outbreak of violence between the same formations at the same Assembly Point, this one spilled over into Ntabazinduna and Connemara Assembly points, resulting in more than 300 deaths. Then in August 1981, the Zimbabwe Defence Forces Inkomo Barracks armoury was sabotaged by South African agents. They started explosions which destroyed $50 million in ammunition and equipment. The government must have seen this as ZAPU action as well. For in the same month, North Korean instructors arrived to begin training the 5th Brigade, which was to later be deployed to combat the dissidents in Matabeleland.

In February 1982, arms caches belonging to ZIPRA were discovered in Matabeleland, this led to the arrest of ZIPRA high commanders and expulsion of ZAPU leaders from cabinet. These arrests and expulsions also led to former ZIPRA fighters defecting from the national army with their weapons in large numbers, which led to an increase of bandit activity in Matabeleland. This resulted in curfews, detentions and weapon searches in Bulawayo. Curfews were imposed in Matabeleland; and troop numbers and detentions were stepped up. In the same month, the Thornhill Air Base in Gweru was sabotaged by South African Agents who destroyed 13 fighter jets, thus rendering the Air Force of Zimbabwe inoperable. All these actions would have created a siege mentality in the security services.

The actions of the dissidents were also very costly in civilian lives. In July 1982, 6 foreign tourists were kidnapped and killed, their deaths were only confirmed years later. Between Nov 1982 and Dec 1983, 33 people were murdered by dissidents on commercial farms. January of 1983 saw the Government allowing white farmers to re-arm, to protect themselves against dissidents after a spate of attacks killed 6 people on commercial farms. In January 1984, an announcement was made in Parliament that, since Jan 1983, dissidents had murdered 120 people, mutilated 25, raped 47 and committed 284 robberies. In July of the same year, it was announced again in Parliament that since January 1984, dissidents had killed 45 civilians, raped 37, and committed 253 robberies.

In July 1985, it was announced in Parliament, that since January 1985, dissidents had killed 45, raped 40, and committed 215 robberies. After the 1985 elections, Dissidents targeted Shona-speaking civilians in an attack in Mwenezi, killing 22. Even in the year that the Unity Accord was signed, Dissident action was still taking civilian lives. In January 1987, it was again announced in Parliament that, during 1986, dissidents killed 116 civilians, raped 57, abducted 20 and committed 210 robberies. All this would have also made Zimbabwe a no go area for tourists, thus affecting tourism's contribution to the economy.

It was to this state of insecurity that the government responded with the 5th Brigade. In December 1982, the 5th Brigade had its passing out parade, ready for deployment. On 26th January 1983, the 5th Brigade was deployed in Matabeleland North, and reports of atrocities began to be received within days. Joshua Nkomo, the ZAPU leader, was placed under house arrest in March 1983, but fled to Botswana. A curfew was placed around Bulawayo leading to thousands of detentions. In the same month, the Zimbabwe Catholic Bishops Conference (ZCBC) and the Catholic Commission for Justice and Peace, spoke personally to the then Prime Minister, Robert Mugabe, and presented him their paper – *Reconciliation Is Still Possible*. Presumably, in response to this, on 5th April, the curfew was lifted in Matabeleland North, and on 22nd July, the 5th Brigade was withdrawn from Matabeleland for a brief retraining session. The Brigade was redeployed to Matabeleland North on 29th August the same year. In September 1983, the Chihambakwe Commission of Inquiry was set up to investigate atrocities in Matabeleland.

In January 1984, the Chihambakwe Commission began collecting evidence of army atrocities in Bulawayo in the same month. On 4th February, a food embargo was imposed on Matabeleland South, and the 5th Brigade was simultaneously deployed in the region. Mass detentions followed, with thousands of civilians being incarcerated at Bhalagwe Camp in Matobo District. On 7th April, the ZCBC expressed deep concern over conditions in Matabeleland South, and on 10th April, the curfew was relaxed, and the food embargo was lifted. In July 1984, The 5th Brigade was also withdrawn from Matabeleland for retraining, and then redeployed in 1985. It is useful to note that the 5th Brigade did not succeed in ending the insecurity, a political settlement still had to be reached for that to happen. On 22nd December 1987, ZANU and ZAPU signed the Unity Accord, merging to become ZANU PF, with all the attendant integrative mechanisms written into the treaty.

A Conflict Map:

What is clear from the foregoing, is that the country was in a state of serious insecurity, and it was to this insecurity that the government had to respond. With the benefit of hindsight, it is now clear to us that there were other actors besides ZAPU in the instability. We are now able to identify all the actors in their multiplicity, something that may not have been possible during the insecurity. In conflict resolution studies, a conflict map is a device for listing all the participating actors, their motivations, and relationships. This helps in clarifying the true nature of the conflict. We can now tease out these various actors, their relationships, and effects on the dynamics that ensured.

There were three groups of actors involved in the disturbances in Matabeleland, but the government treated them as if they were all one entity. Moorcraft records that the three groups were: "bandits feeding on the anarchy; genuine ZIPRA dissidents held together by a disciplined command structure, with support from sanctuaries in Botswana, and loyal to Dabengwa and Masuku, with perhaps only titular allegiance to Nkomo; and Super-ZAPU, supplied by South Africa."[114]

Apartheid South Africa's Total Strategy seems to me to have had a preponderant influence on the insecurity. Total Strategy was South Africa's plan to destabilise all neighbouring States to ensure Apartheid's continuance. First of all, South Africa had white Rhodesians who had stayed on in the new Zimbabwean institutions, committing sabotage on its behalf. Then, in addition to Super-ZAPU, Pretoria also supplied the genuine ex-ZIPRA dissidents with weapons and ammunition. While this was a marriage of convenience for both sides, it still made an impact on the country's security. The genuine ZIPRA dissidents were Apartheid South Africa's adversaries, insofar as they supported South Africa's main black liberation movement – the African National Congress (ANC). Still, the genuine ZIPRA dissidents served Pretoria's purposes, albeit indirectly.

For Apartheid South Africa, the rebellion in Matabeleland undermined Zimbabwe's policy of reconciliation. White farmers left Zimbabwe as 60 white farmers were murdered by dissidents, more than the total killed in the liberation war.[115] Towards this goal, Super-ZAPU agents even killed white farmers to drive them out of the country. The deployment of the Army in Matabeleland also benefitted Apartheid South Africa in another way. It restricted the incursions of African National Congress (ANC) *Umkhonto we Sizwe* fighters into South Africa. Further, the South African destabilization plan was also designed to force Mugabe to overact, as is to be expected in all situations of insecurity. The 5th Brigade obliged that expectation. This last scenario was meant to support the idea that blacks needed white oversight, otherwise they would kill each other. All in all, these problems were meant to prove that a country governed by the black majority, was unviable, thus protecting Apartheid South Africa from scrutiny.

On the government side of the conflict map, the ZRP Police Support Unit, CIO, and some ZNA Special Forces units were the first respondents when the insecurity began. In interviews, former dissidents have said that these units were very effective at targeting the actual dissidents. It was only when the 5th Brigade was deployed, that atrocities started getting recorded. Complicating the conflict map, was what have been called pseudo-dissidents. An example is the axe murders of 16 white farmers belonging to a Christian sect in Esigodini in November 1987. The claim has been made that this massacre, and others, were carried out not by genuine ex-ZIPRA dissidents, but by pseudo-dissidents.

Mkandawire has described this incident thus: "There was a final group of what has been referred to as "pseudo-dissidents," including the gang led by Gayigusu in Matabeleland South, which was responsible for the murder of 16 missionaries in November 1987. This gang was allegedly the personal "hit squad" of politically powerful ZANU officials in this part of the country. They were summoned by local squatters engaged in a land dispute with the missionaries who were trying to evict them. Sixteen men, women and children were axed to death."[116] Such actions are to be expected in a state of insecurity, opportunistic actors will always arise to pursue their own agendas.

Why Gukurahundi Happened?

The main reason in the public imagination for why Gukurahundi happened, is that the Shona were revenging against the Ndebele for the raids that happened in the 19th Century. When the Ndebeles under King Mzilikazi settled on the Zimbabwe Plateau in 1838, they used to raid the neighbouring Shona for grain, cattle, and women. This is supposed to be the Shona grievance that led to Gukurahundi. I know this because I have personally heard some Shona people say the same thing. Andrew Meldrum also records his shock when he heard a Shona acquaintance say: "Those Ndebeles had it coming. They needed to be taught a lesson."[117] Various authors have also recorded that when the 5th Brigade was targeting the civilians in Matabeleland, they brought up the issue of the Ndebele raids of the 19th Century.

This is what conflict theorists call the "ancient hatreds" cause of conflict. The theory is that different tribal groups always remember their conflictual history, and this shapes their relations into the future. The theorists describe this relationship as "fear of the future lived through the past." According to this theory, the Shona would have feared that the Ndebele being the government would result in the persecutions of the past returning. The Ndebele would also have imagined that the Shona being the government would seek revenge for their past experiences. It is a sound explanation, but it has its limits with regards the specificities of what happened in Zimbabwe. Thus, in reference to Gukurahundi, it is my contention that the public imagination is slightly misinformed. There were other factors that intervened and led to Gukurahundi. The public imagination needs to be made aware of those intervening variables.

In my enquiries into the matter, I found out that Gukurahundi happened largely because the State was responding to insecurity. I have chosen to call this the "National Security Perspective" as to why Gukurahundi happened. I have called it that because, every National Security practitioner will respond exactly the same way given this scenario. A study of State dynamics everywhere in the world, will yield that no viable State has ever allowed an armed challenge to subsist on its territory. The very definition of State itself includes having a monopoly on the use of legitimate force in your territory. The State, therefore, cannot allow there to be armed people who are not authorised by the State to do so. It was when the State in Zimbabwe tried to disarm ZAPU that the excesses occurred.

Joshua Nkomo, had he won the first elections, would have reacted the same way to the same insecurity in the country. After that, there is no guarantee that excesses would not have happened. Even the Rhodesian State we fought against, purely from a National Security Perspective, was justified in responding with force to our armed challenge. Excesses then occurred. For peace's sake, we had to forgive the excesses by the Rhodesians. This is how the matter presents itself to anyone who makes an honest enquiry into what happens in conditions of insecurity.

The factor that mainly influenced the Zimbabwean government's response to the insecurity was the competition for political power between Joshua Nkomo and Robert Mugabe. Robert Mugabe and Joshua Nkomo were equally unaccommodating of each other. Joshua Nkomo, having led the first of the truly nationalist movements, had expected to be the first post-independence leader. But by 1980, this expectation was outdated: Mugabe and Nkomo had belonged to different political parties during the whole duration of the armed struggle. In looking further into this matter, I also found some instances that made the Nkomo – Mugabe rivalry quite personal. The most serious instance was when Joshua Nkomo connived to make Mugabe and others Stateless persons with the "Tanganyika Affair." I will discuss this affair in more detail below.

For now, I just want to posit that leadership personality clashes can translate to group fighting. Personal competition between two political leaders, inevitably pits their organisations against each other. The relationship can also happen the other way, with leaders just espousing their groups' quarrels. Theories of conflict call this the "group competition for resources" cause of conflict. Resources and public goods within a country can only be allocated by the State. Security is one such public good. Therefore, ZAPU and ZANU can be seen to have been competing for State power, because they did not trust each other as provider of the other's security.

The Security Dilemma:

The National Security Perspective responds to insecurity with force. This is what the exigent nature of the situation demands. But once this response has been activated, politics should seek to understand the underlying causes of the insecurity. ZAPU/ZIPRA had genuine grievances. To my mind, the underlying cause for the insecurity in our country, was the trust deficit between ZAPU and ZANU. This trust deficit had been nurtured since the 1963 split and throughout the 14 years of the armed struggle. When it came to the end of the liberation struggle in 1980, as I have pointed out above, neither ZAPU nor ZANU could trust each other as provider of the other's security.

When there is such a trust deficit, the tendency is to keep arms for defensive purposes. The same distrust existed between ZANU/ZANLA and the Rhodesians just before the elections. To ensure its security, ZANLA also kept a sizable force and arms out of the Assembly Points during the ceasefire period. I want us to grant that ZAPU/ZIPRA may also have cached weapons in deference to the same logic, and not necessarily because they were planning to topple the government from the onset. Unfortunately, even if this was the case, the outcome is still the same: insecurity. This is what Barry Posen explained is the Security Dilemma: whereby "what one does to enhance one's own security causes reactions that, in the end, can make one less secure."[118]

Once the election outcome had been certified, ZAPU/ZIPRA's possession of arms and usage without State authority, made it a target for disarmament. Robert Mugabe's ZANU, for having won the 1980 elections, had the legitimacy and duty to maintain National Security.

The National Security Perspective:

Professor Ngwabi Bhebhe, a former ZAPU cadre, and now prominent historian, has characterised Gukurahundi in terms of what I have termed here the National Security perspective. He wrote:

> "Moreover, when people discuss our nationalist historiography, they want to pour the worst venom on ZANU-PF (sic) and even

forget the inevitability of post-colonial civil war. Perhaps what was not inevitable were its excesses. But frankly, considering the way we had built our guerrilla armies, I again doubt whether a ZIPRA dominated army would have fought such a civil war any different from the way ZANLA dominated Zimbabwe National Army fought the civil war in the Midlands and Matabeleland. I am aware of the destructive and brutal role of the Korean trained Gukurahundi, but are we certain that if we, as ZAPU, had won the elections, we would not have had our friends to train our own military units to destroy or tame former ZANLA forces. Rivalry between ZAPU and ZANU was simply too much and uncontrollable and only those who were on the periphery of our struggle deserve to misunderstand our post-colonial conflicts."[119]

This is the exact description of what I have called the National Security Perspective, whereby it does not matter who is in power, they would have responded the same way to insecurity.

In responding to the insecurity, Mkandawire thought the government made this mistake: "although there was no secessionist movement, the new government reacted as if the very existence of Zimbabwe as a nation was at stake."[120] Mkandawire misses the point. The National Security Perspective is informed by one rule only: maintaining a monopoly on the legitimate use of physical force in the territory. If a group of people acquired arms of war, even if they have not taken any actions with those arms, the government has to disarm them. Even if the arms are for defensive purposes only, the National Security rule is that those people have to be disarmed. The National Security practitioner must always assume the worst of people who arm themselves without authorisation from the State. In the case of Zimbabwe around 1980, the armed people were already killing civilians with those arms. The duty to protect the citizens was also activated thus.

Perhaps, at this stage, I must rehash the definition of the State given to the world by Max Weber. Writing in Politics As A Vocation, Weber defined the State as a "human community that (successfully) claims the monopoly of the legitimate use of physical force within a given territory."[121] He then pressed the point home by saying; "note that 'territory' is one of the characteristics of the State. Specifically, at the present time, the right to use physical force is ascribed to other institutions or to individuals only to the extent to which the State permits it. The State is considered the sole source of the 'right' to use violence."[122] This is the crux of the matter: the State just cannot allow a challenge to its monopoly on the legitimate use of violence to subsist on its territory.

The 1980 Elections awarded Robert Mugabe's ZANU the legitimacy to be the new State authority in Zimbabwe. ZAPU having lost in the same elections, was for this reason targeted for disarmament. The same would have happened if ZANU had lost the elections and decided to hold on to its arms. In fact, there was a Rhodesian plan to wipe out all ZANLA forces and leaders had Robert Mugabe rejected the election results and taken up arms. This was called Operation Quartz, and it had the tacit approval of Joshua Nkomo, insofar as he had already agreed to form a government of unity with Ian Smith and Abel Muzorewa, to keep Mugabe out of power.

The political aspect of the plan was a coalition government that excluded Mugabe – no one was projected to win an outright majority in the 1980 elections. The military aspect of Operation Quartz would then be announced as a "Countercoup," when Mugabe refused to accept the election outcome and returned to war. The Rhodesians Security Forces would then wipe out ZANLA guerrillas in the Assembly Points, with the (expected) support of ZIPRA.[123] The ZANLA leadership in the country were targeted for destruction, while ZIPRA leaders would be given a chance to surrender if they were in the same buildings as the ZANLA targets.[124] A Muzorewa – Nkomo – Smith alliance was mooted to then run a pro-Capitalist Zimbabwe.[125] As it turned out, the landslide 57 seats for ZANU were so unassailable that even a coalition of Nkomo (20), Muzorewa (3), and the 20 seats reserved for whites would still not form a majority government.

All the threats to the new government we think today were not existential threats, only seem so to us because most of them were thwarted. If they had not been thwarted, the outcomes could have been even more catastrophic for the country. All post-conflict societies are just one successful threat away from catastrophe. In Rwanda, the shooting down of the Presidential Plane was the trigger for the Genocide that killed between 800 000 to 1 Million Tutsis and moderate Hutus. In our own immediate post-conflict situation, every Rhodesian CIO attempt on Mugabe's life was a potential trigger for the same catastrophe that Rwanda faced.

Robert Mugabe was a constant target for assassination by the Rhodesian Central Intelligence Organisation. The CIO, at the last-minute, had aborted an attempt to assassinate him in London during the Lancaster House Talks.[126] There were nine other attempts by the Rhodesians after that. The one that could have impacted the country catastrophically was the last one. This was "on 22 March 1980, when the SAS planned to use a SAM-7 Strela to shoot down a plane carrying Mugabe and 22 members of his central committee as it came in to land at Salisbury airport. Some SAS operators objected to killing the crew as well, and ComOps (Combined Operations) cancelled the plan at the last minute."[127]

Another South African plan that was also thwarted had the potential to have catastrophic consequences for the country. This involved placing roadside bombs in electricity substations and traffic control boxes, which would be detonated when the VIP motorcade for the Independence Eve celebrations was passing.[128] This would have killed Lord Soames, Robert Mugabe and Prince Charles. The expectation was that the black population would go on a rampage killing whites in revenge for Mugabe's assassination.[129] The South African Battle Group Charlie would then intervene in a "humanitarian capacity" against ZANLA, with the (expected) support of ZIPRA, and install a temporary Muzorewa – Nkomo administration.[130] Given what had happened in the Congo, the world would not have been opposed to such an intervention to save lives, but this plan also failed when a CIO operative – Danny Stannard – got wind of it.[131]

Thus, the actions of the new Zimbabwe government, were also informed by the knowledge that their opponents were plotting to destroy them. This would have produced a siege mentality, which, in turn, impacted how the government responded to any National Security threat. This explains the government response, which Mkandawire said was as if the very existence of Zimbabwe was at stake.

Was Gukurahundi A Genocide?

Gukurahundi has now started to be used for political mileage by political entrepreneurs and Non-Governmental Organisations (NGOs). It is these political entrepreneurs and NGOs who have started to declare Gukurahundi a Genocide. The political entrepreneurs and NGOs making such declarations today, have their own agendas which have nothing to do with our reality. The relevance-seeking political entrepreneur, and the funding-seeking NGO, profits from presenting issues in the worst possible light. Still, this distortion introduces a narrative that is detrimental to our nation-building project. It keeps us divided by appealing to our emotions with exaggerations. This is also why I said we should close the Gukurahundi Chapter and all its antecedents so that our nation building can be as strong and unitary as it ought to be by now.

Do not forget that the white settlers also claimed that had they not arrived on the Zimbabwe Plateau, the Shona would all have been killed by the Ndebele. This was just the excuse the white settler used to legitimize their presence in our country, it had nothing to do with the reality. The more unreflecting among us may have believed this lie, and it would have informed their view of Ndebeles. A more reflective attitude would have asked a few questions before accepting this claim from the white settler. Questions like, for example, if the Ndebele arrived on the Zimbabwe Plateau in 1838, and the White Settlers arrived in 1890, why was it taking over 50 years for the Ndebele to complete their "Genocide" against the Shona? This is the same reflective attitude we should use in our thinking about Gukurahundi.

The Shona – Ndebele hatred was never the main fault line between ZAPU and ZANU. When PCC (ZAPU) and ZANU fought each other on the streets of Highfield in the 1960s, the tribal lines had not yet been drawn. It was merely two different political organisations fighting each other. They were killing each other all the same, despite the fact that both formations had Shona and Ndebele supporters. It was the same in the 1980s: ZAPU and ZANU now competing for State power. The Ndebele who were targeted, were only targeted because the operation took place in a geographical area predominantly populated by the Ndebele. If the disturbances had been in Mutare, the civilians in Mutare would have experienced the excesses of the security operation. This would have been because the security forces targeted civilians they thought were giving succour to the Dissidents.

There is also a tendency to quote an even higher number such as 30 000 to 50 000 killed, so as to declare Gukurahundi a Genocide. A Genocide is not merely a numbers game. If it were, then we would say that Ian Smith committed Genocide because 40 000 black people died in the Rhodesian War. I do not call what Ian Smith did a Genocide, because there was no intent. For me, intent is more definitive of Genocide than merely the number killed. Genocide presumes a hatred of a specific tribe who will be targeted for just belonging to that tribe. In this formulation, it does not matter that you do not support a political party, you will be killed. The targeting in Gukurahundi was not tribal or ethnically motivated, it was political. Ndebeles who belonged to ZANU were not targeted. Enos Nkala is a notable example of a Ndebele who was even in the ZANU Executive Committee. Enos Nkala even publicly insinuated that a Shona person, Geoff Nyarota, was now a dissident for exposing government corruption in the 1980s. Thus, there was just no deliberate plan to wipe out all the Ndebeles.

You only need to look at the chronology of events given to us above by the CCJPZ to see that there was just no intention to destroy the Ndebele out of hatred. The government did not just once in power, establish death squads to target the Ndebeles. Mugabe had even included Ndebeles in his government. The trigger for the security operations was dissident activity in Matabeleland and the discovery of ZAPU arms caches. Even then, Robert Mugabe first responded to the insecurity with regular units. The ill-disciplined 5th Brigade was only latterly raised. You also need to look at the responses Robert Mugabe made whenever concerns about the 5th Brigade were raised. The 5th Brigade was withdrawn for retraining twice to try to make it conform with the human rights standards of the time. Curfews and food embargoes were lifted in response to appeals from civil society organisations. It is all these factors that convince me that there was no deliberate plan to wipe the Ndebele from the Map. This is just not what the anatomy of a Genocide looks like.

Contrast that with the Rwandan Genocide to see the machinery and language that was put in place. There were radio stations encouraging militias to murder Tutsis, and even telling them where the Tutsis were taking refuge. Hutus who refused to participate in the killings were also killed. Then there was the Ten Hutu Commandments which unabashedly promoted hatred of the Tutsi. Tutsis were banished from State institutions and business. There was also the mobilisation and arming of civilians to help with "sending Tutsis back to Ethiopia via a short cut – the rivers."

The absence of such mobilisation in Zimbabwe convinces me that Gukurahundi was just a response to insecurity where human rights abuses were committed. This insecurity happened because ZAPU and ZANU were deeply hostile to each other, before, during, and after the liberation struggle. The hostility to each other was not on tribal lines – it was over political differences. What has happened over time is that this has been forgotten. I tried to trace why Joshua Nkomo and Robert Mugabe were so unaccommodating of each other, and this is what I found.

The Mugabe - Nkomo Rivalry:

In January 1982, Joshua Nkomo held a furious press conference where he denounced Mugabe in this way; "Who is this Robert Gabriel Mugabe? Who does he think he is that he can call a One-Party State without consulting me? He is a little man, a sneaky man. Small men will always cheat you, just as Mugabe has tried to cheat me. Never trust a small man."[132] While Joshua Nkomo was justified in resisting the announcement of a One-Party State, the tone raises issues around political communications in post-conflict societies.

"This time Robert Mugabe has gone too far. I will never agree to form a One-Party State with him. If he doesn't have the decency, the sense, to speak to me first about such an important matter, such a critical matter, then I cannot trust him, and I will never form a One-Party State with him. And he cannot have a One-Party State without me, Joshua Nkomo, and without my party, ZAPU, the party that started African Nationalism in this country. We cannot allow it. He cannot have it. He will never have his One-Party State here. Never!"[133] Nkomo was still speaking as if he was equals with Mugabe, but this was no longer the case. The elections had changed this reality.

One of the difficulties of politics, is communicating your anger publicly, without sounding as if you are plotting subversive activities. Joshua Nkomo certainly encountered this problem in his pronouncements in the lead up to his sacking from government. The problem is that you are trying to communicate to different audiences at the same time. On the one hand, you don't want your supporters and enemies to think you are weak, but the same message can be misconstrued as an open threat to a Constitutional order. Especially so, in the context of guerrilla movements that have just assumed power with all the other competitors still having their weapons.

So, while Nkomo was justified in what Meldrum has called a rant, it is interesting to look at what this particular type of communication achieved. Robert Mugabe soon called a press conference of his own in response, where he announced that arms caches had been discovered on ZAPU farms. He accused Nkomo of trying to overthrow the government, then sacked him.

But, what made Mugabe and Nkomo this unaccommodating towards each other? Was it just the competition for State power or was there something more personal? Masipula Sithole has done a great job of tracing all the contradictions that bedevilled all the national liberation struggle formations in Zimbabwe. From his Struggles Within Struggles, we find the source of the distrust between Joshua Nkomo and Robert Mugabe.

The Mugabe – Nkomo rivalry does not really start with Mugabe and Nkomo, it starts with Ndabaningi Sithole pitted against Nkomo. It was only when Sithole was ousted from ZANU in 1974/5, that this competition became a Mugabe – Nkomo rivalry. The competition was always for the control of the biggest nationalist movement in the country. Ndabaningi Sithole, Mugabe, and others initially submitted to Nkomo's leadership. They then became dissatisfied with his leadership over issues relating to the direction the confrontation with the white settler would take. Joshua Nkomo was settling for less than the outright self-determination the other nationalists now wanted. Once they voiced their dissatisfaction with his leadership, Nkomo conspired to have them thrown out of the Party.

Here, Nkomo became a political animal and did his best to outmanoeuvre his political rivals. I think one of those manoeuvres is what made Mugabe always view Nkomo in a poor light. I have called it the Tanganyika Affair. Joshua Nkomo finally succeeded in his manoeuvrers with the PCC/ZAPU Caucus at Cold Comfort Farm in 1963. There, Nkomo was elected unopposed as "the only national leader and Life President" of PCC/ZAPU.[134] Shamuyarira also observes that this title of Life President, made it difficult for these political rivals to reconcile. [135]There was no longer a vacancy at the top of ZAPU, something Mugabe often repeated, in reference to the Presidency, when he later became President of the Country.

Ndabaningi Sithole, Mugabe and others, seeing the difficulties created for them leading up to the PCC/ZAPU Caucus, boycotted that gathering. Instead, they formed ZANU on 8th August 1963, and thus ended any relationship between Nkomo and themselves. The PCC/ZAPU itself was formally established on 10th August 1963. These two organisations would exist separately until the Unity Accord of 22nd December 1987.

The split had nothing to do with tribalism. Even when Ndabaningi Sithole was ousted from ZANU, to be replaced by Robert Mugabe in 1974/5, it was not about tribe. Ndabaningi Sithole had written a letter to Ian Smith from prison, pleading with him, and stating that he had renounced the armed struggle. This is the reason why he was deposed as ZANU leader, not because he was a Ndau. It was the same with Joshua Nkomo, the issue was his competence as a leader at the material time, not his tribe.

We can find the first articulation of Nkomo's limitations as a leader way before the split that created ZANU. This comes from a much earlier time, before the NDP was banned. Michael Mawema's letter of resignation from the NDP was the first instance of public criticism of Nkomo's leadership qualities from people who had close contact with him. Mawema wrote that:

> "I decided to resign from the NDP because of treachery, inconsistency and betrayal of the mandate and demands of our people at the last constitutional conference. We demanded one man one vote, but Nkomo agreed with UFP [United Federal Party] and signed for a qualitative franchise of £720; we demanded a majority representation in parliament, but Nkomo signed for 15 seats in a house of 65; we demanded our land, but Nkomo signed a document which excluded our Zimbabwe… Being a true son of Zimbabwe I made a public condemnation of the Nkomo-Whitehead-Sandys constitution as utterly unacceptable, and I was suspended for having rejected that constitution."[136]

Thus, Nkomo was caving in on demands at a stage when such concessions were inconsistent with the effort to emancipate the black Zimbabwean. A few years earlier, these same concessions would have been acceptable, but at this stage of the struggle, the nationalists' demands were different.

By the time we get to the ZAPU – ZANU split in 1963, the issues against Nkomo were very clear. Shamuyarira explains; "By now opposition to Nkomo had crystallized on four points. Those who opposed him wanted a 'policy of confrontation'; they wanted a new political party to be formed; they were disappointed by his lack of decisiveness as a leader; and they were concerned about the lack of confidence in Nkomo which many Pan-African leaders had expressed to them."[137] We find these accusations from multiple sources, and they are also confirmed by documented Joshua Nkomo actions.

When ZAPU got banned on 20th September 1962, Joshua Nkomo was in Lusaka, the leaders inside the country were detained, and the expectation was that he would return to the country and if arrested, give symbolic leadership to his followers.[138] Instead he went to Dar es Salaam against the advice of even his Zambian hosts.[139] Nkomo's leadership at this point is then characterised by a fear of imprisonment which made his comrades start questioning his commitment and courage. Ndabaningi Sithole, in his letter, titled The Reasons For Our Action, settled on this theme of Nkomo's avoidance of prison, dishonesty, and dictatorial tendencies. He wrote that:

"Mr. Nkomo is very much afraid of going to jail and this fear of jail causes him to evade taking the necessary decisions which any leader in his position is expected to take. The white settlers have exploited this fact to full advantage. Because of this fear, Mr. Nkomo has deserted the people at the time when they most needed bold leadership that does not count the cost. When ZAPU was banned on September 20th, 1962, Mr. Nkomo was then in Lusaka. Much against the advice of UNIP and his supporters Mr. Nkomo fled to Dar-es-Salaam leaving as it were, his sheep to be scattered by the wolf. Mr. Nkomo publicly stated that he did not want to 'rot in jail.' Meanwhile hundreds of his supporters went to jail. When he was finally forced to go back to Southern Rhodesia and face detention, after ten days of chopping and changing, the psychological moment had been missed, and his supporters' confidence in him was greatly shaken and under-mined, and since then the people have been saying: 'how can we get our independence with such a cowardly leader?' While in detention, Mr. Nkomo's fears were also clearly demonstrated. He arranged for a private plane to take all the members of the Central Executive secretly out of restriction, but they refused to jump their restriction."[140]

The "Tanganyika Affair":

The last issue of wanting to form a government in exile was opposed by all the Central Executive, until through dishonesty Nkomo persuaded them all to abscond on their bail conditions and go to Tanganyika (Tanzania).[141] He convinced members of the Central Executive to skip their bail by saying that Julius Nyerere had agreed to host a government in exile.[142] On arrival in Tanzania, Nyerere was surprised to see them and asked; "If you leave the people you are leading, who is going to lead them? Who is going to organize them?"[143]

Ndabaningi Sithole further wrote that; "Last April, Mr. Nkomo under false presentations, induced Mr. Robert Mugabe, who was out of custody on a heavy bail, to jump the bail to come to Dar-es-Salaam. In complying with Mr. Nkomo's wishes, Mr. Mugabe has involved himself in an offence against the law. As if this was not enough, Mr. Nkomo has cabled President Nyerere that he has suspended Mr. Mugabe. This apparently was intended to cause difficulties for Mr. Mugabe so that he is in trouble both in Southern Rhodesia and in Tanganyika."[144] Shamuyarira says that this deception was a point of bitter personal disappointment for relations with Nkomo.[145]

Once deceived into going into exile, Nkomo then suspended the same Central Executive members from the Party, which meant that these people now had no locus standi in Tanzania, as well as unable to return to Rhodesia as they would be imprisoned for violating bail. This deception by Nkomo would seem to have been geared at consolidating his hold over the political party.

Again, Ndabaningi Sithole states as much; "Mr. Nkomo had become a law unto himself, and as such dealt severely with anyone who disagreed with him, who criticized his leadership, and who suggested any radical change in the present leadership. On 6 July, at a rally held in Harare, Salisbury, he publicly named ten hard-core nationalists as his chief enemies. Among these were Enos Nkala, Henry Hamadziripi and Maurice Nyagumbo, all of whom have served terms of imprisonment varying between two and four years for political reasons, and this act has infuriated many people."[146]

This act of branding others chief enemies of the movement is hardly the act of a democrat, and further, his suspension of Takawira, Malianga, Mugabe and Sithole, were taken without consulting the deliberative organs of the party. The leaders in exile then voted to depose Nkomo and replace him with Ndabaningi Sithole, given all of Nkomo's actions. Nkomo then called for a conference to vote for new leadership, charging the exiles to return home and face the people, knowing fully well that they could not return as he had instigated them to violate bail conditions, and so would be arrested on return. Masipula Sithole concedes that this is the meanness of politics, and Nkomo was surely acting in the manner that the field demands. When Sithole and his group finally returned, they were arrested and freed on bail, but declined to participate in Nkomo's Cold Comfort Leadership Conference, alleging the delegates were handpicked by Nkomo.[147] The split was cemented.

When this split happened, ZAPU had the most people in Salisbury (Harare) as well as Bulawayo. Having learnt from seeing the dangers of tribalism in countries that had decolonised earlier than ours, there was a deliberate effort not to recruit on the basis of tribe. Shamuyarira records that; "Despite these clashes (ZAPU – ZANU violent confrontation in 1963), however, the differences between the parties never took on a tribal character. For this ZANU should take credit. Nkomo is a Matabele, while the majority of Sithole's supporters are Mashona: Sithole himself comes from the Ndau tribe, on the Mozambique border. Clearly then ZANU could have organized on tribal lines and had tremendous tribal appeal; but it never did this, because the party leaders realized that once you set yourself on this path, you end up dividing the country into regions."[148]

There were even attempts at reunification, but it had to be on Joshua Nkomo's terms because he led the larger organisation at the time – ZAPU. The OAU had suggested that there be a reunification as resources were misdirected at fighting at each other instead of for independence. But Nkomo held the view that "there had never been any split, all the people were united behind him. He continually invited the ZANU leaders to 'return to the people' where he alleged he was. It was unity on his terms or nothing. He argued that ZANU had never had any support worth talking about; therefore, unity with such a party was pointless. It would be just an admission of the existence of the non-existent."[149] The reunification in 1987 can also been seen as having been on ZANU's terms. Overtime, ZANU had become the stronger party. A question for our nation to think about further, is whether the reunification of ZAPU – ZANU could have been done without that much blood being spilt first.

I have raised all these points of the weaknesses in Joshua Nkomo's leadership in response to distortions that are now entering our history. The historical record between ZANU and ZAPU needs to be discussed as it really happened. The problem I have in mind here is the revisions by the Ethnonationalists. Ethnonationalism is the very anti-thesis to what we are trying to do in Zimbabwe: Nation-building. These points I have raised are also an affront to the cult of personality, there are no infallible people. So, we should not discuss Joshua Nkomo as if he had no faults. Only when all his faults and strengths are taken into account, will our history be more accurate. Thus, I reiterate, the initial disenchantment with Nkomo's leadership, was not because of his ethnicity or tribe, it was about his abilities and propensities.

Setting The Nationalist Record Straight:

One of the falsities that have started to appear in our historical record is a revision of the relationship between Nkomo and Mugabe. If these distortions are not corrected now, they will be believed as gospel truth by our posterity. One of the reasons for these distortions is a revision of history by people who were opposed to Robert Mugabe. Even stalwarts of the struggle, such as Dumiso Dabengwa and Tshinga Dube, have also advanced some revisions of our history. Their motivations, of course, are an understandable rancour towards Robert Mugabe, who they say was the architect of Gukurahundi.

But if we are going to achieve our goal of being one strong nation, these falsehoods have to be corrected. If not corrected, they will become incubators for more hatred in our country. The main misconception these falsehoods introduce, is that Nkomo was cheated out of his God given position to lead Zimbabwe in 1980. This then would make it seem that ZIPRA was justified in taking up arms to correct an injustice.

If we were to boil down the revision to one thing, it is in their agreement that Zimbabwe would have been better off if Nkomo had been its first Prime Minister. These revisions have thus, ultimately, sought to raise Nkomo to the level of an infallible, tolerant and democratic leader, while Mugabe was not. This claim has no merits because no one can prove alternative history. The leader in opposition is no guide to what he will do in power, where he will be faced with the exigencies of National Security for example. Fortunately, we have Joshua Nkomo's record in the political parties he led, and the decisions he made in fighting the Liberation Struggle. Going by his record I touched on above, the claims of being infallible and democratic are clearly unfounded. Below follows a discussion of some of the revisions and the reality of the matter.

The first accusation against Robert Mugabe, in this regard, is that he was too power hungry and ambitious. The charge is that Mugabe should have been subservient to Joshua Nkomo when they went into the elections in 1980. This charge has no basis in reality as Joshua Nkomo and Robert Mugabe had not belonged to the same political party since 1963. They had led their different formations – ZAPU and ZANU respectively – which had prosecuted the liberation war separately.

Dumiso Dabengwa even went further and claimed that Tongogara told him that Mugabe is not good enough to lead, Nkomo should lead. This is interesting, but if we revisit the split that happened between ZAPU and ZANU in 1963, and the war efforts of the two formations, there are no grounds to argue that there should have been an automatic re-marriage at the end of the war. Much less one which automatically gave Joshua Nkomo the leadership position. The contribution of the different forces is clear to see, with ZANU having more fighters, and having fought over 75 percent of the country, while ZAPU had less fighters and fought in 25 percent of the country. There is no logical reason why people who had differences over methods could now hand over power to others they had differed from throughout the 14 years of war, when the success of their methods had now yielded fruit. Dabengwa also introduces a very undemocratic element when he talks as if Tongogara's wishes was the only way ZANU should have proceeded. He does not say by what mechanism Tongogara's wish should have become the decision of the majority in ZANU.

The second charge is that Robert Mugabe was a lesser revolutionary so was installed by the British to protect the Whites' interests after Independence. These revisionist claims even go further and try to claim that Joshua Nkomo was the hard-line revolutionary who was thwarted by British machinations. One of the proponents of this revisionism, has even gone on to claim that it was Mugabe who capitulated on the Land Question at Lancaster House, while Nkomo held firm.[150] The truth of the matter is something quite different. Robert Mugabe was opposed to the 10-year moratorium on the land issue, as was Joshua Nkomo. But Mugabe was more vehemently opposed, while Nkomo was more amenable to accepting the premises of the Lancaster House Agreement for reasons that were factored in by

Lord Carrington into his calculation in running the Lancaster House Conference.

These reasons were Nkomo was now older and belonged to a smaller tribal group and wanted an early chance to influence Zimbabwe's destiny, while Mugabe being younger, and leading the majority tribe, could hold out.[151] Mugabe was even about to leave the Lancaster House talks because of the land question, but Samora Machel demanded Mugabe accept whatever was on the table, as Mozambique was also tired of the war. The same feeling applied to Zambia. Machel said to Mugabe; "we FRELIMO secured our independence by military victory against colonists. Your settlers have not been defeated, so you must negotiate."[152]

Also, those who make it seem as if Nkomo and Mugabe had much choice in the outcomes of the Lancaster House talks, forget that Britain was not negotiating in good faith. Carrington intimates that his trump card at Lancaster, was that anyone who walked away from talks, would have been seen as the one who didn't want peace, thus allowing Britain to recognise the Smith – Muzorewa Regime.[153] The recognition of Rhodesia, which had been illegal since the UDI, would have changed the dynamics unfavourably for the guerrilla armies.

The falsity that Britain installed Mugabe to do their bidding is also clearly belied by the facts. The Rhodesians campaigned hard for Muzorewa and would have even preferred Nkomo instead of Mugabe to take over. There was actually a Rhodesian Operation called Operation Quartz which was all about preventing Mugabe coming into power.

The military aspects of that operation were about assassinating Robert Mugabe. The political aspects of the same operation were about facilitating a Muzorewa or Nkomo led coalition to come to power. The hope was for an electoral outcome that allowed Nkomo, Muzorewa and the 20 reserved white seats to become a coalition government. Of course, Mugabe won an unassailable landslide, and all the assassination attempts failed, so the White Rhodesians and the international community were forced to work with Mugabe by this victory.

Mugabe's landslide victory is easy to explain. It was simply because of the 75 – 80 percent coverage of the country ZANU had in the liberation struggle, translating to electoral votes, hence the landslide victory. Nkomo himself may have thought the voting was tribal after the 1980 elections when he said: "you give them one man one vote, and this is what they do with it."[154] However, this does not mean ZANU had mobilised along tribal lines. I have also not seen any evidence to support the view that Mugabe was helped by the whites. The whites only came on board when he extended the hand of reconciliation to them. As well, you must understand that Britain and the United States came on board only because Mugabe was not persecuting the whites. This is an important detail for our nation with regards the next address which talks about Sanctions.

The further claim that Mugabe was intolerant and unaccommodating, is also not borne out by the facts of the matter. For having won a landslide, he could have formed a government of exclusively ZANU members, but he sought to make Nkomo ceremonial president, which Nkomo turned down. Still, in his first cabinet, Mugabe accommodated Nkomo and some ZAPU ministers, as well as the whites in the spirit of reconciliation. In the spirit of one man one vote, Mugabe had the constitutional mandate to form a government without consulting anyone. Remember, these same people he accommodated, had been recently working hard to keep him out of power. Ian Smith writes that; "Nkomo still believed we could win enough seats to form a government of national unity excluding Mugabe who, Nkomo said, could not be trusted, as was proved by Mugabe's breach of the agreement he had made with him."[155] It is necessary that we all have an understanding of our true history.

Overcoming Our Imaginary Differences:

The fact that the public imagination even accommodates the idea that Gukurahundi happened because of Shona and Ndebele "ancient hatreds," means that we have a misunderstanding of history that can still be exploited by our detractors to divide us. It means that only a few people know our true history. These misconceptions have to be corrected so that the majority of our people know and understand our true history. This will then mean that we do not misdirect our energies towards unnecessary quarrels. Our focus will then be only on the true challenges to our national and public interest.

I am insistent that our tribal differences are imaginary. Yes, we have different languages, yes we have some minor cultural differences, but our experiences under white settler domination should have taught us that to outsiders, only the colour of our skin is what matters. We are really the same. Politically, this is the only way to view the matter if we are going to succeed in our nation-building task. I would also not be surprised, if biology confirms the illogic of tribalism.

You see, because of intermarriages overtime, I think we will be hard pressed to find anyone in Zimbabwe who is pure this ethnicity or pure that tribe. This is why I say our tribal and ethnic differences are now largely imaginary. At this point, I can use myself as an example again. I am supposed to be a Zezuru (Shona), having been born in Chivhu to the Mhofu Clan. By this token, I am supposed to be intolerant of the Manyika (Shona), because they are not Zezuru like me. But my Grandmother is a Manyika from the Nyati Clan, and her maiden surname is Makoni. My home area where we settled permanently is in Mzarabani, and intermarriages with the Korekore people happened with people who moved there with us from all over the country. In my own family still, my brothers and sisters married and had children with Ndebele people. I do not see then, how anyone can still claim to belong to this specific ethnicity or tribe, on account of the intermarriages that have happened overtime.

Our true issues are political, and often times some unethical people will try to mobilise on ethnic and tribal lines. When we were united to fight the white settler, he then tried to introduce the distortion that we were supposed to hate each because of Ndebele raids that would have killed off all Shona people had he not arrived. Some unreflecting people may have believed this. But this was an exaggeration, we lived together for 52 years before the white settler arrived on the Zimbabwe Plateau. The raids of the Ndebele were just what was consistent with that historical period. The extent of their impact was just exaggerated to appeal to people's emotions. We have to ensure that political entrepreneurs and outsiders cannot continue to divide us in this manner. We can ensure this by understanding everything that happened in our history in its true context.

Conclusion: Never Again.

My fellow countrymen and countrywomen, this has been one of the most difficult parts of our history for me to survey. It is a very emotionally disturbing subject, even to just research and discuss it. I truly wish we had never experienced it. Unfortunately, it happened, and it is one of those important topics this volume of Addresses could not ignore. I have tried to explain everything that happened in its true context.

Gukurahundi happened because of the trust deficit and competition for State power between ZAPU and ZANU. The trust deficit led to a situation called the Security Dilemma. Which, in turn, led to insecurity in the country. It was in response to this insecurity that human rights abuses were committed. Gukurahundi was not an attempt to wipe out the Ndebeles, or revenge for the 19th Century raids on the Shona. This idea can only be entertained by Ethnona-tionalists, or by people who are very ignorant of our history.

This misconception needs to be corrected in our nation because it can be an incubator for unnecessary hatred between our people. Our leaders of the time, Joshua Nkomo and Robert Mugabe, who knew the issues first-hand, resolved Gukurahundi with the Unity Accord of 1987. This was the best solution to Gukurahundi. We can only tweak a few things in that solution, such as compensation for victims if none was provided for in the agreement. The Second Republic, under President Emmerson Mnangagwa, has instituted a National Peace and Reconciliation Commission which will be tasked with resolving all the outstanding issues from the 1987 Unity Accord. This is the correct way to approach the matter – through the official channel of government.

What is dangerous is what some political entrepreneurs have started to propose: that we completely discard the whole agreement and pursue retributive justice. To appeal to emotions, these same people have made the exaggeration that Gukurahundi was a Geno-cide against the Ndebele. This appeal to emotions will work to arouse anger and hatred between the tribes that was not really there to begin with. When that happens, we will end up killing each other again, and in a genuine tribal conflict, the killing will only stop when the hated tribe has been exterminated.

.

Address VII.

Sanctions.

"So, if we were to decide to try and work for change in power in Zimbabwe, I would hope that we would have the wisdom to be discrete, to be low-key and to avoid giving those in power there the excuse that foreigners are out to get them. We would treat Zimbabwe basically like a pariah under this option. We would disengage from official government-to-government relationships, programming of any sort, and wait for the pressures to mount, helping them as best as we can" – Chester Crocker, US Assistant Secretary of State for Africa, US Senate Hearings on ZIDERA, 2001.

F ELLOW COUNTRYMEN and countrywomen, in the foregoing
Addresses, I have mostly focused on issues pertaining to our history. At this point, I think we can now turn to our ongoing challenges.
The hope is that the historical issues I have tackled, have provided
us with a common understanding of the true nature of our current
problems. With such a common understanding of our affairs, we can
act in such a manner that, some of the problems that will eventually
need solving, do not even arise in the first place.

For example, one of the major problems currently facing our
country, is the impact of the Sanctions that were imposed on our
country at the turn of the century. A look back to our conduct as a
nation when the Sanctions were imposed, shows that we did not have
a common understanding of what was about to happen. Every nation
is a community of common destiny – what happens to it impacts all
those inside it. If we had had that understanding, none of us would
have even cheered on the imposition of Sanctions. Instead, some
of our co-nationals were very vocal in calling for the imposition of
Sanctions.

Some of these people who called for the imposition of Sanctions,
did so with the expectation that the resultant suffering would help
them achieve power here. This is quite an indictment of the mindsets some of our countrymen still have. It is a very poor mind that
does not look into the future and foresee that some damage can be
irreversible. The Zimbabweans who have died because of the Sanctions just cannot be brought back to life. But I mostly decry these

unreflecting mindsets, because they are impervious to history's lessons. It is these same poor mindsets that allowed the Colonialist to divide and conquer us in the past. It is also exactly this kind of mindset, that saw black people sell their fellow black people during Slavery. Thus, the painful lessons of those shameful periods of our history, have not been learnt.

There is also the possibility that, it was ignorance of what damage Sanctions can do, that made our people call for them upon their own country. Some of our people who were enlisted into calling for Sanctions, may have done so because, they did not fully realise how damaging Sanctions would be. They did not understand that Sanctions would be as vicious in effects, as when a full-scale war has been launched on our country.

What I have learnt in preparing these Addresses, is that most people may not necessarily fully understand what they are signing up to, where most technical matters are concerned. Thus, if our people called for Sanctions because they did not fully understand what harm Sanctions can do, it is incumbent upon the nation to educate them on this count. Mind you, the imposition of Sanctions was also accompanied by a concerted disinformation campaign by our enemies. The nation must, therefore, devise a civic education that gives everyone the ability to identify which things are contrary to the national interest, and which ones are conducive to it.

Thus, our condemnation of fellow Zimbabweans who called for Sanctions on our country must be subject to the distinction of who erred out of ignorance, and who erred because it was expedient. I mention this distinction because, the subject of Sanctions is one whereby, even a liberal like myself, can be intolerant. By this I mean that, if the people who called for Sanctions on our country, and continue to do so, knew fully well what Sanctions entailed, then there can be no reconciling with them. They are fifth columnists: people who would, if actual war came, take up arms against Zimbabwe. These are people who, by their actions, proclaim that they do not want to be part of our polity, and further, that they even want to harm our country at any given opportunity. There just can be no common ground with, those among us, who harbour ill-will for our collective in this manner. In the United States, such collusion with foreign powers, is punishable by law. The takeaway here, is that there needs to be some punishment, to deter those who would take actions that are harmful to their own nation.

To be sure, Sanctions would have been imposed without our own people calling for them – our people who did so, only served as a legitimating tool. They remain an inessential component of the Sanctions imposition decision matrix. The thing to keep in mind here, if we are interrogating cause and effect strictly, is that black Zimbabweans do not really have a vote in our enemies' foreign policy decision-making.

Still, what Thomas Hobbes said about Witches back in 1651, is relevant to the punishment I envisage should be imposed on Zimbabweans who knowingly call for Sanctions on their country. Hobbes said that; "as for Witches, I think not that their witchcraft is any real power, but yet that they are justly punished for the false belief they have that they can do such mischief, joined with their purpose to do it if they can."[156] All this, of course, is subject to the distinction I made above, of people who knew in advance of the inimical effects of Sanctions, and those who did not know.

The countries that imposed Sanctions on us, on the other hand, do not get any benefit of the doubt, for they knew fully well, the deleterious impact Sanctions would have on a country's economy. In fact, their calculation was that these deleterious effects on the population, would help them achieve their regime change goals. Further, they also know about the illegality of these Sanctions, though they pretend otherwise. My task here is not to change their minds, for their conduct throughout history shows us that they are obdurate.

Instead, my task in this Address, is to ensure that my fellow Zimbabweans understand all the arguments around Sanctions. The enemy counts on the ignorance of the target country's population to assist him in his dissembling. The task, therefore, is to make the issues clear for every Zimbabwean who cares to understand this matter. Understanding all the issues clearly, is always a good starting point in countering the enemy's designs.

In this vein, fellow countrymen and countrywomen, dismiss any illusions from your minds, that Sanctions were imposed on us because the sanctioning countries care about the black people of Zimbabwe. This is just one of those dishonest ploys the Western countries have used to hide their true motives since time immemorial. You will recall that Colonisation was packaged as a civilisation mission, wars to acquire resources abroad are continually packaged as promotion of democracy, and regime change programs are claimed to be promotion of human rights.

The fact of the matter is that these countries' approach to international affairs is that of an "our might makes us right." Any pretexts deployed, are just deliberate insults to the intelligence of the people being attacked. Sanctions were placed on Zimbabwe because the government dared to allow landless blacks to dispossess the white farmers. The Sanctions then, were a collective punishment designed to create conditions for regime change in Zimbabwe.

As for consequences, the countries who have imposed Sanctions on us are, indeed, for the time being, protected from any consequences by their positions and current power in the international system. But, in this Address, I will also say something about the conditions that will need to obtain in the international system, to allow us to impose costs on the sanctioning countries. A look to history shows that power transitions do happen in the international system.

Herodotus confirmed the reality of power transitions in his Histories, when he recorded that; "I shall go forward with my history, describing equally the greater and the lesser cities. For the cities which were formerly great, have most of them become insignificant, and such as are at present powerful, were weak in the olden time. I shall therefore discourse equally of both, convinced that human happiness never continues long in one stay."[157] If we take such a long view of international affairs, then redress can always be achieved by the previously disadvantaged countries, if they persevere.

Having posited these preliminary points, I can now go into the subject matter of this Address: Sanctions. The key questions with regards these Sanctions are: were the Sanctions legal or illegal? Why were they imposed? What has been the humanitarian impact of the Sanctions? And what can we do to defeat these Sanctions?

The Illegality Of The Sanctions:

The logic that undergirds international law is the same as that behind domestic law: they both make the existence of a community possible. They do so by establishing acceptable conduct, duties and obligations, and punishments where breaches occur. In domestic law, the supreme law is the Constitution, which sets out how the society will be run. The Constitution is the constant reference document for societal relations. It ensures that the rules are not made up as and when issues arise in society. If a law becomes dysfunctional, or hated, the Constitution must be amended before that law is altered or discarded. A society where the Constitution is not adhered to can hardly function. So, for our purposes here, law is one of the principles that makes any community possible. Though there are important differences between domestic and international law, one parallel still subsists; disorder will ensure from an absence of, or where one exists, the disregarding of the Constitution in both systems.

Until the First "World War" in 1914, the international community did manage to exist for some time without a Constitution.

But with advances in the destructive power of weaponry, it became necessary to have such a Constitution. Just as well, because in an unstable and unpredictable system, even the strongest also face existential threats. Without a Constitution, humanity was now on a path to self-destruction. This is borne out by the fact that, the self-help system that preceded adherence to a written Constitution, resulted in two devastating "World Wars" – mostly fought in Europe, North Africa, and Asia. These wars were costly in human life and materiel, which led to the need for a written agreement, stipulating the rights, duties, and obligations of all members.

The closest the international community now has to such a Constitution, is the United Nations Charter. Thus, it is to the United Nations Charter that we must look, to establish the legality or illegality of any action by a State. The rules codified in this "Constitution" were not accidental either. These codifications were a result of foresight, practice, observations, and compromises arrived at by the most competent people in society. These are what are called the sources of international law. For the discussion at hand, the United Nations Charter is also markedly important: it came about as a result of the observation that, the pure self-help system was driving humanity towards self-destruction.

Yet this same self-help approach to international relations, is what those who have imposed Sanctions on us have started to lean on again. This is diametrically opposed to the major innovation the UN Charter brought to the international system: the abolition of self-help. You see, what the UN Charter did, was to definitively institute multilateralism and a rules-based approach to international affairs. From this postulated multilateralism premise, once Sanctions are taken unilaterally, you can be assured that they are illegal. There is no room for equivocation on this issue: legal Sanctions under international law, are only those issued under a Chapter VII, United Nations Security Council (UNSC) Resolution.

This could be the very end of our current discourse, but because I want everyone in our nation to be able to articulate why Sanctions on Zimbabwe are illegal, I must go into the very nuts and bolts of the international law that govern Sanctions. In this regard, a reading of the UN Charter will further furnish us with what the law says on the imposition of Sanctions. Another thing to also keep in mind, is that even with the domestic Constitutions, there are people who will break the law. If the society is functioning correctly, these people are branded outlaws, and punitive measures taken in accordance with the Constitution.

It is quite different in the international system in the case under consideration, due to their power, the countries breaking the law have instead put out a narrative branding the law-abiding countries as the outlaws. This then is another additional reason that necessitates this current discussion; the Western countries who are now relying on the principle of "might is right," pretend they are following the law. Clearly, they are not. We just cannot allow them to be in breach of international law, and still assume the moral high ground through propagating lies. A look at what actions are permissible under international law will set the record straight. What is permissible can be found by looking at the relevant United Nations Charter Articles.

The Relevant UN Charter Articles:

To understand the relevant articles for Sanctions in the United Nations Charter, we must start with the one prohibiting the use of force in international relations. This is the correct approach, since the United Nations (UN) came into being to "save mankind from the scourge of war." Once the United Nations had legislated against war, it follows that other lesser matters would be legislated for as well. It is in the spirit of the prohibition of war that we find the nature of UN legislation; it prohibits some actions but acknowledges actions allowable based on practical realities. The important thing to still keep in mind is that States were being moved away from the self-help system to a rules-based order.

Article 2 (4) of the UN Charter is the standard bearer in the move away from the self-help system to the rules-based order. It specifically prohibits the use of force and has acquired the status of *jus cogens,* or a peremptory norm, from which states cannot derogate, except in one specific circumstance: self-defence. Article 2 (4) holds that; "all Members shall refrain in their international relations from the threat or use of force against the territorial integrity or political independence of any State, or in any other manner inconsistent with the Purposes of the United Nations."

Showing the wisdom of the framers of the United Nations Charter, Article 51 of the same Charter spells the instances where states can use force: "Nothing in the present Charter shall impair the inherent right of individual or collective self-defence if an armed attack occurs against a Member of the United Nations, until the Security Council has taken measures necessary to maintain international peace and security. Measures taken by members in the exercise of this right of self-defence shall be immediately reported to the Security Council and shall not in any way affect the authority and responsibility of the Security Council under the present Charter to take at any time such action as it deems necessary in order to maintain or restore international peace and security." The pattern then, is clear, aggression and offence are proscribed, while defence is allowed, up to a point.

The most important article where the Sanctions on Zimbabwe are concerned, is Article 2 (7) of the same UN Charter, which reads; "Nothing contained in the present Charter shall authorize the United Nations to intervene in matters which are essentially within the domestic jurisdiction of any State or shall require members to submit such matters to settlement under the present Charter; but this principle shall not prejudice the application of enforcement measures under Chapter VII." The principle herein contained is that of sovereign equality and the non-interference in the domestic affairs of sovereign states. Thus, the reason why Sanctions on Zimbabwe were not issued under a United Nations Resolution, is because the issue at hand was a purely domestic matter, and any UN intervention would have violated Article 2 (7). Invariably, unilateral Sanctions are a violation of Article 2 (7).

If Article 2 (7) were absolute, the countries who are violating it could find refuge behind necessity. As it is, they cannot, because Article 2 (7) has exceptions. The UN Charter allows for the Security Council, under Chapter VII powers, to intervene in the affairs of a sovereign State, but in specific circumstances. Article 39 sets the conditions thus: "The Security Council shall determine the existence of any threat to the peace, breach of the peace, or act of aggression and shall make recommendations, or decide what measures shall be taken in accordance with Articles 41 and 42, to maintain international peace and security." These circumstances are what ought to be satisfied before the non-intervention principle can be set aside. Needless to say, these conditions did not obtain in Zimbabwe, despite claims to the contrary by those who rushed to impose Sanctions to advance their own selfish goals.

Article 41 of the UN Charter states that; "The Security Council may decide what measures not involving the use of armed force are to be employed to give effect to its decisions, and it may call upon Members of the United Nations to apply such measures. These may include complete or partial interruption of economic relations and of rail, sea, air postal, telegraphic, radio, and other means of communication, and the severance of diplomatic relations." Clearly this is the article that authorizes Sanctions in international relations, and any Sanctions ordered under these Chapter VII powers, will be legal and binding on all member States.

Article 25 states that; "The Members of the United Nations agree to accept and carry out the decisions of the Security Council in accordance with the present Charter." Furthermore, these Sanctions so instituted, take precedence over any other commitments States may have towards the sanctioned State. To this end, Article 103 of the UN Charter holds that; "In the event of a conflict between the obligations of the Members of the United Nations under the present Charter and their obligations under any other international agreement, their obligations under the present Charter shall prevail."

Thus, there is no lacunae in international law that necessitated unilateral sanctions against Zimbabwe. The imposition of those Sanctions was a clear disdain of international law by the targeting States, singly and severally. On the question of whether Regional Organizations have the power to impose Sanctions, the short answer is no. In Article 53 of the Charter, we find it stated that; "The Security Council shall, where appropriate, utilize such regional arrangements or agencies for enforcement action under its authority. But no enforcement action shall be taken under regional arrangements or by regional agencies without the authorization of the Security Council."

Let us keep Article 53 of the Charter in mind because, I will return to the subject of Sanctions imposed by regional bodies. First, I must make the important distinction between Retorsions, Countermeasures, and Sanctions. This distinction is necessary because it shows us what in the family of non-forcible measures, is permitted unilaterally by international law.

Retorsions, Countermeasures, or Sanctions?

Sanctions belong to a family of responses to breaches of the law that are allowed under international law. The United Nations Charter was not a suicide pact, where nations would have no means of responding to wrongful acts until a course of action had been determined by the UNSC. This is evident in that the right to self-defence was not proscribed by the UN Charter. It is also from the same logic of the right to self-defence that Sanctions spring from. To come to the point at once, there are still corrective measures countries can legally take when a wrongful action occurs against them. Self-defence when an armed attack occurs, is allowed subject to the considerations of proportionality and notifying the UNSC of the measures being taken at the earliest opportunity.

Other forms of responses allowed when a breach occurs are ones where there is no use of armed force. To this family belong, Retorsions, Countermeasures, and Sanctions. Although the three seem similar at first glance, they are slightly different, and in these slight differences lie the distinction for what is legal and illegal under international law. The thing to continue to keep in mind, as is self-evident in natural law, is that self-defence has never been an offence. It is only the things that go beyond the act of self-defence that are proscribed.

Here, I can give you an example in domestic law so that you can see a ready parallel. Self-defence is permitted when an individual is attacked, but only up to the point that it remains self-defence. Again, in domestic law, there are punishments for murder, but nowhere is it permitted that the relative of a victim can kill the murderer as suitable punishment. The community decides the punishment for each transgression.

The logic that undergirds this idea was best articulated by John Locke, when he wrote that: "it is unreasonable for men to be judges in their own cases, because self-love will bias men in favour of themselves and their friends. And on the other side, hostility, passion and revenge will lead them to punish others too severely."[158] Similarly, the international community has evolved from a wild west, state of nature self-help system, to one with laws. In these codifications, we find what is permissible and to what extent a State can act unilaterally when faced with a wrongful act.

In all this, the principle that is unimpeachable, is that of self-defence is no offence: prohibitions instituted by international law still allow actions to be taken in self-defence. This same principle also applies to the actions a State can take when there has been a breach of international law against it. The victim State is still allowed to take steps to protect itself against the breach, which if it is an armed attack, would be self-defence measures. But as self-defence is circumscribed by law, so too are the other reactions a victim State can engage in, and to what extent. This point of the degree of what is permitted and to what extent, constitutes the difference between Retorsions, Countermeasures and Sanctions, though they exist on the same spectrum.

Retorsions are all those reactions to wrongful acts which do not interfere with the target State's rights under international law. These reactions may just be limitations of diplomatic and other contacts, or withdrawal of voluntary aid programmes.[159] Cassese's definition holds a Retorsion to be "any retaliatory act by which a State responds, by an unfriendly act not amounting to a violation of international law, to either (a) a breach of international or (b) an unfriendly act, by another State."[160]

While reactions that interfere with the target State's rights, are categorised as Countermeasures as explained by the International Law Commission (ILC).[161] The ILC defined Countermeasures as "non-forcible measures, taken by an injured State in response to a breach of international law, in order to secure the end of the breach and, if necessary, reparation."[162] The ILC limits countermeasures to the temporary non-fulfilment of international obligations the injured State owes to the responsible State.[163] They are not punishments, but inducements to the delinquent State to return to legality.[164]

The temporary suspension of landing rights for aircraft registered in the delinquent State, is a typical reciprocal Countermeasure, should the injured State's aircraft have been prevented from landing in the delinquent State in breach of international law. You will recall how Zimbabwe prevented a South African Airways plane from taking off from Harare International Airport, until the then First Lady's aircraft could also be allowed to depart South Africa in 2015.

Sanctions go far beyond the scope of the first two, and therein lies one key difference, and the key to what is legal and illegal under International Law. The distinction was captured well by Zoller, when she wrote that; "as opposed to Countermeasures, Sanctions are very specific measures. A Countermeasure is a measure which has temporary effects and a coercive character, while a Sanction has final effects and a punitive character. Moreover, Sanctions have an exemplary character directed at other countries which Countermeasures do not have."[165] To drive the point home even further, Zoller gives this example: "The imposition of measures designed to achieve regime change in another country is an action beyond the doctrine of Countermeasures, since the original action by the target State may not necessarily constitute a breach of an obligation owed to any of the imposing States."[166]

So, all punitive and coercive measures which go beyond the requirement to just stop the breach of international law as expected of Countermeasures, are best seen as Sanctions.[167] What the distinctions I have made here show is that: States can respond to wrongful acts by other States, but only to the extent that this stops the wrongful act and restores relationships. So, returning to my conception of a spectrum; Retorsions will be in the green zone to denote they are permissible, while Countermeasures will be in the green to amber zone denoting permissibility up to a point, Sanctions would be in the red zone to denote that they are impermissible without a UNSC Resolution authorizing them. This last point of UNSC Resolutions is particularly important as it brings us full circle to discussing the UN Charter's relationship with Sanctions imposed by Regional Bodies.

The Relationship Between United Nations Sanctions and Regional Sanctions Regimes:

It is also useful to recall that regional bodies such as the European Union (EU), the Association of Southeast Asian Nations (ASEAN), and the African Union (AU) are all subservient to the United Nations Charter. Article 53 of the UN Charter is clear on this point. Thus, if the regional bodies take out Sanctions without UNSC authorisation, those Sanctions are still unilateral, and therefore illegal. The relationship between regional bodies and the United Nations, is such that they are empowered to take some actions, being closer to the crises, and understanding the context better as they certainly do. But beyond these caveats, any determination a regional body makes must be approved by a UNSC Resolution to pass the legality test. To this extent, ASEAN and the AU have been exemplary, while the EU is the textbook example in failing the legality test.

The theme running through my discourse is that there are unilateral actions that are permitted under international law, but up to a point. Past that point, the actions become illegal. For example, the AU or SADC has suspended the Membership of its constituent States where they have been found to be in breach of its rules, and this is justified on the basis of consent.[168] Here, the target State has agreed to be bound by its rules.[169] The rule that the AU, SADC and ECOWAS have used to suspend their Member States is the one concerning an unconstitutional change of government. Article 30 of the AU's Constitutive Act, Article 33 of the Treaty of SADC, and Article 45 (1) of the Ecowas Protocol all set out that unconstitutional changes of governments will be punished by suspension.[170] These African regional bodies' actions have been consistent with the United Nations Charter in that they have been a springboard for UNSC Resolution authorised United Nations Sanctions. The African regional bodies have also not sought to sanction countries not bound by their articles of association.

ASEAN rejects the notion of Sanctions altogether and has never imposed them on its members or externally, and even objected to Western Sanctions on Myanmar.[171] This, perhaps, is a reflection of Asian wisdom, as it is clear to anyone who enquires, that Sanctions are a major impediment to development. You cannot say you care about the well-being of the general population, whilst imposing the Sanctions that will retard economic development.

The EU, on the other hand, has been a byword for the imposition of illegal Sanctions. Some have tried to defend the EU by saying it has "only imposed unilateral Sanctions after consensus at the UNSC proved impossible to achieve."[172] This does not make the EU's Sanctions legal. This is the equivalent of taking your case to Court, then when you do not get the judgement you want, you go ahead and execute the punishment you think is appropriate.

To be sure, there are some actions the EU is permitted in response to perceived breaches to international law, but past a certain point, it just becomes naked pursuit of national interest and therefore illegal. For example, arms embargoes can be justified "as necessary to prevent the State or States imposing them breaching their own legal obligations, (under e.g., the law of neutrality) or being complicit in another State's illegal conduct (under international human rights or humanitarian law or the Arms Trade Treaty)."[173] But, again, as Happold observes here, if done within these parameters, these will be Countermeasures – permissible under international law – and not Sanctions per se. I have explained the distinction between Sanctions and Countermeasures above, and shown what can still be legal, even though imposed unilaterally.

Some have also argued that States have the freedom to revise relations as they please, including economic relations.[174] In this regard, some Zimbabweans have felt that the EU is in the right to withhold any development assistance to Zimbabwe, as it was voluntarily given. A closer look at this matter will yield that the EU would be in breach of international law, if this is done in a manner to punish the Zimbabwean government, such as to bring about regime change. It is also worth remembering that the development assistance, is given in lieu of the reparation the EU owes for the theft that occurred during Colonialism. The important thing is still that, unilateral actions by the EU, will only be legal if they remain either a Countermeasure or a Retorsion. Once they cross into the spectrum of Sanctions, they will be illegal without UNSC authorisation.

In any case, if the argument the EU is making that they are protecting a core tenet of the UN Charter is valid, then they should be able to get a UNSC Resolution. If you look at the reasons why the UNSC vetoed an action, often, it will be because the EU was encroaching on the principle of non-intervention in the domestic affairs of other States. It was certainly the case when Russia and China vetoed the EU's attempt to get Chapter VII Sanctions authorised against Zimbabwe in 2008. If you read the grounds for that Veto, you will see that the EU was attempting to have an illegal act passed by the UNSC. Having made this clear, let us now look at the real reasons that led the US and the EU to interfere in the domestic affairs of Zimbabwe as they did. After this brief sojourn, we will then turn to the humanitarian impact of these illegal Sanctions, and what we ought to do to defeat them.

False Equivalence:

It is with dismay that I have heard learned Zimbabweans opine that, as we demanded Sanctions on Rhodesia, so too must we accept Sanctions against ourselves. This is a case of false equivalence, the sanctioning countries know this, but some of our learned people do not seem to know this. Sanctions against Rhodesia were legal in that they were imposed by the United Nations Security Council. They were imposed under UNSC Chapter VII powers, against an unrecognised government, which was existing in defiance of the international norms of self-determination and self-government.

Foreigners subjugating a local population do not qualify as self-government, and Apartheid is a crime against humanity. The Rhodesian government that declared the Unilateral Declaration of Independence (UDI) on 11 November 1965, was an illegal government which never got recognition from any other country, except just the two other Apartheid states of the time, namely, South Africa and Portugal. The Rhodesian regime had been illegal from its inception in 1890, it just so happened that the UDI was also a rebellion against Britain which had sustained this illegality up until 1965.

This break in relations between Britain and Rhodesia offered an opportunity to end Apartheid in Zimbabwe. Britain had refused to do so with its military on the grounds that it did not want to fight its kith and kin. Sanctions against Rhodesia, cognisant of all these factors I have pointed out, were thus issued with a UNSC Resolution under Chapter VII powers – UNSC Resolution 216 of 1965. The UNSC would pass subsequent Resolutions pursuant to the same matter, namely: UNSCRs 217, 221, 232, 253, 277, 288, 314, 388, and 409.

The kith and kin argument declared by Britain in refusing to use force to end Apartheid in Rhodesia, also played its part in the mild application of those Sanctions. The Sanctions against us in 2001 and 2002, on the other hand, were imposed by a group of States without a UNSC Resolution. They are therefore illegal under international law. Let us keep this distinction in mind, so that we are not misled by false equivalence in our analysis.

Protecting White Privilege:

The case of the illegal Sanctions on Zimbabwe is also very instructive for the way that international institutional racism works. It is very instructive that the whole civilised international community did nothing, when an estimated 5 000 to 20 000 black people were killed in Zimbabwe. I have talked at length about Gukurahundi in the Sixth Address. This was when the security services overreacted to insecurity in Matabeleland. Operation Gukurahundi by the 5th Brigade of the Zimbabwe National Army (ZNA) killed that many fellow black people. The insecurity the Zimbabwean government was reacting to, was mostly targeting white farmers and tourists. So, as long as our security services were working to protect white lives, they were given carte blanche.

The same international community was outraged when only 12 white people were killed in the land repossession action in 2000 by war veterans of Zimbabwe's liberation war. They were so outraged to the extent that they took out Sanctions and turned Zimbabwe into a pariah state. So outraged to the extent that they even attempted to put Zimbabwe's internal affairs before the United Nations Security Council under Chapter VII. Russia and China vetoed this Resolution in deference to Article 2 (7) of the UN Charter in 2008.

Tony Blair even contemplated invading Zimbabwe but found no support from Zimbabwe's neighbours. President Thabo Mbeki of South Africa was quite surprised that the situation in Zimbabwe, where 12 white farmers had died, was deemed worthy of an urgent UNSC Resolution, but not the concurrent situation in the DRC, where 5 million blacks were dying.

It is also useful to remember that, even though the Sanctions against Rhodesia were legal under international law, still, because of skin colour, even those who drafted those Sanctions did not fully adhere to them. For all their claims of being resourceful in Sanctions busting, the fact of the matter is that the Rhodesians were helped by the United States, South Africa, and Portugal in Sanctions busting.

An example suffices at this point. Although Britain enforced a maritime blockade of the Port of Beira as Sanctions enforcement action; "Rhodesia was estimated to be receiving 145 000 gallons of oil per day, against its estimated need under rationing of 83 000 gallons. More effective action would have been to invoke penalties against the parent companies, Shell and BP, whose South African subsidiaries were supplying much of the oil."[175] A maritime blockade of countries breaking the Sanctions was also never considered.[176] Britain flatly resisted any attempts to follow through with Sanctions on South Africa for busting the Sanctions on Rhodesia.

The reason given by Britain was that of the interdependencies between the South African and British economies: sanctioning South Africa "would cause widespread unemployment in Britain and worsen the balance of payments by about £300 million a year."[177] The result was still that enforcement of Sanctions had a relief valve, which allowed the Rhodesian regime to survive for 15 years more. I think it was all a well calculated charade. Still, this reason of interdependencies of the economies is also useful in our thinking about the ways African countries can defy the illegal Sanctions imposed on Zimbabwe. It tells us that it is possible for countries to defy implementing the illegal Sanctions, if the imposing countries fear the cost to their own economies.

What is still clear is that Britain itself was not motivated by the plight of black people in Rhodesia. Instead, it was more motivated by the need to reverse the defiance to the Crown that the Rhodesians had made by making their Unilateral Declaration of Independence in 1965. Britain's motivation for imposing the Sanctions then was to ensure that Rhodesia subserved the Crown again. Once subservient, Britain would have given the White Rhodesians a neo-colonial deal that would still protect their privileges. This had been the pattern of decolonisation everywhere in Africa up until then. It was just that the Rhodesian regime was too supremacist to even contemplate being seen under the rule of blacks. It did not matter to the Rhodesians that this would only have been in name.

In the Fifth Address, discussing land reform in Zimbabwe, I have said that this recalcitrance by the white settlers was a mistake. It ultimately made them lose everything. If the Blacks had not fought and died for their rights, their attitude on land reform would have been as flippant as it is in other countries that did not fight wars of liberation. Having lost many black lives in the liberation war, meant that the neo-colonial deal the British finally negotiated for the white settlers in 1979, was 15 years too late. Black Zimbabweans only observed that deal until they had fully disarmed the white settlers, then they still went on to reclaim their land. It is this land repossession from whites that caused Sanctions to be imposed on Zimbabwe.

An Unusual And Extraordinary Threat?

Rhodesian Sanctions busting were facilitated more by none other than the United States. If you look at the framework for US Sanctions busting in Rhodesia, you will see how conversely, it is true that the Sanctions imposed on Zimbabwe today are not motivated by concerns for black Zimbabweans' human rights. Instead, they are an attempt to reverse the substantial gains the blacks won in fighting the white racist regime that oppressed them for nearly 100 years.

United States resistance to Sanctions on Rhodesia was predicated on maintaining white supremacy there. The imposition of Sanctions in Zimbabwe is predicated on restoring the unfair privileges white supremacy awarded itself in Zimbabwe during the 1979 Lancaster House negotiations. The United States has even said that Zimbabwe presents "an unusual and extraordinary threat to United States Foreign Policy."

This is quite a strange thing to say considering the power differentials between Zimbabwe and the US. This can only make sense if viewed with the international institutional racism prism. Zimbabwe has demonstrated that black people can take up arms against white privilege and succeed. The main reason why we went to war was so as to correct our land disenfranchisement by whites. With the Fast Track Land Reform Programme (FTLRP) in 2000, we finally restored the land back to black people.

This had an unacceptable demonstration effect for the United States and white privilege everywhere. Mind you, the United States is founded on the dispossession of indigenous peoples from their land. There are also still a lot of places where whites are still enjoying the unfair privileges precipitant from Colonialism and Apartheid. South Africa, Namibia, Kenya, Colombia, and Brazil are but a few of the countries with imbalances predicated on white privilege.

The way global capitalism is structured, you can also be assured that with these losses of land in Zimbabwe, there were concomitant financial losses for companies and eminent persons in the Western capitals. I know for a fact that there were absentee landlords who held land in Zimbabwe purely for speculative purposes. But we can further understand United States motivation on the Zimbabwe issue, if we look closely at United States Sanction busting for Rhodesia. I see international institutional racism hard at work.

United States' Rhodesia Sanctions Busting:

A former United States Army Officer who recently looked at United States Sanctions busting during the Rhodesia period, returned the following interesting insights. The former Army Officer in question, Danny Sjursen, has talked of the "Rhodesian Lobby – an extensive American alliance of seemingly strange bedfellows sympathetic to the white supremacist state."[178] The most significant success of these people's effort was the passing of the Byrd Amendment of 1971, which allowed U.S. companies to mine and purchase Rhodesian Chrome.[179] The US would buy $212 million worth of Rhodesian Chrome between 1972 and 1977.[180] This made the United States the only nation officially in violation of UNSCR mandated international Sanctions.[181] Sjursen also notes that "America's first and fourth ever United Nations Security Council (UNSC) vetoes were wielded to protect the white Rhodesian regime from the full enforcement of internationally mandated sanctions."[182]

The racist element of Washington's Sanctions busting is uncovered when we explore what Sjursen has called "Jim Crow in Africa." The Byrd Amendment was named after its sponsor, Harry F. Byrd, who left the Democrats in opposition to its civil rights agenda and built his career defending segregation.[183] Sjursen observes that "Rhodesia was an imagined Jim Crow paradise viewed from afar, long after the domestic system Byrd had long protected was in the dustbin of history."[184] He was joined in this venture by other white supremacist Senators. The most committed racists were Strom Thurmond of South Carolina, James Eastland of Mississippi, and Jesse Helms of North Carolina.[185] With James Eastland being recorded as having out-bigoted his racist Rhodesian hosts during a visit there when he admonished them for interracial mixing: "you've inserted the thin wedge by allowing stinking niggers into such a fine hotel."[186]

Even when the support for Rhodesia was not couched in such overtly racist terms, race was still the reason why the Sanctions were undermined. These same people were also hard at work to have the UNSC Resolution mandated Sanctions completely dropped. They were only wrong-footed by the collapse of the racist regime, due to the war of liberation waged by the blacks.

The motivation for the United States was protecting white privilege then, and it still is now. This is very clear from what has been laid out as the conditions for lifting the Sanctions imposed on Zimbabwe. The main condition for lifting Sanctions is when Zimbabwe demonstrates "a commitment to an equitable, legal and transparent land reform which should respect existing ownership of, and title to, property by providing fair, market based compensation to sellers."[187]

Did these white owners buy the land at a fair market price, or they acquired it by violent expropriation from the original black owners?

Why Sanctions Were Really Imposed:

Let us be clear about one thing, the Sanctions imposed on Zimbabwe were not about the rule of law, nor were they about restoring Democracy. They were not about human rights either; instead, they were specifically a response to black Zimbabweans taking back their land from the white settlers. My fellow countrywomen and countrymen, we need to view the world as it really exists. The world is a competition between countries for domination. This competition resolves into blacks versus whites. This is exactly what the distinction between the Global North and Global South entails. The only concern for the West is defending the unfair privileges their white kith and kin have in African countries. It is a white supremacist agenda, and it is what animates the Western countries' foreign policies.

Once this is understood we will spare ourselves a lot of unnecessary grief. In the Sixth Address, I talked at length about when black was killing black in Zimbabwe, with between 5 000 to 20 000 black people estimated to have been killed between 1981 and 1987. Yet no Sanctions were imposed against the Zimbabwean government over human rights abuses. President Robert Mugabe was even awarded a Knighthood by Britain in 1991. But within a few months of land repossession by blacks, the US and the EU found the will to impose Sanctions on Zimbabwe.

This should also be a lesson for black Zimbabweans: we are our brothers' keepers, no one cares if we kill each other. The black Zimbabweans who make the mistake of thinking that outsiders have their interests at heart need to be disabused of this notion. The black Zimbabweans who call for Sanctions on their country, thinking the suffering of their fellow black people will bring Western intervention are mistaken. The suffering these Sanctions cause, is acceptable collateral damage to those who will have imposed them in pursuit of their own agendas.

The Humanitarian Impact Of Sanctions:

Unilateral Sanctions imposed to achieve regime change, aim to create conditions of suffering among the general population so that they turn against their leadership. The hope is that the suffering will cause the population to vote out the leaders in power, civil unrest, or even civil war. The countries imposing the Sanctions will want to replace the leaders with a puppet regime.

Chester Crocker, speaking in the Senate hearings that resulted in the United States imposition of Sanctions, clearly stated that the goal was to change the regime in Zimbabwe. He has often been misquoted as having said; "To separate the Zimbabwean people from ZANU PF, we are going to have to make their economy scream, and I hope you, Senators, have the stomach for what you have to do." I have not found these words in that exact format in my research. This must have been a reading between the lines by our people who know the United States's regime change modus operandi. The "make their economy scream" quote, was actually an instruction by Richard Nixon to the CIA to prevent a democratically elected Salvador Allende succeeding in Chile in the 1970s. Those who know this history, also know that the United States uses economic sabotage to effect regime change.

This was certainly the case when the United States and the EU imposed Sanctions on Zimbabwe with the hope that the population would defect to the Movement for Democratic Change (MDC). The MDC was funded by the White farmers who had just lost land and had the support of their kith and kin in the US and the EU. The arrangement was that the MDC would get political power and restore land to white farmers as their end of the bargain. The calculation was also that discord can be sown in the leadership, so that leaders will defect and cause the government to collapse. Whichever way the Sanctions were made to achieve their aims, the countries who imposed them were not concerned by their humanitarian impact.

If you know where to look, the governments who impose Sanctions know exactly the deleterious impact they have on economies. The Foreign Affairs Ministries of the countries imposing Sanctions will spin them as targeted at a few delinquents. But if you hear the enforcement agencies giving their reports of the success of the Sanctions, you will clearly see that the target is the general population. Take the example of Iran, and what was presented at the 10th Anniversary meeting of the Treasury and Financial Intelligence (TFI) in Washington D.C. The Keynote Speech there was by none other than the then Secretary of the Treasury – Jack Lew. In his presentation, he happily said that: "The Sanctions have deeply damaged Iran's economy, causing its economy to shrink, its currency to drop, its unemployment to jump, and its inflation to skyrocket."[188] These indeed are exactly the effects that Sanctions have on any country's economy, and if you look closely at those stated effects, you will see that they are deleterious to the general population. Any attempts to say care is being take not to harm the general population is just the usual lying the West has been known for since Colonialism.

The impact of Sanctions on the humanitarian situation is exactly as can be expected when an economy is deliberately sabotaged as is admitted in their impact on Iran. I will leave aside the double standard that Iran is being punished for Nuclear proliferation, while Israel which has acquired undeclared Nuclear weapons is left alone. The United States can only boast about damaging Iran's economy because the Iran Sanctions are justified by a UNSC Resolution. Those who imposed Sanctions on us have not been able to boast about the damage they are doing, because then it would show that they are white supremacists concerned only with white privilege. It would belie their claim that the Sanctions are in place to serve the black people of Zimbabwe. Their pretence however does not alter the facts.

Black Zimbabweans have suffered the humanitarian impacts of Sanctions. We have to contend with 100 children dying everyday due to preventable diseases. 8 women are dying every day in childbirth due to chronic shortage of drugs and underfunding of the health sector. The lack of medicines, hyperinflation, 90% unemployment, and lack of water purification have led to a situation where lives have been lost unnecessarily. The economic dilapidation and stunted growth will impact Zimbabwe for many years to come.

What Ought To Be Done?

Clearly, Zimbabwe cannot afford to adhere to the terms that the West has set for lifting Sanctions. The terms the West wants Zimbabwe to adhere to involve reversing the Land Reform completely. This will be a total surrender, so unacceptable to Zimbabwe, given the number of lives we sacrificed fighting the racist regime that stole our land in the first place. There is also the number of deaths we have suffered during the Sanctions period; all this adds to the death toll in defence of our birth right. All the sacrifices and hardships we have faced in the past 22 years will have been for nothing if we surrender to these terms. We have no choice but to be self-sufficient under these Sanctions. Surrender is just not an option.

There is also a demonstration effect, whereby we will let down other oppressed peoples if we capitulate now. South Africa and Namibia are the examples closest to home. Apartheid having ended there later than in our own country, means they still have to deal with the same issues of land ownership imbalances. In fact, Zimbabwe was also sanctioned as a demonstration to South Africa what proceeding with land reform would entail. But South Africa and Namibia could have helped affairs by also coming to Zimbabwe's aid more. These countries who are in the same danger as us, of being sanctioned in defence of white privilege, could have done more. I envisage a "civil disobedience" to all Sanctions without UNSC authorisation.

I am quite dismayed by the way countries of the South have allowed countries of the North to put Sanctions on their sister countries without revolt. They did not protest or refuse to comply with the Sanctions. This docility is the same docility found among sheep; it is the same docility that saw us get colonised in the first place. Countries who are in danger of being arbitrarily sanctioned have a duty to band together and defy Sanctions imposed without a UN Security Council Resolution. A duty to resist. Sooner or later, they too will be turned into basket cases anyway when the sanctioning countries have destroyed the first target country.

A Global South Rebellion?

Hope for a rebellion against US Sanctions lies in the very real possibility of overreach we started witnessing under Donald Trump. Sanctioning China or Russia severely could award the Global South rebellion a much needed leader. The Global South needs a country with the necessary economic clout to lead the rebellion against Western whimsical Sanctions. China could be that country if the West continues to overstep the boundaries of civility in international relations.

At a seminar at the Graduate Institute in Geneva, Samanth Subramanian explored the possibility of countries treating the United States as the rogue State it has become. His insights are useful for a discussion on how the countries in danger of being sanctioned by the United States, can defy, or even sanction, the United States. Subramanian made the mistake of envisioning the European Union (EU) being the first group of countries that will impose Sanctions on the United States. He thought this could happen over an issue like the United

States reneging on the Paris Climate Accord. He is wrong in thinking that the EU could ever sanction the United States. In his formulation, he underestimated how racist the EU is; they will never take any action that will award China world supremacy. Sanctioning the United States and damaging its economy implies that the US will fall in the rank of nations. This can only benefit China, which is on the cusp of overtaking the United States as the predominant economy.

Regardless of this mistake Subramanian made, we can still use his analysis to understand what it will take to break free of the current US led global economy. Being at the centre of the global economic web, has allowed the United States to impose Sanctions on a whim. Subramanian observes that the interconnectedness of the world's economies to that of the United States, has allowed it "to unilaterally enforce sanctions in a consistent way, punishing not only receiving countries but other states and corporations that deal with them."[189] The reason for this power, he adds, is the might of the dollar, the world's reserve currency.

The U.S. dollar lies on one side, or the other, of 88 percent of foreign exchange transactions, which means that the world's banking networks all home in on America as well. If you go to an ATM in Bangalore, or anywhere else, it is very likely that some of those bits of data will, at some point, go through New York: ... It's like the financial system is a sewer, and all the pipes run through New York."[190] The example he gives to drive this point home is that; "For companies and banks, being banished from the U.S. pipes is a fate akin to death. In 2015, the French bank BNP Paribas paid a penalty of nearly $9 billion for violating U.S. sanctions on Cuba, Sudan and Iran."[191] BNP Paribas was willing to do anything not to be frozen out of the United States Banking System.[192]

While this is one reason the United States is difficult to sanction or defy, Subramanian concedes another one: "Consider, for instance, that Amazon and Microsoft hold nearly half of the cloud storage used by companies and institutions around the world. If American companies came under the kind of sweeping blacklist that applies to Iranian firms, the BBC, Fujitsu, Novartis, Samsung, Maersk, Lufthansa, HSBC, the London Tube and the European Space Agency would all have to find other cloud providers in a hurry."[193] So, to give the devil his due, the United States is also a force to reckon with in tech and innovation. Unlike other Empires in the past, United States world leadership has not been guaranteed only by fear of its military. Instead, International Relations Scholars have even called it "Empire by Invitation." This denotes what an attractive and a benevolent force for good it was at its inception.

The United States was accepted as the country that underwrote the world order that ensured after the Second "World War." Subramanian's article only arose because the United States itself has now become a threat to that same order. These discussions that have arisen now, are only arising because the United States has started acting like a rogue State, even towards its own allies, especially under Trump. It is an inevitable consequence of power that it corrupts. For this reason, I have also cautioned the Global South, in the Fourth Address, to expect China to act the same way when it becomes the pre-eminent global power. Of course, the EU and other allies of the United States have only started to notice the United States' rogue tendencies now. Other people have been at the brunt of the United States's rogue behaviour for years now.

To this end, Subramanian mentions a time when the United States was sanctioned in the past. The instance Subramanian brings up is when, in 1973, the Arab States imposed an oil embargo on America for arming Israel during the Yom Kippur War. This inflicted genuine pain in the form of long queues at gas stations, truckers' strikes, the start of a two-year recession, and the US even considered invading Saudi Arabia to restore supplies.[194] This successful Sanctions action is summed up thus in Subramanian's theorising: "the Arab oil embargo remains the best example of surmounting "the classic 'collective action problem.'

Not every country in the world has to unite to constrain the U.S. What made the embargo possible was that a small set of states controlled a commodity that America relied upon, making a sanction easier to coordinate. So, the question becomes: What is the structural weakness of the U.S. that you need to target, and what's the coalition of actors that you then need to put together?"[195] This is an important insight for everyone involved in planning the censure of the United States. The Global South should also always remember this insight for use against whoever will be installed as world leader after the United States.

I will admit it here, that defying United States Sanctions is currently very difficult. This is because of the position it commands by mere fact of the US Dollar being the world's reserve currency. A promising avenue in circumventing the United States's preeminent position is China and Russia's prowess in tech and innovation. For example, these two countries already have their own Global Positioning Systems (GPS). If this is replicated in the banking sector, it will soon be possible to circumvent United States whimsical behaviour. An alternative to SWIFT, the most common banking protocol, will allow whoever produces it, to become an alternative to United States world hegemony in the financial sector. I will leave the modalities of that discussion to the experts in tech and finance among us.

But, even if all-out countersanctions against the United States do not happen, at least "civil disobedience" should be on the cards for countries in danger of illegal Sanctions. There are ready examples of what actions can be taken by those exercising this "civil disobedience." Subramanian records that Britain and France exercised this civil disobedience when they refused to send troops to replace Americans for Trump's plan to withdraw from Syria.[196] African countries should just be more creative with their "civil disobedience" to illegal Sanctions against a sister country.

Of course, the greatest threat that African countries face in coming to Zimbabwe's aid is the problem of fifth columnists. They are people in every African country who are willing to do anything to get validation from the West. These divisions on matters of national importance have always made Africa susceptible to exploitation. I have already pointed out with regards Zimbabwe, that there are people who are standing ready to serve foreign interests. This sell-out mentality is what allowed Slavery to take place as blacks sold fellow blacks into Slavery. It also allowed Colonialism to occur, as black people took arms to oppress fellow blacks in service of foreign masters. This problem occurs on an intra-country level as well as inter-country level. Take Gabon under Omar Bongo, for example, which helped the white settlers in Rhodesia bust sanctions, thus prolonging the oppression of fellow blacks. There are also countries in Africa willing to go to war against other African countries at the West's behest. Thus far, in not giving back its land, Zimbabwe has so far shown what defiance to Sanctions looks like.

Conclusion:

The question I really wanted to tackle in this Address was the question of the legality or illegality of the Sanctions imposed on Zimbabwe. By looking at the closest thing the international community has to a Constitution – the UN Charter – I found that the Sanctions imposed on Zimbabwe are illegal under international law. For Sanctions to be legal they have to be issued under a United Nations Security Council Resolution. As the situation in Zimbabwe around Land Reform was purely a domestic matter, the United Nations was prohibited from intervening by Article 2 (7).

But due to international institutional racism, the United States and the EU then imposed Sanctions on Zimbabwe unilaterally. They couched their rhetoric in the language of human rights violations and democracy, but the truth is that they wanted Zimbabwe to stop its Land Reform. They were just trying to protect white privilege, despite the clear injustice of land ownership in Zimbabwe.

I also found it necessary to discuss Sanctions that were placed on Rhodesia and contrast them with Sanctions that were placed on Zimbabwe. I wanted you my fellow countrymen and countrywomen, to rid yourself of the notion of false equivalence. This notion says that as we wanted Sanctions against Rhodesia and Apartheid South Africa, we must also accept Sanctions against ourselves. Sanctions against Rhodesia were issued under a UNSC Resolution, so were therefore legal. Sanctions against us are manifestly illegal. I also discussed how the United States was involved in Sanctions busting on behalf of Rhodesia because it was sympathetic to the white settlers.

The world is a racist place, I want you my fellow countrymen and countrywomen to be aware of this. This knowledge will ensure that we cannot be pitted against each other by foreigners. The MDC was used by foreigners because it may have mistakenly believed that superpowers like the United States of America cared about black people's rights. This is simply not true, the white countries only wanted to impose a puppet government to protect white privileges. If they cared about human rights, they would have acted during Gukurahundi. I mention this specifically so that we do not find ourselves killing each other again in service of white people's causes.

In terms of what needs to be done, clearly, we cannot give back our land as the United States wants. This is non-negotiable, but the current government has started making concessions that may be palatable to nationalists. They are paying compensation for the improvements on the farms but not for the land. This is in line with our Constitution, so slightly acceptable to us. Beyond this, everything will have to be down to our ingenuity and honesty. In the next Address, I will talk about Corruption, which has had as much a deleterious impact on our economy as the Sanctions. If we get to solve Corruption, we will have solved the part of the impact to our economy that is within our control.

Address VIII.

Corruption.

"In the developing world, corruption is public enemy number one. Every dollar that a corrupt official or a corrupt business-person puts in their pocket, is a dollar stolen from a pregnant woman who needs health care; or from a girl or a boy who deserves an education; or from communities that need water, roads, and schools. Every dollar is critical if we are to reach our goals to end extreme poverty by 2030 and to boost shared prosperity" – Jim Yong Kim, World Bank President, 2013.

"A minimum of comfort is necessary for the practice of virtue" – Patrice Lumumba, First Prime Minister of the Democratic Republic of the Congo.

My FELLOW COUNTRYMEN and countrywomen, continuing in the same vein as the preceding Address, that of discussing our polity's current problems, so as to articulate pathways out of them, I must now turn to a problem that is very contiguous to Sanctions: Corruption. How could it not be? We have seen how destructive Sanctions are to an economy. Surely, it must follow that, in an economy made dysfunctional by Sanctions, corrupt practices like bribery, will proliferate as people try to offset the hardships.

Sanctions cause corruption, but this linear causal relationship is not absolute. The absoluteness of the linear causal relationship is refuted by the fact that countries not under Sanctions also experience corruption. In fact, before we came under Sanctions ourselves, there were already many instances of corruption in our country. Thus, the discussion of our economic problems, must encompass more than just blaming Sanctions for all our problems.

While Sanctions have negatively affected our economy, our own acts of corruption have greatly aided and abetted them in this damage. We should equally be concerned by our own "unforced errors." What I am calling our unforced errors, are all the things that we have done out of greed and, with no regard for the second and third order effects of such actions. For example, misappropriating funds meant for medicines will result in deaths. There should be no amount of appealing to Sanctions as a justification, that can make such a selfish act acceptable.

This, too, is what I want this Address to steer us towards; knowing and avoiding taking any actions that are harmful to our society.

The long term success of our country depends on people maturing enough to realise that what is best for the country, is also, in the final analysis, what is best for them.

One of the problems with corruption, is that it is also one of those terms people use to delegitimize their political opponents. Care has to be taken then when we hear accusations of corruption levelled against individuals. To be sure, our legal system acknowledges this fact, and therefore demands that there be concrete proof against anyone accused of being corrupt. It is the public opinion that needs to be made to also adhere to this principle of burden of proof. For this reason, I want us to understand corruption as it really is, and not just in the politicised manner it is bandied around in beerhall discussions. I want us to do this so that we do not get misled by political entrepreneurs when they appeal to our emotions. A few years ago, in our country, the mere cry that someone was a thief was enough to bring about mob justice. 'Lynching' someone on the false allegation that they are corrupt, will be as much a vice as corruption itself. The thread running through all my Addresses in this volume, is that we should try to have a true understanding of all the issues that affect us.

What I am going to do in this Address then, is to discuss the causes, nature, and effects of corruption on our country. I want us to be very clear on which acts count as corruption and their effects, so that we can, individually and severally, avoid being perpetrators or accomplices to corruption. My instinct tells me that changing the individual's attitude towards corruption, is the most important first step in tackling corruption. If every individual is revulsed by corruption, society will self-regulate, and corruption will become frowned upon as much as child marriages are frowned upon now. As it is, the corrupt are admired by society, which acts as an enabler for them. To be sure, this cheerleading is not what causes corruption. So, we still have to explore what exactly has caused corruption in our country, if we are to suggest sensible mitigants.

As Old As The Hills:

"Do not accept a bribe, for a bribe blinds those who see and twists the words of the innocent," so says the Bible in Exodus 23:8. As the Bible is one of the oldest written texts we have in the world, this tells us that the problem of corruption is not unique to our epoch. Corruption is as old as humanity itself. From this fact, it follows that, corruption is, indubitably one of humanity's frailties, but so is the propensity to kill. As we have not tolerated murder as a human frailty, just because Cain killed Abel in the first book of the Bible, so too should corruption not be tolerated. Instead, every human society has proscribed murder and punished offenders. It should be the same with corruption, subject to our understanding of all its causes.

The fact that corruption is explicitly described as a vice in the Bible, also raises questions about our claims of being a God-fearing nation. If we are such an avowedly Christian and God fearing nation, why is there such a high prevalence of corruption in our country? This is exactly the same question I posed in the Second Address, whether religion does any good for our society. If corruption is widespread amongst us like this, when we are an 84% Christian country, then religion has not impacted us in a positive way.

But, perhaps, the prevalence of corruption in our country just speaks to the fallibility of Christianity. With its message of love for sinners, and limitless forgiveness for transgressions, Christianity may just be another enabler for corruption. Transgressors can engage in corruption in the full expectation of forgiveness once they ask God for it. Contrast this with religions that stone thieves, and you will find that those religions have an extra layer of deterrence for most vices. Our current subject matter is not religion however, so I will come to my point at once. The value of this very brief look into religion, is that the fear of God is not a deterrent against corruption, so other means to deter must be produced by our society.

Aeschylus had an insight which we can use as a guide in this regard. Writing in The Oresteian Trilogy, he said that; "From your polity, do not wholly banish fear, for what man living, freed from fear, will still be just?"[197] There is a hint in this statement that cruel and unusual punishments may be needed as a deterrent. Some heart-breaking cases of corruption surely demand that as proper punishment. In some countries, the death sentence is applied for corruption. In China, Lai Xiaomin, was sentenced to death, and executed on 29th January 2021, for bribery and embezzlement involving nearly US$280 Million. We, however, still have to work within the parameters of the Constitution of Zimbabwe. Indeed, the law in Zimbabwe already has punishments clearly defined for cases of corruption, what is needed is consistent application of the laws.

What Is Corruption?

Transparency International defines corruption as "the abuse of entrusted power for private gain."[198] Society only works because everyone has tasks assigned to them that they have to carry out according to set rules. There is a principal – agent relationship in the assignment of these tasks. Society, through its various institutions, is the principal, while any person occupying a position in any institution, public or private, is the agent. It is the abrogation from agreed upon rules, for personal gain, which is corruption.

For example, a policeman who asks for a bribe to let a motorist off who has broken a traffic law, is an agent who is abrogating from the rules set for his task by his principal – society. Such actions have harmful consequences for society, and this is why corruption matters. If a policeman takes a bribe to let a drunken driver continue with his journey, the driver may cause an accident which will maim or kill an innocent person – someone who will actually be driving in adherence to society's rules. This is the crux of the matter where corruption is concerned – it causes harm to society.

Some corrupt actions are not as clear cut as the policeman taking a bribe example above. But a framework can be devised that shows the corruptness, or otherwise, of the ambiguous acts. To this end, James Scott proposed a framework with these three standards that can be used to decide whether a public official's action was corrupt. The three standards are: the standard of public interest; the standard of legal norms; and the standard of public opinion, and Scott saw that the three often coincide.[199] He found corrupt acts often breach all three standards. I, instead, think the first two standards, that of the public interest and that of whether the action is legal, are defensible as objective measures we can use in deciding if an action is corrupt or not. The standard of public opinion is problematic for me as public opinion can be swayed by propaganda and sensationalised reporting.

Thus, in this Address, the acts I will think of as corruption, are those that can be proved to fail the standard of the law, and also that of the public interest. Therefore, in my conception, corruption encompasses all those acts that are illegal, as well as those that are inimical to the public interest, though not necessarily thought illegal in the statute books. Thus, for me, keeping money in an offshore account for reasons of paying less tax, while not thought of as corruption, is corruption if it is harmful to society.

I therefore agree with Fisman and Golden, when they said, corrupt acts can be illegal but need not necessarily be so.[200] Another typical example would be that of business leaders who pay themselves millions despite their performance not creating value for their shareholders.[201] In Zimbabwe, there are many examples of when Directors of State Owned Enterprises paid themselves millions, despite not creating any value for the taxpayers. One recent such example is when the Director of Premier Service Medical Aid Society (PSMAS)

– a Parastatal – was paying himself a US$250 000 monthly salary, when the Company was US$38 Million dollars in debt.

There is just no justification for that salary, when one is a Director of such a poorly performing public entity. From this expansion of the definition, it follows that morally questionable actions can be seen to be corruption despite not being subject to punishment by law. I say this because my hope is that public-spirited people in our country, will hold themselves not just to the legal standard, but to the moral one as well.

Complicating the discussion about corruption a bit more, Ha-Joon Chang has pointed out something he called "noble cause corruption," and the example he gave was that of Oscar Schindler bribing Nazi officials to save Jewish lives.[202] This should just make us aware that there are some acts which are illegal on paper, but that are legitimate given the context. The analogy often given in the social sciences is that of an ambulance breaking the speed limit in an emergency. This is just something to keep in mind, it does not really affect the definition of corruption.

Corrupt Acts:

The list of corrupt acts then, includes bribery, extortion, exchange of favours, nepotism, cronyism, judicial fraud, accounting fraud, electoral fraud, public service fraud, embezzlement, kleptocracy, influence peddling, and conflicts of interest. The very dictionary definitions of these terms proclaim their wrongness. Nepotism is defined as the hiring of a family member instead of a more qualified but unrelated candidate. Embezzlement is the stealing of public funds. These two examples also show the difficulty of enforcement action against corruption. Nepotism is not strictly illegal, so there will be nothing to enforce, but it still affects society negatively in that the less qualified person will not be competent on the job so can only achieve suboptimal results. Embezzlement is illegal, but difficult to enforce because the perpetrators always covers their tracks, and even when caught, can have the wherewithal to pay off the police, judges, and whosoever is in authority. A further problem that complicates enforcement is that corruption is an institution and actually fights against those who are trying to stop it.

Corruption As An Institution:

Scott cautioned against taking political systems at face value, arguing that corruption can be seen as an institution in its own right. In that regard, he said that: "Corruption, after all, may be seen as an informal political system. Whereas party manifestos, general legislation, and policy declarations are the formal façade of the political structure, corruption stands in sharp contrast to these features as an informal political system in its own right. Here coalitions that could not survive the light of day, government decisions that would set off a public outcry, elite behaviour that would destroy many a political career are all located."[203]

The dictionary definition of an institution holds that it is an established organization or corporation especially of a public character. What we know about public institutions is that they have personnel, buildings, equipment and constitutions. Where corruption has been long established, it should also be thought of as an institution – an informal institution. Thus, though you will not see its personnel or written constitutions, they exist and come into play in defence of the continuation of this informal institution.

I also mention this point because I do not want us to be naïve and think that corruption has no force and vitality of its own. Nuhu Ribadu speaking at TEDx in Berlin, talked about how corruption in Nigeria fought back when he was made Head of the Economic and Financial Crimes Commission – an anti-corruption organisation. In carrying out his duties, he says he ended up arresting the Inspector General of the Federal Police for corruption. He also says that in the process he arrested 49 Chief Executives of Banks. The case that stands out for me from his presentation, is that of James Ibori, who was Governor of Delta State when Ribadu began investigating him for Corruption. Ibori first tried to bribe Nuhu Ribadu with US$15 Million not to arrest him, and when that failed, they removed Ribadu from his position, in addition to trying to assassinate him. This was possible because, Ibori was friends with Umaru Musa Yar'Adua, who became President of Nigeria during the time when Ibori was being investigated.

The other way corruption also fights back, is if all the powerful in society are corrupt themselves. In such a situation, the first among the elites who tries to go after corruption, compromises his power. Let us take the example I gave above of nepotism, and let us also be very clear that, with this example, I am not accusing anyone specifically. The job functions I have chosen are just for illustrative purposes. Let us say, for argument's sake, that the Chief of Defence gives his nephew a position in an important public company, and the nephew is corrupt. If the President of the Country, depends on the Chief of Defence for his power, he cannot go after the corrupt nephew without compromising his position.

If he were to arrest the nephew of the Chief of Defence, the Chief of Defence might withdraw his political support for him. The only way that type of corruption can be attacked, is if all the elites are against corruption and have even warned their relatives that if they are corrupt they will go to prison. This idea I am proposing to you here is not fantastical either. I have seen this kind of thing in Rwanda, where if your case is being investigated by the police, everyone stands clear and allows the police and the judiciary to finish their processes. For this reason, I will talk about Rwanda below, for I think we can learn much from it on how it has minimised inducements to corruption.

What Causes Corruption?

If paying bribes is widespread in society, everyone is likely to engage in it, because those who do not pay bribes will not get the services they want.[204] This is what Fisman and Golden explained as contingent behaviour: people will do what they expect others to do in a given society.[205] They further say that, due to contingent behaviour, anyone whose behaviour deviates from the norm, will find it too costly.[206] So, in a society where corruption is widespread, everyone must participate in corruption or else they will not access required services or business opportunities.[207]

It follows then, that in a society where corruption is not the norm, anyone who tries to engage in corruption will also find it costly to do so.[208] This is exactly what I was driving at when I mentioned earlier that if our country disapproves of corruption, there will be a time when it will be unpopular. But contingent behaviour is not an explanation of what causes corruption, it is only an explanation for why people engage in corruption when, ultimately, society is harmed by it. We must still find an explanation as to why society becomes widely corrupt or not corrupt in the first place.

Rose-Ackerman and Palifka think that the causes of corruption can be found in these three broad categories: institutions, incentives, and personal ethics. Under the category of institutions, they say that if formal institutions like law enforcement are not strong, informal ones like bribery and influence peddling will proliferate.[209] As for incentives, again where strong organizational stances against corruption, monitoring and punishment do not exist, incentives for corruption arise.[210]

Personal ethics just refers to people having no scruples about engaging in corruption.[211] This last cause of corruption is also the one I think we can tackle by appealing to our people's better natures. The same authors also acknowledge contingent behaviour in this category when they say, "perceptions of corruption can help shape personal ethics: the more an individual perceives corruption to be the norm, the more the person is likely to engage in corruption."[212]

Fisman and Golden have also proposed a further framework that I think is very applicable to Zimbabwe as to why corruption happens in the first place. They have proposed an explanation they called the "modernization argument." According to them, people in developing countries demand more services than the authorities can supply, those with money then resort to bribery to access the few services.[213] What also facilitates the bribe taking and paying, is that the institutions of governance will also be weak in developing countries.[214] So, this is an explanation that says there is competition for few resources, and those who are willing to pay extra will get the services. This is in reference to such public services as health.

For bribes, Rose-Ackerman and Palifka, suggest some incentives. The first incentive is when there are benefits that are short in supply, and which the government awards on legal criteria other than payment, paying a bribe will act as a substitute for nonmonetary qualifications[215]. Secondly, low paid officials demand bribes to do their jobs, as without getting the bribes they deliberately delay doing their jobs.[216] Thirdly, business people are also incentivised to pay bribes because, they can lower costs for them as they will not pay taxes and duties.[217] So, if these are some of the incentives for bribes, then fighting corruption must also involve removing the incentives here cited.

The role of pure greed in the causes of corruption must also be factored in, for there are some people who are not deprived but who will steal at a grand scale. Sani Abacha who stole an estimated US$1 Billion - $4 Billion in Nigeria is a case in point. For such cases where there is no obvious need, it would also be interesting to explore psychological explanations for corruption, such as those that pertain to kleptomania.

The Black Tax And Corruption:

Some people have tried to say that it is only through Western lens that African traditions like gift giving can be mistaken for corruption. James Scott refutes this protestation by asking how a 10% rake off an airport contract fits into these gift giving explanation?[218] But still, the strong familial links and cultural practices we have in Africa should be factored in when we are discussing corruption. Western societies with their impersonal relationships have some marked differences with our societies. It is a common refrain that, life in the West is so stressful because there are no family support systems. But the same familial support systems we extol as a virtue in Africa, introduces some instances that favour corruption which are not there in the West.

For example, the black tax is not a feature of Western life, but it is very much one in Zimbabwe. The black tax is simply all those amounts that the bread winner of a Clan has to pay to support his extended family. In such a set-up, even nepotism can be explained away as an attempt to lighten the burden of the black tax on the bread winner in question. The person will employ a relative in a company where he has influence, or else he has to pay out of his pocket to support the relative. An equivalent of this in Western societies could be the school network. What is important about the problem of the black tax is that, if we understand how it causes corruption, we can mitigate it. The mitigant I suggest is that whoever employs a relative, should also make sure that the relative is the most competent.

Is All Corruption Harmful?

Transparency International is unequivocal that corruption is harmful to society. I take the same view. Take the example I used above of a policeman accepting a bribe to allow a dangerous motorist to continue on his journey. The motorist will likely maim or kill someone who is following the rules. This is how I view all corruption, the way it harms society when rules are flouted for private gain by individuals. In the banking sector for example, something like influence peddling is harmful for the constitution of banking. Palifka and Rose-Ackerman argue that; "Personal influence and corruption lead banks into high-risk lending – sometimes to borrowers with no intention of repaying the funds."[219] Banks have rules that ensure those who are credit worthy can borrow, if these rules are abrogated from, people who cannot pay back the funds, will get loans to the detriment of the banks.

But as with all ideas, there have been other thinkers who have argued that not all corruption is harmful to society, and that some types of corruption are actually beneficial to the economy. This other view's argument is that things like bribes sometimes speed up the pace of a transaction. I think we should also be aware of this competing view, as it helps explain why countries like China, that are also corrupt, have managed to develop. Yuen Ang has argued that China did so by engaging in the least harmful forms of corruption. These differences in types of corruption, has helped her explain why China has managed to develop despite having rampant corruption. If we cannot root out corruption completely, if human nature is so flawed that it just must engage in corruption, perhaps engaging in its less harmful forms could be an acceptable alternative. This seems to be the lesson from China.

Corruption, Lessons From China:

Since I have said corruption has impeded our economic development, it is tempting to think that countries like China that have developed, did so because there was no corruption there. This is a mistaken view, there was corruption in China throughout its development. But Yuen Ang has made an argument that essentially says that China developed because it engaged in the right type of corruption. The picture would have been different had China engaged predominantly in the most harmful forms of corruption such as grand theft.

In this vein, Yuen Ang takes a qualified approach to the harm that corruption causes to an economy. She uses the analogy of drugs in her view of the effects that the different types of corruption have on society: some are very harmful, and some are less harmful. She introduces these two dimensions to corruption: a dimension which involves pure theft, and another which involves exchanges. She then introduces two categories in each dimension, and each category corresponds to corrupt activities by either elites or by non-elites. In the dimension of corruption that involves theft, we have petty theft and grand theft as practiced by non-elites and elites respectively. In the dimension that involves exchanges, we have speed money and access money, again, as practiced by non-elites and elites respectively.

In her theorising then, "petty theft and grand theft are equivalent to toxic drugs – they are the most economically damaging as they drain public and private wealth. Even worse, such corruption subverts law and order, deterring investors, tourists, and even foreign aid donors."[220] Speed money, whereby businesses and citizens pay petty bribes to speed things up, is less harmful than petty theft and grand theft.[221] In the drugs analogy, she views "speed money as painkillers: although they lessen pain, they do not give health benefits, and consuming them in excess is harmful."[222] In the same drugs analogy, access money is seen as steroids: it is growth enhancing but comes with serious side effects.[223] Access money refers to those huge sums corporations and individuals pay to have access to policy makers. In the United States this happens in the form of lobbying, while in the UK, donations to political parties are the equivalent.

On corruption in China, Ang further says that: "access money, on the other hand, is the steroids of capitalism. Steroids are known as growth enhancing drugs, but they come with serious side effects. And countries both rich and poor, in the West and the East, can fall prey to its temptation. From a businessperson's point of view, access money is less tax than an investment. For example, Chinese entre-preneurs are willing to bribe their way into legislative congresses because the benefits of networking with Party-state bosses more than offset the expense. Likewise, in the United States, big corpora-tions sink billions of dollars into lobbying every year because returns exceed costs. By enriching capitalists who pay for the privileges and by rewarding politicians who serve capitalist interests, access money can perversely stimulate commercial transactions and investment which translates into GDP growth."[224]

To those who may have thought corruption is only in poor coun-tries, she says; "Wealthy economies may have low quantities of aggre-gate corruption, as measured by standard cross-national indices, but it does not mean that they have no corruption; rather, their corrup-tion may be of a different quality – concentrated in access money, which is difficult to capture and not immediately growth-retarding. Contrary to popular beliefs, the rise of capitalism was not accompa-nied by the eradication of corruption, but rather by the evolution of the quality of corruption from thuggery and theft toward sophisti-cated exchange of power and profit."[225]

So, what China did was to also deliberately steer its people from harmful forms of corruption such as theft and extortion, into the beneficial ones.[226] According to Ang again: "These forms of corrup-tion – petty theft, grand theft and speed money – were brought under control through an ambitious program of capacity building, which began in 1998 under Premier Zhu Rongji and is still being expanded. The programme includes a Civil Service Law, standardizing tax rates, strengthening oversight through budgeting and accounting reforms, replacing cash payments of fees and fines with direct electronic deposits, and consolidating public bank accounts."[227] This is what China did, and it is there for us to copy, should we find ourselves so hopeless that we cannot avoid corruption. Again, this is the point I was making above, that if we cannot eradicate corruption, we should only engage in the less harmful forms.

The other distinction she introduces which may be lacking in Zimbabwe but is there in China, is the corrupt but competent distinction. With this distinction I picture that even nepotism hires should defer to the logic of competent people before any other consideration. It is no use to give your dimwit cousin the position of CEO in a company, for that company will be run into the ground. So, even nepotism hires should be given positions congruous with their competencies.

Corruption In Zimbabwe:

I hope by now that it is clear to everyone that, there is corruption in every country on the planet, the main difference is just in extent and types. Corruption has indeed been with us for as long as we have been a nation, and even earlier. There was corruption in Rhodesia, but I do not care about corruption in Rhodesia, because I do not hold people who practice Apartheid to any high moral standards in the first place. The very act of Rhodesia excluding people from employment positions because of skin colour is corruption worse than nepotism. I only mention this because some of our countrymen and countrywomen who have not thought about corruption systemically, tend to say that the white settler in Rhodesia was not corrupt.

I also only care about corruption in other countries insofar as we can compare its effects there with corruption's effects in Zimbabwe. Case in point is what I have just said above about China. Corruption in Zimbabwe is what I care really about. I also know much about it personally, having worked in institutions in the country where corruption occurred. From my own experiences, I think I can describe corruption in Zimbabwe as having occurred in these two distinct stages, the "Elite Entitlement Corruption" of the immediate post-independence era, and the "Pre and Post-Sanctions Widespread Corruption," where everyone got involved in the act. Elite Entitlement Corruption can be seen in the major scandals such as the Willowvale Motors Scandal.

This Elite Entitlement Corruption soon after independence, is best characterised by what Robert Mugabe said while speaking at the Heroes Acre, at a funeral of one of the liberation war heroes – Maurice Nyagumbo. He had committed suicide because of the Willowvale Motors Scandal. With the crowd applauding and ululating, a clearly emotional Robert Mugabe eulogised that: "*Nhaiwe Nyagumbo shamwari yangu, wadarirei kuzviuraya, riri Jeri ripi rawaipinda ini shamwari yako ndichiri mupenyu?*" Translation: "Nyagumbo, my friend, why have you taken your life, which prison could you have faced when I, your friend, was still alive?" This is the epitome of Elite Entitlement Corruption, when an all-powerful executive President, announces publicly, that his friends should not fear getting jailed for corruption!

So, as far as I can see, in the first years of our independence, there was a permissive environment when those who had fought in the liberation war felt entitled to do, or take, whatever they wanted. There was no accountability as the general population felt indebted to them, and among themselves, as evinced by Mugabe's eulogy above, they were above the law. Geoff Nyarota, one of the reporters who broke the Willowvale Motors Scandal was even accused of now being a ZAPU supporter (essentially a dissident), at a public gathering by Enos Nkala – a ZANU Central Committee Member and Cabinet Minister.

What compounded this problem was the fact that our people who took over from the Rhodesian government we had just defeated, were not technocrats, having inherited a system that had denied them educational opportunities. So, some of the corruption was also down to the fact that these people did not know better how to run the new system they had inherited. Even what I posited above as a solution - nepotism that defers to competent people - would not have worked because, there were few people who were competent at the time. Still, this permissive environment is how corruption took root in our country in the first place. If those at the top are also engaged in corruption, it follows that the ones at the bottom will also engage in corruption because of contingent behaviour. Some elements of our mismanagement of the economy, and the effects of our inherited problems, also meant that hardships were already being experienced in the economy, forcing more people to engage in corruption

I would be lying if I say that corruption was not proscribed. I worked for some time at Harare International Airport, and I witnessed the corruption that was happening there in all the government institutions that were stationed there. I also saw the rotation of Customs Officers to different ports to ensure that they did not become familiar with each other and so have a regular roster to engage in corruption. No one openly advertised their corrupt activities because the fear of imprisonment was there, so this tells me that there was never a time when corruption was accepted as legitimate conduct. All I can say is that corruption is a difficult problem to eradicate. President Mnangagwa who announced that he would fight corruption on taking over in 2017, has since lamented how deep rooted corruption is in Zimbabwe.

But all the reasons that have been given as a cause of corruption, and the difficulties of eradicating corruption in poor countries, fall on the side when we think about Rwanda. The idea that nothing can be done about corruption in developing countries, is refuted by Rwanda.

Corruption, Lessons From Rwanda:

As part of my research for these Addresses, I travelled to Rwanda and stayed there for 7 months observing for myself, the positives I have heard about Rwanda. This field trip, as it turned out, was very useful in seeing how a fellow African country has decisively dealt with the problem of corruption. I must also admit to you that, this was the main reason why I supported the military assisted transition in Zimbabwe in 2017. I expected that the Second Republic would be able to deal with corruption with the same vitality as it has been dealt with in Rwanda. So far this has not been the case.

I lived in Rwanda for 7 months in 2021, while I was there I drove to every corner of the country, and my experiences with the police in those 7 months is my entry point into the corruption in Rwanda debate. There was not a single time when the police asked me for a bribe. Being a motorist is surely the quickest way to get asked for a bribe in developing countries. The assumption is that if you are driving you are wealthy and can afford to pay a bribe. Even when nothing is wrong with your vehicle, the police will either contrive something, or ask for "money for a drink." None of this happened to me while I was in Rwanda.

There were even opportunities to solicit a bribe from me. Take for instance the time I drove to the Twin Lakes in the Volcanoes National Park, about 120 Kilometres West of Kigali. On this visit, I was driving a top of the range VW Teramont vehicle that I had hired from VW Mobility Solutions. In countries where corruption is rampant, such a vehicle is a signal that you must have money to spare. If they do not ask for a bribe, the Police will ask for money as a gift at least. I came across a roadblock where the police were checking vehicles for unpaid penalty charges. As it turned out the vehicle I was driving had an unpaid penalty charge incurred by a previous customer. The procedure was that they should have impounded the vehicle, which would have greatly inconvenienced me. But when I explained the situation to the officer, he said to me: "I am going to let you go, but do me a favour, when you hand back this vehicle make sure you tell VW to pay this outstanding penalty notice." I am very good friends with the people at VW Rwanda, so when I got back to Kigali, I insisted they pay the penalty charge. I also suggested to them ways they can ensure their customers do not burden them with these charges when they hand back the car.

Still, this last encounter with the Rwanda National Police (RNP), left me curious as to why they do not ask for bribes when the opportunities to do so surely arise. The unpaid penalty notice on my vehicle was 75 000RWF (US\$75), the minimum wage in Rwanda is 80 000RWF (US\$80), it is not what the police get paid, but the way bribes work, the policeman should have asked for at least 40 000RWF (US\$40) to let me go on my way. This 40 000RWF in a country where the monthly minimum wage is 80 000RWF must go a long way for anyone who has it in his hand. This did not happen, so I asked my friends in some of Rwanda's institutions why this was the case.

The answer when it came, was the antithesis to what I called Elite Entitlement Corruption in reference to President Robert Mugabe's announcement that if his friends were corrupt, they needed not fear jail. In contrast, I was told the reason why this has been the case, is because President Paul Kagame himself, is very intolerant of corruption. By not being corrupt himself and ensuring that none of his circle engage in corruption, he has led by example. People at all levels of society who have engaged in corruption have been arrested and imprisoned, their names, their corrupt acts, station in society and prison sentences have also been published in national newspapers. This has hammered home the message that corruption will not be tolerated at any level. In Rwanda if you are being investigated by the RNP, you become an untouchable until you have cleared your name. In some countries, if the police is investigating you, the powerful interfere by demanding that the police drop the investigation.

The people I asked about the non-existence of bribery at the street level in Rwanda, also told me that deterrent sentences are the reason why there is zero street level corruption. There was a time when if you bribed a police officer with 5 000RWF (US$5) and he accepted, and you were caught, both of you would get 5 years in prison each. How this was made to work was that people from the intelligence services would deliberately try to bribe the police officers, or masquerading as police, ask for bribes from people who had contravened a traffic regulation. In time, because people could not be sure whether someone who is offering, or asking for a bribe, is not from the intelligence services, bribe taking and offering stopped.

In deference to the quotation from Patrice Lumumba that opened this Address, I asked my Rwandan friends whether the Police were being paid salaries that made them comfortable enough that they did not need bribes. Lumumba said: "A minimum of comfort is necessary for the practice of virtue." I have taken this to mean that no amount of appeal to morality, will make a person experiencing hardships be a virtuous person. I have also admitted in the section covering the causes of corruption above, that people take bribes to offset the hardships that come from earning too little. My friends in Rwanda told me that the RNP does not pay exceptionally well, but it tries to support its members with medical aid, and discount on shopping in some stores. This is also a very important understanding of how to mitigate corruption. Punishment is needed yes, but the street level officials also need to be insulated from hardship through official channels.

Rwanda has also made sure that no one pays any fines or service charges to individuals, another inducement to corruption. Instead, all the payments for government services are electronic. But what ensures that Rwanda is corruption free is that when all this money has been collected, the government led by President Paul Kagame ensures it is all used for public services. No one skims some of the amounts for their personal use, this ensures there is confidence in the government and serves as an example for street level officials, who would soon flout the rules, if the leadership did not lead by example. This is the main lesson we can take from Rwanda, that the people at the top do not engage in Elite Entitlement Corruption.

Of course, no country is corruption free, but at the levels I was able to investigate and to interact with, I found zero corruption. There must be some corruption in Rwanda, because while speaking at the launch of the 2021 – 2022 Judicial Year, President Paul Kagame himself said that: "People go to Courts hoping that the judges will listen to them, make judgements based on evidence presented, and as provided by the law. But we hear that some in the justice sector still ask for bribes. This is unacceptable and must be stopped."

The Cost Of Corruption To Society:

The crux of the matter for me, is that those who engage in corruption need to understand that it is harmful to society, and some of that harm can very well befall them personally. Take an example where buildings are constructed in violation of legal codes, because bribes have been paid. These buildings will collapse or will be fire hazards. The person who paid the bribe and the one who facilitated the illegal construction may well be in the building when it collapses. But even if they take precautions never to enter those buildings, no one should produce a building that may kill fellow human beings. This is the idea of public-spiritedness I will talk about in the Eleventh Address.

Conclusion:

My fellow Countrymen and Countrywomen, I have had to discuss corruption because it is another issue I want us to truly understand.

The damage that corruption causes to society is what I find abhorrent. My hope, in discussing corruption, is that we can all know exactly what it is and how it harms society. I would then like all of us to be revulsed by corruption. Having surveyed the causes of corruption and found them to exist on a psychological as well opportunistic level, I think changing individuals' attitudes towards corruption is the major step that will reduce it. If enough of us refuse to participate in corruption, it will soon be viewed with the same revulsion we reserve for murder in our society.

Corruption is a vice that has plagued humanity for all its existence, what we can try to do in our country is to not give it ready succour. Rwanda has managed to do this; we can copy some of the things they have done there. In other countries, they just steered their population towards the less harmful forms of corruption. This is the lesson from China and the developed countries in the West. Control of corruption also requires our leaders be incorruptible themselves, thereby leading by example.

Address IX.

The Fourth Industrial Revolution And Us.

"Concern for man and his fate must always form the chief interest of all technical endeavours. Never forget this in the midst of your diagrams and equations" – Albert Einstein.

I N COUNTRIES LIKE OURS, where one of our distinctive features, is the high rates of unemployment, I think any clamouring for the adoption of the Fourth Industrial Revolution (4IR), is misguided at this stage. In Europe, it has been estimated that by 2034, 47% of all human jobs will have been lost to one or another aspect of 4IR, chiefly Artificial Intelligence (AI) and Automation. For this reason, I have a problem with the Fourth Industrial Revolution: I do not share the enthusiasm some people have about us adopting 4IR. In fact, I am opposed to us adopting 4IR right now. Where unreflecting people see only opportunity, I also see the challenges it contains.

One of the longstanding problems in Zimbabwe, and Africa in general, is our high unemployment rates. In Zimbabwe, during the height of our problems with Sanctions, the unemployment rate was invariably pegged at 90%, I do not see the wisdom then, of rushing to embrace an industrial revolution that will likely make 47% of our paltry 10% employed redundant. I, instead, think we are better off focusing all our efforts on succeeding in the previous three industrial revolutions, which we still have not yet fully achieved. As evinced by China, succeeding in the first three industrial revolutions, creates employment and can lift millions out of poverty. This is what we need more than anything at the moment. Only after the same success as China in the first three industrial revolutions, can we then focus on 4IR.

In any case, it is not possible to start constructing a building without first putting the foundation in place. We, therefore, must also realise that our efforts are misguided, if we try to adopt just aspects of 4IR, without having succeeded in the first three industrial revolutions. I see the first three industrial revolutions as compulsory steps in a country's development journey. Some have suggested that underdeveloped countries can leapfrog the first three industrial revolutions. To my mind, this idea is manifestly false.

The idea is also plain contrary to the tenets of development. If we do not own the processes that enabled 4IR to emerge in the world, our countries will still remain consumers to countries whose 4IR adoption rests on their success in the first three industrial revolutions. Those countries first built their factories that now produce civilization's essential goods, so their economic development rests on solid foundations. Thus, we should also go through the first three industrial revolutions so that we own all our processes. Not owning those processes will keep us at the mercy of the whims of the countries that do. For this reason, if it were up to me, I would actually outlaw the adoption of 4IR by all countries that have not yet mastered the First, Second, and Third Industrial Revolutions.

My contention here, is also that, our competitor countries had acceptable standards of life even at the point when they had succeeded just up to the Third Industrial Revolution. All their current successes are predicated on those foundations. At this point in time when they are adopting 4IR, we still have sections of our society who do not have access to innovations that were brought in by the First Industrial Revolution. Large swathes of our population still rely on Ox-drawn ploughs for their farming. Access to electricity is also very limited, with capacity lacking even in our urban areas. Why then are we even talking about 4IR, when we have not given everyone in our society basics like access to running water? Everyone has running water in Switzerland, so there, they can talk about adopting 4IR without looking ridiculous. We, on the other hand, have not put the foundations in place to even think about 4IR.

I am also further concerned by the dangers that 4IR will bring, but I think when we do decide to adopt 4IR, our backwardness in this field could be a blessing in disguise. The industrialised nations are really at a stage when they are being compelled by their opening of "Pandora's Box," to adopt technology and innovations that will likely cause them as many problems as they will be solving. In this regard, I have this romantic idea that we are uniquely positioned to lead from behind. We will do this by correcting all the mistakes the developed countries are making in adopting dangerous things like AI. We can learn from their mistakes and chart a better 4IR path. All we need to do, when the time comes, is adopt the positive aspects of 4IR without the harmful consequences. In this sense, our current underdevelopment can work to our advantage. Of course, the main fear where AI is concerned, is that it will enslave and ultimately destroy all humanity. On that count, the matter is quite out of the hands of the developing countries.

What Is The Fourth Industrial Revolution?

Tshilidzi Marwala defined the Fourth Industrial Revolution as "the confluence of cyber, physical and biological technologies."[228] This is to say, 4IR is the point at which all of humanity's earlier and current inventions are now interacting at a greater extent than before. For this reason, to understand the Fourth Industrial Revolution alright, we need to understand the three industrial revolutions that preceded it. The fact of the matter is this, 4IR is predicated on the three previous industrial revolutions. From my vantage point then, countries that have not succeeded in the first three revolutions, have no business even talking about adopting 4IR.

Of the revolutions that have gone before 4IR, the first major shift was the agrarian reform, when people domesticated animals and began production, transportation and communication that allowed for settled communities to emerge.[229] This Agrarian Revolution was the platform on which the First Industrial Revolution stood. For the First Industrial Revolution was essentially a transition from muscle power to mechanical power.[230] It started in England in the 18th Century, triggered by the invention of the steam engine and construction of railroads. The First Industrial Revolution saw the introduction of machines in factories to produce goods, which, hitherto had been made by hand in cottage industries.[231] This shift to machine production, raised opposition from the Luddites – named after Ned Luddite – who took to smashing the machines as they feared losing their jobs to machines. I have the same job losses concerns with regards 4IR.

The Second Industrial Revolution happened in the 19th Century and was brought about by the advent of electricity generation, and the means of production it allowed to take place. The assembly line was introduced, thereby ushering in the mass production of goods. The Third Industrial Revolution happened in the 20th Century, specifically in the 1960s, and it is also called "the computer or digital revolution because it was catalysed by the development of semi-conductors, mainframe computing (1960s), personal computing (1970s and '80s) and the Internet (1990s)."[232] The Fourth Industrial Revolution which is currently unfolding before our eyes, is a logical confluence of all these prior developments. This confluence is even changing what it means to be a human being, with genetic engineering even making it possible to create superhumans.

Can Underdeveloped Countries Leapfrog A Stage?

The rapid adoption of Information and Communications Technology (ICT) everywhere, has often been cited as an example that developing countries do not need to go through every stage that the developed countries went through: they can skip a stage. The people who are promoting this idea, take pictures of rural farmers in underdeveloped countries holding cell phones, as evidence that these countries have skipped the stage of landline telephony. In this, I think these people are mistaking the shadow for the substance. As long as the actual technical knowhow and manufacture of the cell phones is not done by the developing countries themselves, nothing about the adoption of cellular telephony proves leapfrogging a development stage. Instead, the developing countries are just kept in that dependence cycle where they are still exporting raw materials cheaply, and then getting sold the expensive finished products. No one should celebrate this as the skipping of a stage in the industrial revolutions journey. Thus, as long as we have not ourselves become proficient in turning our raw materials into the products that are making 4IR possible, any claim that we have leapfrogged an industrial revolution is a manifest falsehood.

The example set by China is what we should follow. In the past 40 years, China has lifted itself from being essentially a Third World Country, to a hyperpower now poised to overtake the United States as the pre-eminent economy in the world. China did so by mastering all the three previous industrial revolutions for itself. There was a time, in the past four decades, when large swathes of the Chinese population were peasants still using animal drawn ploughs on their land. As of 2022, China is now the world leader in 5G technology and the manufacturing of High Speed Trains. It also domestically produces very competitive smart phones and Aircraft. China did all this by first succeeding in the first three industrial revolutions. Its participation in 4IR is therefore justified and stable.

The Advantages Of 4IR: Paradise Realised?

If you have ever worked with someone who is so lazy, so insufferable, and who misses work with a different excuse every time, you will appreciate industrialists' enthusiasm for replacing human beings with machines. I have never owned a production company, but I have worked with some people who I knew I definitely would not employ, if I owned a company. From a company owner's perspective then, machines are more efficient because they do not have any of the human being's fallibilities. The whole logic that undergirds Artificial Intelligence, is that at some point, it will do all tasks better than human beings, and more consistently.

According to this logic, the advantage of the machines will be that they will produce better products, will not get tired, and also will not miss work for social reasons. There are also some jobs that are so dangerous that it is best if they are delegated to automation. But there is an internal inconsistency to this advantage: I wonder who will buy the products that the machines will have efficiently produced, if all the consumers have no money owing to their losing their jobs to these machines?

But if we look past this messy initial stage to the long term, there is a case to be made that 4IR could be a version of Paradise that humanity has dreamed of since time immemorial. I talked at length about God in the Second Address. In that Address, I mostly focused on the questions that the authors of scriptures were trying to answer. These questions were: how we came into existence, who created us and why, and how our Creator wants us to live on this Planet. In that Address, I said that all the scriptures are just theories trying to answer those questions. I neglected to specifically talk about the theories of the afterlife contained in those same scriptures. Most scriptures have a picture of Paradise – a beautiful place where all the good people will spend eternity in happiness. There is also a Hell in some religions where the wicked get punished for eternity. As far as Paradise is concerned, one of the main features is that there will be no hard labour there. In just that aspect of Paradise, I see a possibility of 4IR realising Paradise for humanity. Machines will do all our labour, leaving humanity with much free time to pursue leisure.

Although, human nature being what it is, I doubt very much that the owners of the means of production, will allow the majority to partake in leisure when they have not helped produce the goods and services thereof. In this regard again, 4IR is actually likely to exacerbate inequality as the unemployed majority will not be able to afford to pay for even their basic needs.

So, the best advantage of 4IR, as far as I can see, will have to be the practical day to day problems it solves for us. For example, government service delivery is generally positively impacted by some automation where capacity is lacking. In this regard, adoption of some aspects of 4IR has certainly helped service delivery in Rwanda. Also, the problem of corruption has been mitigated by automated payment systems.

Ultimately though, with regards corruption mitigation from automated payment systems, it is the human leaders of Rwanda who are not corrupt when the revenue has been collected. They have used the revenue collected for the right service delivery purposes. So, automated payment systems just reduce incentives for bribery and petty theft. Incorruptible leadership is still the core component in the mitigation of corruption realised from those automated payment systems.

The Luddites:

Even though I accept some of the advantages I listed above, the gist of my argument in this Address, is still against the adoption of 4IR. What I am saying and feeling about 4IR, has also already been said and felt about earlier industrial revolutions. As it turned out, those earlier people were wrong. The example that quickly comes to mind is that of the Luddites, who take their name from Ned Luddite. They went around smashing looms in 17th Century England. This was during the First Industrial Revolution, and these people were opposed to machines replacing them in the factories. The main machine they were opposed to was the Loom. The Luddites were violently suppressed by the State, and many of them were executed. As it turned out, that industrial revolution the Luddites were opposed to, mainly brought about advantages and general prosperity to the world. So, I want us to be aware that there is the possibility that 4IR may just be humanity adopting the tools whose time has come. Humanity's great distinction from other animals is our ability to use tools.

Still, 4IR is problematic for me insofar as it will give all employment to machines and lead individuals into destitution. This is a qualitatively different problem for the one that was feared by the Luddites. Then, the industrial revolutions managed to create a lot of semi-skilled jobs which got filled by human beings. With 4IR, the only jobs I can envisage are highly skilled jobs which will make the majority of the population unemployable. I opened this Address with a quote from Albert Einstein to the effect that the fate of man should be the chief interest of all technical endeavours. It seems to me that with 4IR, the profit margins are the chief interest in the company owners' minds.

Also, for our purposes, the impoverishment that will come from job losses to 4IR, will be felt differently in the developed countries than in the developing countries. This is where context matters. The developed countries will have some capacity to introduce Universal Basic Income (UBI) and are already trialling this in anticipation of mass unemployment from 4IR. UBI is the amount that will be paid to every adult in the country and should be able to cover the monthly cost of living. These countries are able to do this because their 4IR adoption rests on solid foundations. Developing countries on the other hand, have already shown that they are not prepared for such disruption to current employment models.

This difference in shock absorption capacity was demonstrated to us by the Covid19 Pandemic which occurred in 2020. Western countries were able to shield their workers from extreme want with Furlough Schemes. For nearly 2 years, Western Governments paid 80% of wages of the workers who were kept out of employment by the pandemic. African countries were not in a position to do the same. From this example, it is clear to me then, that 4IR will be more impoverishing in developing countries, than it will be in developed countries that have some shock absorption capacity.

A Refusal To Embrace Progress?

But, having extolled the virtues of embracing the scientific paradigm and progress in preceding Addresses, do I not contradict myself now, when I implore us not to adopt these scientific tools that will make life easier? I quite think I do contradict myself, and I am very conflicted about it. In fact, in making the points I am making in this Address; I do very much feel like the King that was encountered by Gulliver on his travels to Brobdingnag. At the time I read Gulliver's Travels, I thought the King was foolish not to embrace every advantage science brought his way. But I find myself now taking his side in the principled rejection of destructive advantage as he did when it was offered.

Wanting to ingratiate himself with the King, Gulliver told the King of Brobdingnag of an invention that had been discovered 400 years ago – gunpowder – which he explained to the King would give him mastery over his neighbours because of the destructive power of weapons fashioned from it. Gulliver offered to direct the King's workmen into making those weapons since he knew "the ingredients very well, which were very cheap and common; and I understood the manner of compounding them."[233] In his refusal to accept these destructive advantages, the King was surprised at "how so impotent and grovelling an insect" as Gulliver was, "could entertain such inhuman ideas, and in so familiar terms as to appear wholly unmoved at all by the scenes of blood and desolation," he had painted.[234] The King concluded that such ideas could have only come from an enemy of humanity.[235] While he extols the King and the Brobdingnagians' other virtues, Gulliver himself concluded the King's refusal to take this advantage as down to ignorance; "I take this defect among them to have risen from their ignorance, they not having hitherto reduced politics to a science, as the more acute wits of Europe have done."[236]

Given our history with Colonialism, there is always a niggling feeling that perhaps I am allowing my humanity to argue for a situation that will cause us to be overpowered again in this age, as we were in the Colonisation period. The Brobdingnagians would certainly have been destroyed by Europeans aided by gunpowder if they ever ended up meeting them on the battlefield. In fact, the story of the Brobdingnagians is our story with Colonisation. Our Colonisation was aided by the Maxim Gun, when all we had were Spears and Cowhide Shields. The tools of the Fourth Industrial Revolution will also impact what militaries can do on the battlefield. President Vladimir Putin has already intimated that whoever masters AI first, will rule the world. Therefore, in the field of national security, not adopting 4IR, will be the equivalent of unilateral disarmament.

A Variegated Approach:

To this threat posed to our national security by 4IR, I think we can have a variegated approach. In the civilian sector, we will concentrate on achieving the industrial revolutions in a linear manner, while allowing the national security sector to skip stages and adopt some aspects of 4IR. The logic undergirding this will be that, for very dangerous jobs, we should automate anyway. Still, as far as AI is concerned, we are never going to be in a position to compete with foreign armies of the West any time soon. We do not even need to match these countries in defence spending to be able to defend our sovereignty successfully. Afghanistan has shown us that even a hyper-power can be defeated by a skilful and dedicated opponent relying on low tech weapons. The United States, with a military budget of £700 billion per year failed to win in Afghanistan over a period of 18 years. The doctrine that informed Afghanistan's ability to fight the United States until it withdrew was Anti-Access and Area Denial (A2/AD) Doctrine. African Armies can, instead, also only invest in the low tech methods often used by A2/AD Doctrine adherents.

The Dangers Of 4IR: Humanity's Last Invention?

The more serious problem with AI is that it could be the last invention humanity ever makes. This concept of the last invention has two connotations. The two connotations are that it will either destroy us or, it will give us unlimited leisure time since it will anticipate all our needs and invent the requisite machines to fulfil those needs. I think the former is the more likely scenario. Those who have thought about this matter longer than me, have called this "the problem of control."

With AI, the envisaged problem is not when AI surpasses human weakness, for that will be quite useful, it will be when AI surpasses human strength that our problems will begin. Will we be able to control a superintelligent machine? This problem of control was stated as far back as 1965, by I.J. Good thus: "Let an ultra-intelligent machine be defined as a machine that can far surpass all the intellectual activities of any man howsoever clever. Since the design of machines is one of these intellectual activities, an ultra-intelligent machine could design even better machines; there would then unquestionably be an "intelligence explosion," and the intelligence of man would be left far behind. Thus, the ultra-intelligent machine is the last invention that man need ever make, provided, that the machine is docile enough to tell us how to keep it under control."[237] In this statement, we find contained the two connotations I mentioned above that the superintelligent machines could either enslave us or free us. I am pessimistic about which one will be the likely one of the two scenarios.

Klaus Schwab takes a more optimistic view towards these possible negative effects of 4IR, but he still leans towards regulation as what will produce the positive outcome. He says that; "Technology is not an exogenous force over which we have no control. We are not constrained by a binary choice between "accept and live with it" and "reject and live without it.""[238] He sees a role for regulation, as I will also reluctantly accept as a compromise, if it turns out that the world cannot outright postpone the adoption of 4IR. He thinks that: "shaping the fourth industrial revolution to ensure that it is empowering and human centred, rather than divisive and dehumanising, is not a task for any single stakeholder or sector or for any one region, industry or culture."[239] This then places the issue on the agenda for the United Nations General Assembly (UNGA), in the same manner that the Climate Change Crisis has had to be debated there. For ourselves, I still counsel that we focus on achieving the First, Second, and Third Industrial Revolutions first, and only debate the Fourth Industrial Revolution in anticipation for the time when we will have established firm foundations for it.

Conclusion:

My fellow countrymen and countrywomen, for me, the time for us to participate in the Fourth Industrial Revolution has not yet quite come. I am mostly worried about the job losses to machines when we already have the highest unemployment rates in the world. Secondarily, I am concerned about Artificial Intelligence's potential to enslave and ultimately destroy humanity. We do not have any control on my secondary concern, but on the first concern we can do something about that situation. Perhaps, what will exercise our minds and unite us more, is that 4IR will not only affect blue collar jobs. Everyone's job is at risk: Journalist, Lawyer, Accountant, News Anchor, Professor, Soldier, Driver, Pilot, Author, and Factory Hand are all threatened alike by Artificial Intelligence and Automation.

My solution for us as a developing country, is to deliberately focus all our efforts on achieving the First, Second, and Third Industrial Revolutions first. The Fourth Industrial Revolution is premised on success in those first three revolutions. For just one example, the hyper internet connectivity that will make driverless cars possible (Fourth Industrial Revolution), cannot happen in a country that has not yet achieved 100% electricity coverage (Second Industrial Revolution). I also know that quality of life was quite acceptable when our competitor countries had just achieved the Third Industrial Revolution. So, personally, I would be quite content living with just the innovations of the first three industrial revolutions. I also know that achieving those first three industrial revolutions, will give large parts of our populations a quality of life they have never experienced before. China lifted 300 million people out of poverty in just the four decades it went from being essentially a Third World Country to fully developed country.

It would seem here then, that what I advocated for in the Second Address, has been turned on its head. In the Second Address, I extolled the virtues of the scientific paradigm, yet it is science that has brought us to our current precarious existence under the shadow of the threat of nuclear annihilation. It is also science that is bringing us closer and closer to a predicted destruction by Artificial Intelligence, once it achieves superintelligence. The solution, however, is not to abandon the scientific paradigm for the superstitious paradigm that was the religious paradigm. We should stay with the scientific paradigm, because it looks for solutions to the problems it has created, while the religious paradigm would now be telling to just await the second coming of Jesus Christ as the solution to our problems. The people who are working in the hard sciences, can certainly think of better solutions to "the problem of control," than me. What I have done in this Address, is to suggest the Social Sciences' answer to our problem with the Fourth Industrial Revolution: regulation. I have suggested we postpone its adoption until a time when we have achieved for ourselves the first three industrial revolutions. This will allow us to have the solid foundations needed to deal with the vagaries that 4IR will bring to our polity.

Address X.

The Military In Zimbabwe.

"We wish to make it very clear to all Zimbabwean citizens that the security organisations will only stand in support of those political leaders that will pursue Zimbabwe's values, traditions, and beliefs for which thousands of lives were lost... Let it be known that the highest office on the land is a strait-jacket whose occupant is expected to observe the objectives of the liberation struggle. We will therefore not accept, let alone support or salute, anyone with a different agenda that threatens the very existence of our sovereignty, our country, and our people" – General Vitalis Zvinavashe, Zimbabwe Defence Forces Commander, March 2002.

"The military is the most outstanding institution in every country, for it alone makes possible the existence of all civic institutions" - Field Marshal Helmuth von Moltke The Elder, 1890.

WHAT FIELD MARSHAL Helmuth von Moltke, The Elder, wrote about the military in 1890, has remained incontrovertible to this date. The military is still the one institution that truly allows civil society to exist. This is because, force, is the final arbiter in all human affairs. Anyone who has not thought about the matter systematically, would look at proceedings in a Court of Law for example, and not see how the military underwrites that process. But it does.

In a Trial in the most democratic country in the world, when a Judge strikes down his gavel to signal the finalisation of the Court Case, he is only able to do that because, his decision is underwritten by the military of the country. If this was not the case, the criminal and his friends could decide they were not happy with the final judgement, and free their friend from custody. It is the fear of the military that will dissuade them. If they go ahead anyway, and free their friend from custody, it is, ultimately, the military that will be called upon to enforce the Court's judgement. This is one way the military underwrites our social contract.

Society is also threatened by covetous outsiders. The military's other remit then, is to ensure that the country remains secure from such aggression from abroad. In these Addresses, I have conceived every nation's highest aim as economic development and prosperity. If you prosper, but are unable to protect your prosperity, outsiders will come and take away the fruits of your prosperity, and even enslave you if they so wish.

This is what Niccolo Machiavelli was referring to when he said, "Good institutions without the help of the military, are not much differently disordered than the habitation of a superb and regal palace, which, even though adorned with jewels and gold, if it is not roofed over, will not have anything to protect it from the rain."[240] Restated then, the indispensable role of the military in society is: underwriting society against domestic and foreign disturbances.

I make the tedious points above because, I have heard some idealists opine that countries could forego having standing militaries. They think that militaries are a drain on economic resources as encapsulated in the "Guns vs Butter Debate." To that suggestion, the answer has already been given by history: those who did not have a standing military of their own, always ended up feeding a foreign one.

I should also mention that there was a time in history, when armies were only raised when a campaign was about to be undertaken, but rationalization of society has since given the answer that having standing armies is best practice. The question of whether we need a standing military, therefore, does not arise for me. What I find worthy of discussion here instead, is explaining to outsiders and posterity, why our military seems aligned with the Ruling Party in Zimbabwe. For our military has been accused of being a partisan military.

This only seems to be the case because, our military defends Zimbabwe's national interest as it is dictated to us by our nation's history. The struggle for Independence from British white settler Colonialism, is the predominant factor in that history. For not having a standing military in the colonization period, we were enslaved by foreigners on our own territory for 90 years. All attempts to dislodge the white settler by force in the 1890s failed. It was only the attempt in 1966 that succeeded as it forced the white settlers to concede to our Independence demands in 1980. As our military was only formed after successfully fighting that Colonialism, it is very sensitive to anything that seems like a reversion to the earlier situation.

While white settler Colonialism refused all black people human rights, the domination was most acutely felt in the land disenfranchisement of blacks. For this reason, it is often the land question that presents itself as the most important issue in the discussion of our national interest. Still, when our military says it will not support people who want to reverse Land Reform, implied in that statement, is the protection of the population from subjugation by foreigners, as was the case during Colonialism.

The Ruling Party enjoys the military's support because, it was the political formation that devised and prosecuted the liberation struggle. It created the guerrilla army that fought the liberation struggle. The same guerrilla army then morphed into our national army at Independence. But, as it was during the armed struggle, so it is after Independence, our military is empowered by our civilians to act independently in the protection of our Constitution, national interest, and values. The national Constitution states that the gains of the liberation struggle are sacrosanct. To that end, the Ruling Party does not have carte blanche: it enjoys the military's support only as long as it is adhering to that precept of the national Constitution.

The Opposition, on the other hand, cannot count on the military's support, as long as it is seen to be acting against the same liberation struggle gains. People forget that there were black people in our country, who fought in the liberation struggle on the side of the white settlers, to perpetuate the same system that denied all black people their human rights. As there were people who actually fought on the side of the foreign oppressor then, the military is justified in concluding that there are people amongst us today, who would be similarly used by the former colonizers. This is what causes the military to reject any civilians seen as representing anti-liberation struggle positions.

With regards the other functions of the ZDF, there have been successes and missteps as happens in all countries. The Deployment to the Beira Corridor in the 1980s is a good example of our military being used correctly in the national interest. The DRC Deployment from 1998 to 2002, on the other hand, was a misuse of the military. I have discussed these two deployments at length in the Fourth Address. The other deployments we have had under the United Nations (UN) flags, are defensible on the basis of national prestige and UN obligations. The funding for UN deployments usually comes from the UN itself, and so are not a drain on national resources. This makes those deployments compatible with the national interest.

As for our territorial defence, the knowledge that we have a military, has been a sufficient deterrent. No one has dared to invade Zimbabwe, even at the height of our Land Reform programme, as some countries had wanted. Also, no one dared to pick up arms domestically to try and reverse Land Reform, as would have been the case if we did not have a military. The ZDF, thus, has largely been very successful in its mandate of protecting the country from domestic and foreign disturbances.

Partisanship or Patriotism?

Most people who have looked at our military, complain of its alignment with the Ruling Party in our country – the Zimbabwe African National Union - Patriotic Front (ZANU PF). They have concluded that this is partisanship. I contend that these people have not understood what is before their very own eyes. This misunderstanding has happened because they have deified the theory of military and society, whilst forgetting that context is equally important in all things. The context that sufficiently explains our military's posture, is our history. Our history with Colonialism has defined what we consider as vital to us. This history with Colonialism, being so recent, still has a preponderant effect on our conception of the national interest.

This is the context some people forget with regards the Zimbabwe Defence Forces (ZDF). In the Third Address, I talked at length about how our nation came into existence. It came into existence through nationalists fighting for our independence from foreigners who had enslaved us on our own territory. This fight for independence, still holds primacy in our conception of the national interest. In that conception, the gains from our liberation struggle are sacrosanct. It is that conception of the national interest, that our military subserves.

This, then, so soon after Colonialism ended, is the essence of patriotism in our context. As a comparator, patriotism, in the American context, could very well mean supporting the subjugation of other countries, and the American military will subserve that function. Our military, therefore, is also orientated to subserve patriotism as it is conceived by nationalists. This then makes our military stand against those who are opposed to the nationalist conception of the national interest. Especially so, when those same people are seen to be taking their directions from the former colonizers we went to war against.

This is exactly what General Vitalis Zvinavashe was referring to in his straitjacket thesis I quoted from above. Our military will only take its orders from civilian leaders pursuing the values of the liberation struggle. This is really all that our military is doing when people accuse it of partisanship. It is just defending the national interest as it is dictated to us by our history. The three examples that will help me show that this is the case in this Address, are the Mgagao Declaration of 1975; the 2008 Presidential Elections; and the Military Assisted Transition of 2017.

Zimbabwe Military History:

The recognition of General Mtshana Khumalo as a hero and master strategist by the Second Republic in Zimbabwe on 20th November

2020, links our current military to our ancestors. General Khumalo was the Imbizo Regiment Commander who ambushed and annihilated the Alan Wilson Patrol that was pursuing King Lobengula, at Pupu, just north of the Shangani River on 4th December 1893.

In our long history under Colonialism, Alan Wilson who was defeated, has been feted and memorialised as a hero. There was even a public holiday proclaimed for him during the days of Rhodesia, and to this day, there is still a school named after him in Zimbabwe. This just speaks to our oversight in not memorialising all our own heroes in the 4 decades we have been independent. I talked about this subject at length in the Third Address, so I will not rehash those arguments here. I only raise the case of General Khumalo here, to put the point across to you that, the uprisings of the 1890s were the nascent stages of our current military.

So, although the current Zimbabwe military was formed in 1980, we should be aware of the linkages we have with our progenitors who fought the white settlers in the original colonization period. The people who fought in the Anglo – Matabele War of 1893 – 4, Chimurenga/Umvukela I of 1896 – 7, the uprisings by Chief Mapondera in 1900, and those who fought in Chimurenga/Umvukela II of 1966 – 1980, are very much a part of Zimbabwe's military history. What they were fighting for – keeping us from being subjugated by foreigners – is one of the main functions of the Zimbabwe military today.

Through force of arms, our territory was annexed by foreigners, and through force of arms we managed to reclaim our independence. Again, through force of arms, our military must stand in defence of our territory and independence. But because there have been changes in the way Colonialism works, our military must, of necessity, also stand against Zimbabweans who would do the former colonizers' bidding.

The former colonizer does not necessarily need to physically conquer countries anymore, they can just install local people to carry out their instructions. It is in this vein, that the military has declared that it will not subserve civilians who take their instructions from the former colonial powers. This then, is where people who rely too much on theory, have misunderstood the Zimbabwean military. Given our recent history, the defence of our territory and values demands that the military only support those who are aligned with the nationalist conception of the national interest.

This is often mistaken as the military being partisan, when in fact, if the Opposition would outdo the ruling nationalist party in nationalist values and ideology – read patriotism – the military would also support them. Instead, the opposition prefers to take sides with our former colonisers, inviting opprobrium from the military thus. This, more than anything else, is the reason why the military views the opposition with suspicion. Around 2011, the military was vindicated in this suspicion, by the discovery of information in the Wikileaks documents, that the Opposition MDC was even asking the United States to invade Zimbabwe and topple the government.

The Zimbabwe Defence Forces:

The Zimbabwe Defence Forces is comprised of the Zimbabwe National Army (ZNA) and the Air Force of Zimbabwe (AFZ). It came into existence through the integration of the three main forces that had fought each other in the liberation struggle – the Rhodesian Security Forces (RSF), the Zimbabwe African National Liberation Army (ZANLA), and the Zimbabwe People's Revolutionary Army (ZIPRA) Forces – in 1980. This integration was one of the agreements that had been reached at Lancaster House in 1979.

The Military was integrated on an equitable basis between these former belligerents. To the extent that, even the Fifth Brigade, had former ZIPRA fighters in it, despite that it went on to target ZIPRA in Matabeleland. It was only the Selous Scouts of the Rhodesian

Security Forces that were banned from integration. This was because the nationalist negotiators at the Lancaster House Conference, found their conduct in the war to have been so egregious.

The British Military Advisory and Training Team (BMATT) trained and integrated the three former belligerents. This happened for convenience's sake because, the military and State we took over, were premised on British institutions. Thus, the ranks, units, and organisation of the Zimbabwe military corresponds with the British military. The Fifth Brigade, however, was trained by the North Koreans and, essentially, stood outside the Chain of Command of the Zimbabwe military during the disturbances in Matabeleland in the 1980s.

The early period of our integration was a dark period for our history. The suspicions between ZANLA and ZIPRA that had existed since the split of the two nationalist formations in 1963, continued and even led to exchange of gunfire between the two, during the armed struggle, and after independence. The Zimbabwe African National Union (ZANU) and the Zimbabwe African People's Union (ZAPU) had split in 1963 over leadership differences.

The two nationalist formations then remained suspicious of each other throughout the liberation struggle between 1966 and 1980. Even when independence came, the suspicions were still there, to the extent that ZAPU/ZIPRA having lost the elections, cached weapons for its own defence once ZANU/ZANLA came into power. This created the Security Dilemma, and was the background to Gukurahundi, which I discussed at length in the Sixth Address.

At this point of our military integration, the former Rhodesian Security Forces element in the Zimbabwe Defence Forces, even had to play umpire between the ZANLA and ZIPRA element. Supporters of the RSF have gone on to claim that this was evidence of the RSF's professionalism. I, instead, think that this was just down to the fact that the Lancaster House Agreement had favoured the white settler:

the Security Dilemma was not felt by them. It was only felt between ZANLA and ZIPRA, and it was only after the Unity Accord of 1987, which brought ZANU and ZAPU back together, that the Security Dilemma was dealt with decisively.

Ever since the Unity Accord of 1987, the Zimbabwe military has been exemplary in dealing with our imaginary differences: the current Commander of the Zimbabwe Defences Forces – General Philip Valerio Sibanda – is a former ZIPRA Combatant. In this regard, I think the Zimbabwe military has been quite the graduate school for our Integration Nationalism. Those who re-enter civilian life from this institution, will be a model of the lack of prejudice that we want in our polity.

The Military And National Security Policy:

The Zimbabwe military is the critical component of our national security policy. National security policy is the technical name for everything that I said above about how the military underwrites our society. It is defined as the attempt to "enhance the safety of the nation's social, economic, and political institutions against threats arising from other independent states."[241] And it exists on these three levels: Military Security Policy, Internal Security Policy, and Situational Security Policy.

According to Huntington, "Military security policy is the programme of activities designed to minimize or neutralize efforts to weaken or destroy the nation by armed forces operating from outside its institutional and territorial confines. Internal security policy deals with the threat of subversion – the efforts to weaken or destroy the State by forces operating within territorial and institutional confines."[242] While "situational security policy, is concerned with the threat of erosion resulting from long term changes in social, economic, demographic, and political conditions tending to reduce the relative power of the State."[243] The military has a role in all these iterations of every country's national security policy.

Military Security Policy:

Military security policy is the exclusive preserve of the ZDF. It is our military's mandate to guard against invasion by other States. This is our military's primary role. All the training and exercises that the ZDF conducts are for the purposes of defending the country against external aggression. This is because the Zimbabwe Military Doctrine is defensive and need not be otherwise, as long as we live in a neighbourhood of friendly States. This would change to pre-emptive/offensive if neighbouring States started posing national security threats to Zimbabwe.

During the height of our Land Reform in the early 2000s, the then British Prime Minister – Tony Blair – asked his Chief of Defence Staff to draw plans to invade Zimbabwe. These plans did not come to fruition because, South Africa, Namibia, and other Southern African Development Communities (SADC) countries, made it clear that they would not allow such an invasion to occur. This is because we live in a neighbourhood of countries led by former Liberation Movements who fully understand our conception of the national interest.

But, if that invasion had come, it would have been the ZDF's primary task to repel it. Also, should any of our neighbouring countries ever be willing to be a bridgehead for an invasion of our country, our military doctrine may start to incorporate pre-emptive/offensive elements.

Internal Security Policy:

The goal, had the invasion come during our Land Reform process, would have been the toppling of the Government of Zimbabwe and the installation of people who would take their instructions from the West. The West calls this Regime Change. Having failed to get the invasion off the ground to reverse our Land Reform and restore white privilege, our detractors resorted to Plan B. What they could not achieve with a direct attack, would now be achieved indirectly. Sanctions, which I talked about at length in the Seventh Address, were the primary tool in Plan B. The Sanctions and sabotage of Zimbabwe's economy were designed to create economic hardships that would force the population to rise up against the government.

The Opposition was the intended beneficiary. The countries that imposed the Sanctions still wanted it to look like any regime change outcome was a popular local solution. The Opposition, once in power, would reverse Land Reform and make other concessions to the Western countries. The current Western regime change playbook relies heavily on the protest potential of the population. The Arab Spring and the colour revolutions in East Europe are very instructive on how this playbook works.

Evincing that the Zimbabwe Defence Forces was well aware of this playbook, in June 2011, Major General Douglas Nyikayaramba, restated the military's position with regards protecting the national interest. Speaking about the MDC leader of the time, he said that: "… he does not pose a political threat in any way in Zimbabwe, but he is a major security threat. He takes instructions from foreigners who seek to effect illegal regime change in Zimbabwe. This is what has invited the security forces to be involved because we want to ensure we protect our national security interests… Daydreamers who want to reverse the gains of the liberation struggle will continue daydreaming." The point Major General Nyikayaramba made here, was that the opposition had no political clout, but was just being used to foment civil unrest by outsiders.

This matter then, whereby groups within the confines of the State, are used to subvert the government, either through armed insurrection or violent protests, is what Huntington called internal security policy. Under this aspect of our national security policy, our military has had to react quickly, to even the violent protest potential of a very small section of the population.

The intervention of the military against the protests of 1st August 2018 and 14th January 2020 are just two examples of action now demanded of the military under the precepts of internal security policy. Ordinarily, the military should not get involved in such matters, but not getting involved at the outset now means them having to fight a larger fire a few days later. Thus, the ZDF's instinct of intervening early, is vindicated as inaction would cost more Zimbabwean lives and cause greater infrastructural damage. Syria and Libya, in 2011, are prime examples of what happens when protests are allowed to get out of control.

The Gerasimov Doctrine?

The internal security policy exigencies for the military, may not be so obvious to people who have not thought about national security systematically. But a look to what has been called the "Gerasimov Doctrine" by Western commentators, can show us why the military must react very quickly even against violent civilian protestors. The West has deliberately misnamed Gerasimov's description of the West's regime change methods as his Doctrine, to make it seem as if Russia also does regime changes. The truth is otherwise. The Chief of the General Staff of the Russian Federation – Colonel General Valery Vasilyevich Gerasimov – was actually describing how the West was now using the protest potential of civilians to effect regime change.

Writing in the Military – Industrial Courier in February 2013, General Gerasimov said: "In the 21st century we have seen a tendency toward blurring the lines between the states of war and peace. Wars are no longer declared and having begun, proceed according to an unfamiliar template. The experience of military conflicts — including those connected with the so-called coloured revolutions in North Africa and the Middle East — confirm that a perfectly thriving state can, in a matter of months and even days, be transformed into an arena of fierce armed conflict, become a victim of foreign intervention, and sink into a web of chaos, humanitarian catastrophe, and civil war."[244] This is exactly what happened in Libya and Syria.

He continued: "Of course, it would be easiest of all to say that the events of the "Arab Spring" are not war and so there are no lessons for us — military men — to learn. But maybe the opposite is true — that precisely these events are typical of warfare in the 21st century. In terms of the scale of the casualties and destruction, the catastrophic social, economic, and political consequences, such new-type conflicts are comparable with the consequences of any real war. The very "rules of war" have changed. The role of non-military means of achieving political and strategic goals has grown, and, in many cases, they have exceeded the power of force of weapons in their effectiveness."[245]

It is exactly for the above reason – that the protest potential of the civilian population can now be harnessed in such a manner that it can achieve the same goals as an invasion – that our military is now overtly involved in the internal security policy domain. Ordinarily, this should be the preserve of internal intelligence services and the police forces, but the new implications described above, now draws the military to intervene very early on.

Situational Security Policy:

Again, according to Huntingdon, "Situational security policy is concerned with the threat of erosion resulting from long term changes in social, economic, demographic, and political conditions tending to reduce the relative power of the State."[246] In this aspect of national security policy, lies greater justification of civilian control of the military.

To my mind, the military's logics and temperament are not best suited to deal with the long term changes in the social, economic, demographic and political domains. The lead the politicians will take in this domain, however, will still be subject to the rule that the civilians are working in the national interest as defined by our history of fighting Colonialism. All those people who died in the liberation struggle will have died in vain, if we do not protect the gains of the national liberation struggle. This is the reason, again, why you will have heard the Zimbabwe military repeat that, they will not salute civilians without liberation war credentials.

Of course, with the passage of time, there will be no civilians with liberation war credentials. This fact is contained in the definition of situational security policy, when it states that it deals "with the threat of erosion coming from long term changes." It is, therefore, incumbent upon the current nationalist politicians and military leaders, with liberation war credentials, to create conditions that will allow the nationalist conception of the national interest to remain preponderant despite the passage of time.

The Herbert Chitepo School of Ideology is a welcome development insofar as inculcating the young generation with the ethos of the liberation struggle is concerned. But concrete action should be taken to consolidate the gains of the liberation in the economic empowerment of all previously disenfranchised black people. The most important thing the current leaders, both military and civilian, can do to ensure that the liberation struggle brand remains attractive, is to be morally upright. When all those who fought in the liberation struggle are long dead, we still want our military to stand in defence of the nationalist conception of the national interest. This can only happen if the path set for the country by the nationalists, remains defensible as the true national interest.

Civil Military Relations In Zimbabwe:

In a Constitutional democracy like ours, the assumption is civilian control of the military, but this civilian control of the military is qualified. It is predicated on the civilians managing the affairs of the country in adherence to the Constitution and national values. When that adherence is compromised, the military may reject the civilians' authority. When this rejection occurs, the Constitution becomes suspended.

Again, people who have not thought about the matter systematically, will not realise how often this could happen if the military does not show restraint. You see, even in relation to the Constitution alone, the set of circumstances whereby the military is justified in rejecting civilian authority are very wide.

David Chuter gives this example, that, where the Constitution insists on a separation between Church and State, the military will be acting legally and legitimately, if it intervenes and prevents a Religious Party from coming to power, even though the religious party has just won free and fair elections.[247] From this postulation, we can also work out all the instances that our own armed forces can intervene in politics in defence of our Constitution, values, and national interest.

Let's take the 2008 Elections for example, as it is one of the often cited examples when people talk about our military intervening in civilian leadership affairs. Given David Chuter's postulation above, this intervention can be seen to have been defensible on the basis of the defence of our values and national interest. A political party opposed to the nationalist concept of the national interest, had won the first round of the Presidential Elections, and was expected to reverse our Land Reform. This expectation was the only reasonable conclusion, considering this Opposition Party was being openly funded by white farmers who had just lost land during our Land Reform.

Two Constitutional Contexts:

If we recall what I said above about context, you will also find that our military can intervene in civilian leadership affairs in two Constitutional contexts: the national Constitution, and the Ruling Party Constitution. The military can intervene in civilian leadership affairs when there has been an abrogation in either Constitution. Intervening when there has been an abrogation in the Ruling Party's Constitution, just happens to also has an effect on the national Constitution.

By way of examples then, the 2008 Elections intervention would have been in protection of the national Constitution and values therein declared, while the 1975 Mgagao Declaration and 2017 Military Assisted Transition interventions, were specifically due to an abrogation to the ZANU Constitution and values. These two last examples happened when ZANU was the government in waiting (1975), and when it was the government in power (2017). As the 2017 intervention directly impacted the national Constitution, rightly, that intervention was quickly made to conform to the national Constitution.

Master Or Servant?

In these same examples I have given above, to some people, the military seems to have too much power, so the master – servant question arises in our civil-military relations. I can assure you that the Zimbabwe military is subservient to the civilians, but subject to one caveat. The caveat is that the civilians will be adhering to the rules they wrote down and created the military to enforce. It is the civilians who wrote their Constitution, and then entrusted their military with the defence of that Constitution.

The military once given this task, can then act independent of civilian direction, when the same civilians who wrote the Constitution are deviating from the rules. It is like when you create a device that prevents your car from starting when you are drunk. When that device does exactly that, it has not become your master, it is just carrying out your instructions. This is the truest form of the civil-military relations in Zimbabwe, despite what you may have heard from the Zimbabwe military's detractors.

To understand this point better, we can now look at the times when the deviation from the Constitution and values I mentioned above occurred, forcing the military to intervene overtly in civilian leadership affairs.

The Mgagao Declaration:

In 1975, from the Zimbabwe African National Liberation Army (ZANLA) Military Base at Mgagao, a group of ZANLA officers wrote a document that became known as The Mgagao Declaration. This declaration became the basis for Ndabaningi Sithole's ouster as the Zimbabwe African National Union (ZANU) leader, and the ascension of Robert Mugabe to the same position. The Mgagao Declaration was made at the time when all the political parties were operating under the umbrella of the African National Congress (ANC).

The ANC was an organisation that had been encouraged by the Organisation of African Unity (OAU), to ensure a united front in the liberation struggle. The ANC thus brought the political parties led by Joshua Nkomo, Abel Muzorewa, and Ndabaningi Sithole under one umbrella. But instead of these leaders working hard to further the objectives of the liberation struggle, the authors of the Mgagao Declaration noted that:

"... the relationship between them is characterized by mutual mistrust and intrigues which divorce them from the realities of the struggle. In our opinion the three leaders are incapable of leading the ANC. An Executive Member who has been outstanding is Robert Mugabe. He has demonstrated this by defying the rigors of guerrilla life in the jungles of Mozambique. Since we respect him most, in all our dealings with the ANC leadership, he is the only person who can act as a middleman. We will not accept any direct discussions with any of the three leading members of the ANC we have described above. We can only talk through Robert Mugabe to them."[248]

These three leaders' authority was rejected on the basis that they had deviated from the values of the liberation struggle. Joshua Nkomo and Abel Muzorewa moreso as they were seen as both competing against each other for a compromise with Ian Smith. Abel Muzorewa's compromise version was the one that succeeded, as it got him the Premiership in the short-lived Internal Settlement of 3rd March 1978. For ZANLA, Ian Smith was trying to forestall their imminent victory by negotiating this settlement at that stage of the war. Hence the Mgagao Declaration which stated that the guerrilla fighters no longer recognised the authority of those who were now compromising on the objectives of the armed struggle.

The Mgagao Declaration had a more direct impact on Sithole, who was the leader of ZANU, of which ZANLA was the military wing. The declaration directly accused him of having deviated from the Constitution and values of the liberation struggle.

"We also level deep criticism against the Chairman of the ZLC [Zimbabwe Liberation Council], Reverend Ndabaningi Sithole for the following reasons: (a) In practical terms he has done nothing to promote the Armed Struggle... ... d) He was given funds from America and Britain for the maintenance of the families of ZANU leaders now in Zambian prisons, but not a penny of them has been used for this purpose. He remarked that he would never feed the families of murderers. He was also given funds for the defence of the ZANU leaders, but not a penny of them has been used for the purpose."[249]

Ndabaningi Sithole's commitment to the armed struggle had started to be questioned even while the ZANU leadership was still in prison. Then, he was accused of writing a letter from prison "to Ian Smith, pleading with him that he had given up the struggle."[250] Even though the letter has not been produced as evidence, on release from prison, his conduct still did not do him any favours in the eyes of the guerrillas.

When Zambian Authorities killed and injured some guerrillas at Mboroma, in the aftermath of the Chitepo Assassination, instead of visiting the injured guerrillas, Sithole went to the United States to see his daughter who was ill. Ndabaningi Sithole's wife, Vesta, in her memoir – My Life With An Unsung Hero – disputes that the visit to the United States was to see her ill daughter. She only says it was an outstanding trip and Sithole had to go, but she does not say why the visit was so important. In the light of prevailing circumstances, it still looked like he was no longer committed to the armed struggle. Latterly, Sithole's case is also further not helped by the fact that he was one of the signatories of the Internal Settlement of 3rd March 1978. The guerrillas saw the Internal Settlement as Ian Smith's ploy to save the white settlers from their imminent defeat.

So, the essence of all the charges against Sithole, is that he had abrogated from the agreement to pursue the armed liberation struggle. Pursuing the armed struggle until victory was a value that had been declared by the political institution – ZANU. The same political institution then set up the military wing – ZANLA – to prosecute the armed struggle. To answer those who tend to see a "Chicken – Egg Dilemma" where our civilians and the military are concerned, in that relationship, the political institution – ZANU – clearly came first. ZANU then created ZANLA, when the decision was taken to wage an armed struggle to free Zimbabwe.

From just this timeline, the politicians were the senior partner in that relationship, but they empowered the military to act independently when a deviation from the Constitution and set values occurred. It was in this context that the Mgagao Declaration was made. The Mgagao Declaration would be invoked again in November 2017, by General Constantino Chiwenga – the then Commander of the Zimbabwe Defence Forces.

The 2008 Elections:

The 2008 Presidential Elections were held on 29th March, but results were withheld until 02nd May. When the results were finally released, they showed that the MDC Presidential Candidate had won the Elections, but not by the requisite 50+1%. President Robert Mugabe, the incumbent and ZANU PF Candidate, had only garnered 43.2% of the vote, against 47.9% for the Opposition MDC Candidate. So, a runoff was slated for 27th June the same year.

The runoff was won by President Mugabe as the MDC Candidate pulled out of the race over claims of violence. Since the Joint Operations Command (JOC) presided over the delay in the results' announcement, many have accused the military of carrying out a "Coup" by preventing the MDC from taking over, when they had "won the Elections." The best information I have is that the MDC Candidate did not garner the 50+1% threshold required by law. But even if he had achieved the required threshold, we could still talk about the military's involvement in terms of its role of preserving the national interest as it is dictated to us by our history.

So soon after our Land Reform, an Opposition that was founded and openly funded by those who wanted to reverse Land Reform, could not have been allowed to come to power. This would have been the equivalent of surrendering our territory to outsiders again. Given what I said above about our national interest as conceived by nationalists, the military would have been justified in preventing the MDC from becoming the government. The example that suits here is the one given above by David Chuter, that the military is justified in preventing a Religious Party that has won free and fair elections from assuming power, if the Constitution insists on the separation of Church and State.

The 2017 Military Assisted Transition:

The Military Assisted Transition that caused President Robert Mugabe to resign after 37 years in power, is another instance when our military has overtly intervened in civilian leadership affairs. The issue in 2017 was that an aging leader, who had been captured by his over ambitious young wife – Grace Mugabe – had started to denigrate and purge some people with liberation war credentials from the party and government. The ambitious young wife was surrounded by even more ambitious young politicians – the Generation 40 (G40) – who wanted to succeed Robert Mugabe.

The deviation from the ZANU PF Constitution here then, was a circumventing of the party's seniority succession model. Concomitant to this circumvention of the Ruling Party's Constitution, was a belittling of the liberation war fighters' contribution to Zimbabwe's Independence. Initially, the Zimbabwe National Liberation War Veterans Association (ZNLWVA), through its leadership, signalled to Robert Mugabe that ZANU PF was not a dynasty where he could just decide to hand over power to his wife or children. This warning was not heeded, owing perhaps to Robert Mugabe's advanced age. The attack on liberation war veterans who were seen not to be subserving Grace Mugabe's ambitions continued.

This purging of the liberation war fighters in 2017, followed exactly the same pattern as that of 2014, when Joyce Mujuru and others with liberation war credentials, were ousted from the Party and government. Rallies were held throughout the country, where Grace Mugabe dressed down and denigrated the then Vice President of the country – Emmerson Mnangagwa. The same false accusations of plotting the downfall of Robert Mugabe, as had been made against

Joyce Mujuru in 2014, were also thrown at Emmerson Mnangagwa. This happened until the point when Robert Mugabe felt that enough denigration had happened to fire Emmerson Mnangagwa without consequence.

On 6th November 2017, Robert Mugabe fired Emmerson Mnangagwa from the Vice Presidency, triggering this blowback: the military's intervention. The people who had captured Robert Mugabe in his old age had miscalculated, and that action of firing Emmerson Mnangagwa was the red line the military would not allow to be crossed. Operation Restore Legacy was activated – a reference to the restoration of the liberation struggle values.

The firing of Emmerson Mnangagwa was supposed to be accompanied by the arrest of the Commander of the Zimbabwe Defence Forces to neutralise the military's response. On 12th November, an attempt to arrest General Chiwenga at Harare International Airport on his return from a work visit to China, was foiled by his charges in the Zimbabwe Defence Forces. Flanked by senior military officers, on 13th November, General Chiwenga warned the civilians that the military would intervene to stop the counter-revolutionary shenanigans that were now happening. He invoked the Mgagao Declaration and the Zimbabwe Constitution in that address.

When the national broadcaster was prevented from reporting this development, the Zimbabwe Defence Forces went into action on 14th November 2017, just eight days after Emmerson Mnangagwa had been fired from the Presidium and ZANU PF. As Robert Mugabe had been elevated to the leadership of ZANU by the Mgagao Declaration for being the only one who was still embodying the values of the liberation struggle, Operation Restore Legacy also opined that Emmerson Mnangagwa was the senior civilian leader now embodying the same values.

The President was placed under protective custody, while all the other people associated with Grace Mugabe's faction, went into hiding, with some eventually fleeing the country. When it came to the actual operation, not killing Robert Mugabe was also a stroke of genius considering the reverence he was held in as a Pan-Africanist icon. No doubt, the military temperament would have wanted to kill the factions and their figurehead to ensure no challenges to the military operation. Credit to the military leaders who understood the need for continued civilian control of the military, even at a time when the military was rejecting the authority of one civilian leader. The civilian leaders the military kept in the loop of the operation, ensured that Robert Mugabe was not harmed. The civilian element also ensured that the other Constitutional processes ran alongside the military operation.

In terms of making Operation Restore Legacy adhere to the national Constitution, a joint sitting of Parliament to impeach Robert Mugabe was convened on 21st November 2017. Seeing the odds stacked against him in this manner, Robert Mugabe resigned at 1000am on the same day, paving the way for Emmerson Mnangagwa to replace him on 24th November – until Presidential Elections were held in July 2018. It is for this reason that the African Union (AU), and SADC, did not place Sanctions on Zimbabwe for an unconstitutional change of government, as is usually the case. This is where the understanding of civilian control of the military allowed the Military Assisted Transition to happen smoothly.

Conclusion:

My fellow countrymen and countrywomen, the main thing I wanted to explain in this Address, is why the military in Zimbabwe seems to align itself with the Ruling ZANU PF Party. This happens because of our history with the liberation struggle against Colonialism. At this stage of our history, and our military having come into existence because of our Anti-Colonialism Nationalism, it can only be orientated towards defending the gains of the liberation struggle. For this reason, our military cannot support anyone who is opposed to that conception of the national interest. To my mind, the independence and dignity that was restored to black Zimbabweans by the liberation struggle, is one of the things that are objectively in the national interest. The preamble to our Constitution incorporates this fact.

So, while casual observers may think that the Zimbabwe military is partisan, the reality is that it is actually subserving patriotism as it applies in our context. Some people have also raised questions about the master-servant relationship in our civilian-military relations. They think the military is now the master, and the civilians the servants. I think the reverse is true. While the three examples I have used here do show the few times that the military has rejected the authority of civilian leadership, they are but exceptions that just prove the rule. The rule is that civilians lead the soldiers, it is only when the civilians are deviating from the Constitution and its values that the soldiers can intervene to correct that anomaly.

The charge that our military is partisan is mostly made by those do not subscribe to the nationalist conception of the national interest. These people tend to also take their direction from foreigners with their own self-interested agendas. If the Opposition really wanted to prove that our military is partisan for no defensible reason, they should outdo the ruling nationalist party in espousing, and defending, the values and gains of the liberation struggle.

Also, I should mention that post-Independence, except in 2017, the military has always been deployed on the instructions of the civilians. So, even in the cases I mentioned above under the precepts of internal security policy, the military has been called upon by the civilians to assist law and order before it breaks down irrevocably. Even our foreign deployments to the DRC and Mozambique, were deployments that were done on the instructions of the civilian leaders. Thus, the master-servant relationship in our civilian-military relations has not yet been inverted.

We should still be concerned though, in general, about the military's potential to reject civilian leadership authority, even when the civilians have not deviated from society's Constitution and values. The military, being the strongest branch of any society, always has the potential to threaten society that way. In our case, the ready remedy I can think of to this problem, is making sure that the military is the repository of all our national values. The system of training and education in the military should be designed to continue producing ethical officers and general duty soldiers. These values that the military should always espouse, were already known during the liberation struggle, and are encapsulated in the song that has been transmitted through the years to today's military – *Nzira dzeMasoja.*

Address XI.

Public-Spiritedness.

"Society grows great when old men plant trees whose shade they know they shall never sit in" – Greek Proverb.

"So, live that thy rule of conduct can be adopted as law by all rational persons" – Immanuel Kant.

"The best time to plant a tree was twenty years ago, the second-best time is today" – Chinese Proverb.

"You are never wrong to do the right thing" – Mark Twain.

MY FELLOW ZIMBABWEANS, having considered most of the problems that have beset our polity, the main cure I can think of, is a simple one: public-spiritedness. I define public-spiritedness as the mindset that always thinks about whether any actions one is taking will benefit our nation. While education is essential for our development, it is public-spiritedness that will guide individuals to act in the interest of our polity. I have been alluding to this throughout all my Addresses in this volume. Take our corruption problem for example, relying on education alone, a highly educated Accountant, can use his skillset to steal money from the public purse with ease. It will be his public-spiritedness which will prevent him from doing so. This is because, his public-spiritedness, will force him to ask himself if his actions will benefit the nation.

This mindset change is much needed in our country. If I were to suggest some metrics for public-spiritedness, I would say it must be the number of opportunities to do wrong, and gain at the expense of the country, one has foregone even when there was no possibility of being caught. It must also be the number of people one has helped selflessly. This can be done by one as a company director creating employment, or by companies engaged in genuine Corporate Social Responsibility (CSR), and not just the tax evasion tokenism. For my part, as a rural boy, contributing to solving the major problems of our rural areas suffices.

The general public can also help in this shift of mindset to public-spiritedness. In the Eighth Address, I said that admiration for the corrupt has been an enabler for corruption, I want us to start admiring selfless people instead. In this regard, we should not hold people in the highest esteem just for their material possessions, but for the number of people they have helped selflessly. Their material possessions should also have been acquired legally. For, the ultimate determinant of actions taken in a public-spirited manner, is that there was no criminality involved at any point.

I also said in the Second Address that, the people who wrote the Bible, wanted to organise their society for the better. It has always been one of religion's core functions, to ensure people act in the interest of the community, as I am imploring us to do here. But because throughout history, the Church itself has been corrupt, the congregants have also fallen short of this required standard. The prevalence of corruption in our country when we are an 84% Christian country, also proves that religion has lost its potency to inspire good conduct. I think the fault for this lies in the flaw in the Christian doctrine of limitless forgiveness. People can do as much wrong as they want knowing that they can always ask for forgiveness and get it. I want us to hold ourselves to a higher standard than what this Christian doctrine implies.

I also know that many factors are needed to influence people to become public-spirited, and so I am well aware that this Address is not the magic bullet. But even if I manage to make just 100 other people aware that there is another way of conducting oneself, this will be a satisfactory achievement for this Address.

Still, this task is not Herculean, because in Zimbabwe, we already have a ready example of someone who embodied public-spiritedness: Jairosi Jiri. My understanding is that he used his meagre personal resources to start the Jairosi Jiri Association – an organisation that helped the disabled in our society. He did this to genuinely help his disadvantaged compatriots. This was genuine public-spiritedness, considering that most people now only do these acts to avoid paying taxes, or to get grants from wealthy donors. I also know that there is quite the philosophical debate about whether altruism can ever be selfless, but we will leave that debate for another day.

For now, let me just posit that this concept I am advancing in this Address, is not alien to us either. All African societies I have been in contact with, have variations of the same concept: Ubuntu in the South African context, Hunhu in Shona, and Ubumuntu in Rwanda. These concepts essentially mean the same thing: understanding our interconnectedness and acting in a manner that, instead of impeding our society, benefits it.

Ubumuntu: Lessons From Rwanda.

In Rwanda, during the 1994 Genocide, Ubumuntu manifested itself in the Hutu people who gave shelter to the Tutsis who were being targeted for extermination. The Hutus who did this, did so at extreme risk to themselves, because anyone who was caught sheltering the Tutsis was also massacred. But because of their humanity, the Hutus took that risk. If some people could do this, at great risk to their lives, there is no reason why someone faced with a simple decision to accept a bribe to the detriment of society, should not just say no, for reasons of public interest.

To be sure, the Genocide was an example of humanity at its worst. It was the very anti-thesis of the public-spiritedness whose virtues I am extolling here. The exclusion of a whole section of society from participating in the economic and social life of Rwanda that went before the Genocide was contrary to Ubumuntu. But since this dark period ended, there has been an impetus to do everything in a public-spirited manner in Rwanda.

Two examples come to mind: the first one is the way President Paul Kagame has insisted that everyone puts Rwandans first in all their considerations. This is buttressed by his leading by example in not being implicated in Corruption. This leading by example inspires great acts of selfless in the general population. The second example is how ordinary Rwandans acts in a selfless manner there as a result.

The best example I came across when I travelled there to take a closer look at Rwandan society, is that of a Public Sports Event Director who has foregone the Event Director's salary for the Kigali Marathon, so that it can be used for society's other needs. I sat down to speak to him, and I was astounded to hear such public-spiritedness despite that I have thought about it most of my adult life. He chooses to forego his payment for managing the Marathon so that it can, instead, be used to support victims of the Genocide. Instead, he relies only on his monthly salary from his normal job. The trend worldwide, is that an Event Director gets paid a separate amount just for staging the Marathon.

The other public-spirited conduct they have in Rwanda is Girinka, whereby the government has given every rural homestead a Milk Cow so that they can benefit from the nutrition thereby provided. While this government programme can be seen as service delivery and not worthy of commending as public-spiritedness, I also visited a private cattle farm where the owner has made sure that all the bull calf he gets, he gives away for free to rural farmers so that they can sire their own herds. This has to be seen as public-spiritedness if you know there is a thriving Stud market in the world. In South Africa, the record bull that I know of, sold for around ZAR2.1 Million. This farmer thus, is foregoing at least a US$100 000 each time he gives away a bull calf to rural farmers.

In Zimbabwe, we once had this practice, but the harsh economic climate may have made it impossible to observe it. You will recall the Shona saying that *"Mombe yekuronzera ndeye kukama wakaringa nzira"* – *(You have to milk a leased cow while watching out that the owner may come to reclaim it back).* This was exactly what was happening, rural people lent their cattle to those who did not have so that they could get draught power and nutrition as well. The only point of caution in the above saying, was that the owner could repossess it whenever they wanted, even while you are in the middle of milking it. Thus, I do not completely discount the possibility that the hardships put on our population by Sanctions, have been the cause of the dearth of public-spiritedness amongst us.

Contrary To Public-Spiritedness: Zimbabwe.

While there are examples of people who have acted in a public-spirited manner in our country, the self-serving spirit seems to me to be preponderant amongst us now. In speaking to my fellow Zimbabweans, I have not had a conversation that astounded me as the one I had with a Rwandan Sports Event Director who forewent his entitled payment for the sake of the public good. Most people I have spoken to, dream of cutting corners and succeeding at the expense of their fellow countrywomen and countrymen. It is as if our national psyche has zoned out of the *Hunhu* idea that should inform our conduct. We really need to try and return to that ideal.

If I look at our history, I see the first instance that public-spiritedness was discarded to be when Colonialism happened. The people who colonized us shot themselves in the foot when they decided to enslave us on our own land, and later, ensure by legislation that they suppressed our development. Colonel (Rtd) Kembo Mohadi, when he was Vice President of Zimbabwe, once complained that whites had erred in not teaching us economics. In our polarised society, in this age of trial by Social Media, people were quick to mock him, but the truth is that he was right in what he said. When the colonialist took over our polities, he introduced a new system that was different from what we had before.

By excluding the black person from learning about this new system, the colonialist shot himself in the foot. I have talked at length about how discrimination prevented black people from accessing education and high positions in the systems they would inherit. By design, literacy rates were very low among the colonised. For example, the Democratic Republic of Congo only had five black university graduates at the time it attained its independence. If he were public-spirited, the white settler in our own country, would have seen that it was to his advantage to have a system of meritocracy from the outset, where all people – black and white – had equal access to educational opportunities. It would have followed that majority rule would have ushered in a team that was already competent in governance. Instead, the racist regime run by Ian Smith, insisted that it would take black 1 000 years to become civilised, meanwhile they were doing everything to prevent black people from accessing the so-called civilising opportunities. This racism and lack of public-spiritedness came back to haunt these same people between 1980 and 2000.

Thus, whatever downturn in fortunes our country went through due to lack of governance capacity when we attained independence, can be blamed squarely on the white colonialist's lack of public-spiritedness. This is not a matter for idle speculation either, the effects are quite measurable. Zimbabwe was bankrupted largely because, the first 15 years of our independence involved massive government expenditure on educating our previously disadvantaged black people. There were adult literacy campaigns to help those adults who had not been educated. There was also free education for most black kids who had been placed in a situation by Colonialism where education would have been impossible for them. Overall, this resulted in the bankrupting of our treasury, but also the highest literacy rates in Africa of around 90 to 98%. This high literacy rate has not resulted in benefit for the country because other factors intervened, and brain-drain ensured. Our expertise, gained at great expense to the national treasury, has thus benefitted economies other than ours.

A further example of the lack of public-spiritedness by the same white settlers can also be seen in their conduct shortly after independence. Robert Mugabe, aware that we lacked technical experience in the running of a modern State, appealed to the white settlers to stay on in a spirit of national reconciliation. Some of the white settlers who stayed were only interested in undermining the new black establishment. Whites in the National Railways were deliberately sending goods trains to the wrong locations just to show that the black people were incompetent. Those who stayed in the military were even involved in sabotaging expensive Air Force equipment such as the 13 Fighter Jets that were destroyed in 1982.

The full exhibit of their lack of public-spiritedness and the effects of such an attitude can also be seen in the land question. If the white settlers had been public-spirited, they should have done everything to ensure they transferred large tracts of land to the demonstrably land hungry blacks who had been disenfranchised by the historic injustice that was Colonialism. Instead, they blocked any effort to resolve the land issue, the result was that they lost everything when the land redistribution happened by force on the instigation of the land hungry masses.

A further show that these white settlers had not learned the lesson of public-spiritedness is that, instead of working to support the new Black farmers, they lobbied foreign governments to Sanction and sabotage Zimbabwe's economy. Unless there was a way that the foreign governments were paying them money to cushion them against the economic hardships that ensured, they too must have suffered for living in a country under Sanctions.

Of course, some of these people had farms in South Africa so could easily cushion themselves from such harm. We could even say that perhaps these people are exempt from our demand that our people be public-spirited. To our polity, the original sin, the one we cannot forgive is Colonialism. As descendants of the Colonialist, perhaps these people do not consider themselves a part of our polity, citizenship is just a convenient ruse, they really still belong to the nations they came from originally. In such a case then, these people are not under the same obligation of public-spiritedness I am demanding for true Zimbabweans.

But on the same land issue, we also find instances when the true Zimbabweans did not act in the public-spirited manner I am demanding of them. The issue of multiple farm ownership is my first gripe with our political leaders. Land Reform was done to address land hunger, anyone who ended up with multiple farms acted contrary to the public interest nature of that exercise. As well, after the land redistribution exercise, people of means, should have foregone receiving any inputs or money from public institutions aimed at capacitating the new farmers. Land Reform will only succeed when the worst-off financially new farmer, has the resources to maintain production, and this cannot happen if the same resources are monopolised by the well-off. Worse still, when some of the well-off decide to sell the inputs they will have received free of charge. Abuse of these agricultural inputs that could make our Land Reform succeed is one matter where I think we have not understood the mission. There are similar examples of this lack of public-spiritedness by Zimbabweans in most of our major issues. There needs to be a change of mindset in all those aspects too.

Public Spiritedness And Leadership:

Even when absolute monarchs were the form of government, it was never advisable to deliberately pursue policies inimical to the public good. It has always been understood that what is good for the polity, is what is also good for the ruler. The idea of Enlightened Despotism, advanced by Frederick the Great of Prussia, held that; "the sovereign is attached by indissoluble ties to the body of the State; hence it follows that he, by repercussions, is sensible to all the ills which afflict his subjects; and the people, in like manner, suffer from the misfortunes which affect their sovereign. There is but one general good, which is that of the State... ... The Prince is to the nation he governs what the head is to the man; it his duty to see, think, and act for the whole community, that he may procure it every advantage of which it is capable."[251]

So, even without democratic pressures such as protests and the threat of being voted out of office, the leader has always been advised to act in a public-spirited manner. Even in Dynastic China, the same principles held. The concept of the "Mandate of Heaven," meant leaders could only retain their authority if they were acting in the public interest. When they stopped acting in the public interest, they were said to have lost the "Mandate of Heaven." While the concept had its limitations, such as when natural disasters were misinterpreted as a sign of a loss of the "Mandate of Heaven," my argument, that leaders had to act in a public-spirited manner to be worthy of their position, still holds.

This is what I hope any leader in a public capacity will use as a benchmark for their own conduct. It does not matter which level of leadership a person has, there should always know that their legitimacy depends on good results. For a CEO working for public companies, they should understand the fiduciary nature of the role. This is why I lamented, in the Eighth Address that the Premier Service Medical Aid Society (PSMAS) CEO was paying himself US$250 000, while leading a parastatal that was US$38 million in debt. There is no justification for such a salary for someone leading a company that is not bringing any value to the public.

It is the same for the leader of the country. He or she should be morally upright and do everything in his or her power to act in the public interest. Resources should not be wasted, but efficiently distributed to where they serve the public interest best. The leader who buys luxury vehicles for himself, but not much needed healthcare equipment, weakens his own country. The leader of an underfed military threatens the country's security, since a well-fed, well-equipped army will defeat our own. It is in all these ways the leader should understand that the head suffers the same calamity as the body. There are innumerable treatises on leadership, I would advise anyone who wants to lead to read them and internalise them. For the purposes of these Addresses, my exhortation for public-spirited conduct, is more on where those of us who benefited from education after independence, can do more to benefit our communities. I expect that these efforts will translate to an advantage for the whole nation.

Everyone's Debt To Society:

I opened this volume of Addresses with a quote from independent Tanzania's first black president – Julius Nyerere. In that quote, he said words to the effect that everyone has a debt to society. He said that everyone who has received the privilege of education has "a duty to repay the sacrifice which others have made. They are like the man who has been given all the food available in a starving village in order that he might have strength to bring supplies back from a distant place. If he takes this food and does not bring help to his brothers, he is a traitor. Similarly, if any of the young men and women who are given an education by the people of this Republic adopt attitudes of superiority or fail to use their knowledge to help the development of this country, then they are betraying our union."

This quote is quite literally what happened in Zimbabwe. The country itself, and every family, sacrificed a lot to get us all educated. I think the public-spirited thing to do, is for everyone who received this education, to repay their debt by contributing to solving society's problems. We all have to use our acquired skills and talents to develop our communities. I know for a fact that the elders in my community had their wishes and visions they could not realise themselves.

But they sent their children to school with the expectation that they would solve those problems.

For example, my Grandparents, and the other elders in our community, were always talking about solving about problems like water supply, grazing for the livestock and efficiency in farming on their small plots. All these things I can now contribute to my own community in fulfilment of their wishes. A development practitioner like myself can solve this problem with ease. Some will say it is the government's task, I say it is the task of every public-spirited person to develop their community. Moreso when the government educated us so that we could solve our communities' problems.

In a way, I also think that fate has also gifted Zimbabwe an opportunity to gain from the talents of her people who were forced out of the country by circumstances. The economic and political problems that led to our exodus from Zimbabwe can have a positive side effect. Again, speaking from a personal point of view, having received such poor treatment in the host country I ended up in myself, has made always me think of Zimbabwe and how I can contribute to a country where my belonging is assured. I have not been made to feel that I belong in the country where I ended up when Sanctions destroyed our economy. My focus thus, has always been to contribute to my country so that I never have to leave it again on my return. I expect there are many people in that same situation as me.

The advantage our country can accrue from all of us, is from the work experience and university education we have pursued despite our being treated like second class citizens in the countries we moved to. I can only speak about Development because I received formal training in it, others who have been formally trained in Law, Education, Civil Engineering and other branches of knowledge can think of ways to contribute in a public-spirited manner to our country. What needs to be done is to harness the skills of returning individuals. But even if there is no official government programme for this, the returning individual can still contribute by using the skills he has gained abroad to give back to the community. I have pictured the most impact being made by us when we do projects to uplift our rural communities. The rural areas are neglected in development and would be the low hanging fruit that can benefit quickly from those who have gained development and other skills abroad. The minimum acceptable is that we should use our skills we have gained over time to develop our communities in a true spirit of giving back to the community, not as politicians, leveraging their skills for political votes. This, for me, is the essence of public-spiritedness.

Conclusion:

We have serious problems in our country, what country does not have its problems? But I think that what can mitigate some of our problems is public-spiritedness. This refers to people putting the public interest ahead of any other consideration in their actions. People must have integrity, which equates to doing the right thing every time, even when no one is looking. I have tried to use the example from Rwanda to show what public-spiritedness looks like. Make no mistake, in our own country at the moment, there are people who are public-spirited, but I think they are in the minority. I have not done a quantitative study of this phenomenon, but the instances of corruption and malfeasance in our public services paints a picture of mostly self-serving people in our polity.

Public-spiritedness can also take root if our politicians and captains of industry lead by example. This is what has happened in Rwanda. President Paul Kagame has been serious about public-spiritedness, he acts in service of that ideal and the rest of the country follows his example. To our difficult problem such as corruption, I think a change of mindset to that of public-spiritedness is the only solution at the moment.

Address XII.

Concluding Remarks.

"Investigate what is, and not what pleases" – Johann Wolfgang von Goethe, 1792.

MY FELLOW ZIMBABWEANS, thank you for indulging me for this long. My main task here was trying to provide more precise information about our nation. I took up this task when I noticed that most of the information in the public imagination was wrong. This has happened because of deliberate distortions by the enemies of our nation, as well as through what the "Telephone Game" has demonstrated about information distortion, even when there is no intention to distort. I thus wanted to set the record straight on all the topics that are within my competence. I wrote this volume mainly for posterity, but anyone who presently wants accurate information about our nation, now also has such a source.

My main hope is that, having more precise information about our nation, will also aid us in playing our part to ensure we bequeath a worthwhile nation to our posterity. Those who fought in the armed struggle to get us opportunities for advancement that we were being denied, played their part. They were uneducated so they could not write their record. We have been accorded education by their efforts, our debt to society is to write our stories on their behalf, and to also continue learning useful things and to implement them for the betterment of our polity.

But if conditions do not allow us to develop our country now, at least we can document the difficulties we are facing, so that posterity will know how to tackle those problems. I cannot emphasize enough how much I really want our posterity to know our points of view, especially that of nationalists. If we leave our understanding of our polity to be written by others, it will be very much distorted.

It is important that our viewpoints, rich or poor, right or wrong, be written by more of us.

I very much lament that our ancestors at Great Zimbabwe did not leave a written record of their daily lives and world view. Our history has been poorer for this. But we who can read and write, should now leave a written record, no matter how elementary. These are our thoughts, and they will count when posterity looks at them. I thus implore fellow Zimbabweans to write as much as possible, so that our corpus will be there for everyone 700 years from now. The more outsiders have preponderant content about our polity, the more drowned out our points of view will be for posterity. We have to leave a written record which says we were here.

Notes

Address II

1. Richard Dawkins, *The God Delusion* (London: Transworld Publishers, 2006), 31.

2. Richard Dawkins, *The God Delusion*, (London: Transworld Publishers, 2006), 31.

3. Norman Davies, *Europe: A History* (London: Random House, 1997), 479.

4. Norman Davies, *Europe: A History* (London: Random House, 1997), 471.

5. Norman Davies, *Europe: A History* (London: Random House, 1997), 471.

6. Max Weber, *The Protestant Ethic and the Spirit of Capitalism* (London: Unwin & Hyman, 1918).

7. Bruce L. Shelley, *Church History In Plain Language* (Netherlands Antilles: Word Pub, 1995).

8. Norman Davies, *Europe: A History* (London: Random House, 1997), 596.

9. Adele Berlin and Marc Zvi Brettler, *The Jewish Study Bible* (Oxford: Oxford University Press: 2004), X.

10. Adele Berlin and Marc Zvi Brettler, *The Jewish Study Bible* (Oxford: Oxford University Press, 2004), X.

11. Adele Berlin and Marc Zvi Brettler, *The Jewish Study Bible* (Oxford: Oxford University Press, 2004), 9.

12. Adele Berlin and Marc Zvi Brettler, *The Jewish Study Bible*, (Oxford: Oxford University Press, 2004), 9.

13. Stephanie Dalley, *Myths From Mesopotamia*, (Oxford: Oxford University Press, 1989), XVIII.

14. Yuval Noah Harari, *Homo Deus: A Brief History Of Tomorrow* (Vintage: London, 2016), 203.

Address III

15. Hugh Seton-Watson, *Nations and States* (London: Methuen, 1977), 1.

16. Hugh Seton-Watson, *Nations And States* (London, Methuen, 1977), 1.

17. Josef Stalin, "The Nation," in *Nationalism,* ed. John Hutchinson and Anthony Smith, (Oxford: Oxford University Press, 1994), 18 – 21.

18. Anthony D. Smith, *National Identity* (Harmondsworth: Penguin, 1991), 73.

19. Umut Ozkirimili, *Theories of Nationalism: A Critical Introduction*, (London: Macmillan Press, 1999), 182.

20. Umut Ozkirimili, *Theories of Nationalism: A Critical Introduction*, (London: Macmillan Press, 1999), 182.

21. Michael Billig, *Banal Nationalism* (London: Sage Publications, 1995), 5.

22. Michael Billig, *Banal Nationalism* (London: Sage Publications, 1995), 6.

23. Engelbert, P., S. Tarango, and M. Carter, "Dismemberment and Suffocation: A Contribution to the Debate on African Boundaries," *Comparative Political Studies* Vol. 35, no. 10 (2002): 1093-1118.

24. Grove, Andy (1998), Academy of Management Annual Meeting, Intel Keynote Transcript. Available online: https://www.intel.com/pressroom/archive/speeches/ag080998.htm Accessed 16.04.2018

25. Chapman, Gary, (2003), An Introduction to the Revolution in Military Affairs. LBJ School of Public Affairs University of Texas at Austin. Amaldi Conference on Problems in Global Security. Available online: http://www.lincei.it/rapporti/amaldi/papers/XV-Chapman.pdf Accessed 16.04.2018.

26. Aime Cesaire, *Discourse On Colonialism* (New York: Monthly Press Review, 1972).

27. Scott Burchill, *The National Interest In International Relations* (Basingstoke: Palgrave Macmillan, 2005), 23.

28. Sabelo Gatsheni-Ndlovu, *Do Zimbabweans Exist? Trajectories Of Nationalism, National Identity Formation and Crisis in a Postcolonial State* (Oxford: Peter Laing, 2009).

29. Sabelo Gatsheni-Ndlovu, *Do Zimbabweans Exist? Trajectories Of Nationalism, National Identity Formation and Crisis in a Postcolonial State* (Oxford: Peter Laing, 2009).

30. Jefferson Murphy, *The Bantu Civilization Of Southern Africa* (New York: Thomas Y. Crowell Company, 1974), 17.

31. David Beach, *The Shona And Their Neighbours* (Oxford: Blackwell Publishing, 1994), 34

32. Eric Hobsbawm and Terrence Ranger, *The Invention Of Tradition* (Cambridge: Cambridge University Press, 1983).

33. Alois S. Mlambo, *A History of Zimbabwe* (Cambridge: Cambridge University Press, 2014), 128.

34. Alois S. Mlambo, *A History of Zimbabwe* (Cambridge: Cambridge University Press, 2014), 144

35. Alois S. Mlambo, *A History of Zimbabwe* (Cambridge: Cambridge University Press, 2014), 128.

36. Patrick O'Meara, *Rhodesia: Racial Conflict or Co-Existence?* (London: Cornell University Press), 91.

37. Patrick O'Meara, *Rhodesia: Racial Conflict or Co-Existence?* (London: Cornell University Press, 1975), 92.

38. Patrick O'Meara, *Rhodesia: Racial Conflict or Co-Existence?* (London: Cornell University Press, 1975), 93.

39. Patrick O'Meara, *Rhodesia: Racial Conflict or Co-Existence?* (London: Cornell University Press, 1975), 93.

40. Patrick O'Meara, *Rhodesia: Racial Conflict or Co-Existence?* (London: Cornell University Press, 1975), 94.

41. Patrick O'Meara, *Rhodesia: Racial Conflict or Co-Existence?* (London: Cornell University Press, 1975), 94.

42. Patrick O'Meara, *Rhodesia: Racial Conflict or Co-Existence?* (London: Cornell University Press, 1975), 92.

43. Patrick O'Meara, *Rhodesia: Racial Conflict or Co-Existence?* (London: Cornell University Press, 1975), 94.

44. Patrick O'Meara, *Rhodesia: Racial Conflict or Co-Existence?* (London: Cornell University Press, 1975), 98.

45. Patrick O'Meara, *Rhodesia: Racial Conflict or Co-Existence?* (London: Cornell University Press, 1975), 98.

46. Patrick O'Meara, *Rhodesia: Racial Conflict or Co-Existence?* (London: Cornell University Press, 1975), 99.

47. Patrick O'Meara, *Rhodesia: Racial Conflict or Co-Existence?* (London: Cornell University Press, 1975), 99.

48. Patrick O'Meara, *Rhodesia: Racial Conflict or Co-Existence?* (London: Cornell University Press, 1975),99.

49. Patrick O'Meara, *Rhodesia: Racial Conflict or Co-Existence?* (London: Cornell University Press, 1975), 100.

50. Patrick O'Meara, *Rhodesia: Racial Conflict or Co-Existence?* (London: Cornell University Press, 1975), 101.

51. Patrick O'Meara, *Rhodesia: Racial Conflict or Co-Existence?* (London: Cornell University Press, 1975), 102.

52. Patrick O'Meara, *Rhodesia: Racial Conflict or Co-Existence?* (London: Cornell University Press, 1975), 110.

53. Montserrat Guibernau, *The Identity Of Nations* (Cambridge: Polity Press, 2007), 11.

54. Montserrat Guibernau, *The Identity Of Nations* (Cambridge: Polity Press, 2007), 11.

55. Alois S. Mlambo, *A History Of Zimbabwe*, (Cambridge: Cambridge University Press, 2014).

56. Anthony D. Smith, *Nationalism: Theory, Ideology, History* (Cambridge: Polity Press, 2001), 26.

Address IV

57. Steven Lamy et al., *Introduction To Global Politics* (Oxford: Oxford University Press, 2018), 122.

58. Charles Beard, *The Idea of National Interest* (New York: Macmillan Company, 1934), 22.

59. Alexander Wendt, *A Social Theory Of International Politics* (Cambridge: Cambridge University Press, 1999).

60. Joseph Frankel, *National Interest* (London: Macmillan, 1970), 39.

61. Joseph Frankel, *National Interest* (London: Macmillan, 1970), 18.

62. Joseph Hanlon, "Destabilisation And The Battle To Reduce Dependence," in *Zimbabwe's Prospects: Issues Of Race, Class, State, And Capital*

In Southern Africa, ed. Colin Stoneman (London: Macmillan Publishers, 1988), 32 – 42.

63. Joseph Hanlon, "Destabilisation And The Battle To Reduce Dependence," in *Zimbabwe's Prospects: Issues Of Race, Class, State, And Capital In Southern Africa*, ed. Colin Stoneman (London: Macmillan Publishers, 1988), 32 – 42.

64. Joseph Hanlon, "Destabilisation And The Battle To Reduce Dependence," in *Zimbabwe's Prospects: Issues Of Race, Class, State, And Capital In Southern Africa*, ed. Colin Stoneman (London: Macmillan Publishers, 1988), 32 – 42.

65. Joseph Hanlon, "Destabilisation And The Battle To Reduce Dependence," in *Zimbabwe's Prospects: Issues Of Race, Class, State, And Capital In Southern Africa*, ed. Colin Stoneman (London: Macmillan Publishers, 1988), 32 – 42.

66. Joseph Hanlon, "Destabilisation And The Battle To Reduce Dependence," in *Zimbabwe's Prospects: Issues Of Race, Class, State, And Capital In Southern Africa*, ed. Colin Stoneman (London: Macmillan Publishers, 1988), 32 – 42.

67. Sheila Rule, "The Guerrilla Fight In Mozambique Also Takes A Toll On Zimbabwe," *The New York Times*, February 21, 1988, https://www.nytimes.com/1988/02/21/world/the-guerrilla-fight-in-mozambique-also-takes-a-toll-on-zimbabwe.html Accessed 03/08/2022.

68. Sheila Rule, "The Guerrilla Fight In Mozambique Also Takes A Toll On Zimbabwe," *The New York Times*, February 21, 1988, https://www.nytimes.com/1988/02/21/world/the-guerrilla-fight-in-mozambique-also-takes-a-toll-on-zimbabwe.html Accessed 03/08/2022.

69. Sheila Rule, "The Guerrilla Fight In Mozambique Also Takes A Toll On Zimbabwe," *The New York Times*, February 21, 1988, https://www.nytimes.com/1988/02/21/world/the-guerrilla-fight-in-mozambique-also-takes-a-toll-on-zimbabwe.html Accessed 03/08/2022.

70. Sheila Rule, "The Guerrilla Fight In Mozambique Also Takes A Toll On Zimbabwe," *The New York Times*, February 21, 1988, https://www.nytimes.com/1988/02/21/world/the-guerrilla-fight-in-mozambique-also-takes-a-toll-on-zimbabwe.html Accessed 03/08/2022.

71. Sheila Rule, "The Guerrilla Fight In Mozambique Also Takes A Toll On Zimbabwe," *The New York Times*, February 21, 1988, https://www.

nytimes.com/1988/02/21/world/the-guerrilla-fight-in-mozambique-also-takes-a-toll-on-zimbabwe.html Accessed 03/08/2022.

72. Sheila Rule, "The Guerrilla Fight In Mozambique Also Takes A Toll On Zimbabwe," *The New York Times*, February 21, 1988, https://www.nytimes.com/1988/02/21/world/the-guerrilla-fight-in-mozambique-also-takes-a-toll-on-zimbabwe.html Accessed 03/08/2022.

73. Sheila Rule, "The Guerrilla Fight In Mozambique Also Takes A Toll On Zimbabwe," *The New York Times*, February 21, 1988, https://www.nytimes.com/1988/02/21/world/the-guerrilla-fight-in-mozambique-also-takes-a-toll-on-zimbabwe.html Accessed 03/08/2022.

74. Martin R. Rupiya, "A Political and Military Review of Zimbabwe's Involvement in the Second Congo War," in *The African Stakes of the Congo War*, ed. John F. Clark (Basingstoke: Palgrave MacMillan, 2002), 93 – 105.

75. Martin R. Rupiya, "A Political and Military Review of Zimbabwe's Involvement in the Second Congo War," in *The African Stakes of the Congo War*, ed. John F. Clark (Basingstoke: Palgrave MacMillan, 2002), 93 – 105.

Address V

76. Nathan Shamuyarira, *Crisis In Rhodesia* (London: Andre Deutsch, 1965), 90.

77. Herbert Chitepo, Address To The National Press Club, Canberra, Australia, 17th July 1973.

78. Herbert Chitepo, Address To The National Press Club, Canberra, Australia, 17th July 1973.

79. Herbert Chitepo, Address To The National Press Club, Canberra, Australia, 17th July 1973.

80. Herbert Chitepo, Address To The National Press Club, Canberra, Australia, 17th July 1973.

81. Herbert Chitepo, Address To The National Press Club, Canberra, Australia, 17th July 1973.

82. Herbert Chitepo, Address To The National Press Club, Canberra, Australia, 17th July 1973.

83. International Crisis Group, "Blood And Soil: Land, Politics, And Conflict Prevention In Zimbabwe And South Africa," *ICG Africa Report No 58*, https://www.crisisgroup.org/africa/southern-africa/zimbabwe/blood-and-soil-

land-politics-and-conflict-prevention-zimbabwe-and-south-africa 06. 10. 2022.

84. Joseph Hanlon et. al., *Zimbabwe Takes Back Its Land* (London: Kumarian Press, 2013), 31.

85. Prosper B. Matondi, *Zimbabwe's Fast Track Land Reform* (London: Zed Books, 2012), 38.

86. International Crisis Group, "Blood And Soil: Land, Politics, And Conflict Prevention In Zimbabwe And South Africa," *ICG Africa Report No 58*, https://www.crisisgroup.org/africa/southern-africa/zimbabwe/blood-and-soil-land-politics-and-conflict-prevention-zimbabwe-and-south-africa 06. 10. 2022.12. Nathan Shamuyarira, *Crisis In Rhodesia* (London: Andre Deutsch, 1965), 80.

87. Nathan Shamuyarira, *Crisis In Rhodesia* (London: Andre Deutsch, 1965), 80.

88. Joseph Hanlon et. al., *Zimbabwe Takes Back Its Land* (London: Kumarian Press, 2013), 33.

89. International Crisis Group, "Blood And Soil: Land, Politics, And Conflict Prevention In Zimbabwe And South Africa," *ICG Africa Report No 58*, https://www.crisisgroup.org/africa/southern-africa/zimbabwe/blood-and-soil-land-politics-and-conflict-prevention-zimbabwe-and-south-africa 06. 10. 2022.

90. Quintus Curtius Rufus, *The History Of Alexander* (London: Penguin Books, 2004).

91. Quintus Curtius Rufus, *The History Of Alexander* (London: Penguin Books, 2004).

92. Quintus Curtius Rufus, *The History Of Alexander* (London: Penguin Books, 2004).

19. International Crisis Group, "Blood And Soil: Land, Politics, And Conflict Prevention In Zimbabwe And South Africa," *ICG Africa Report No 58*, https://www.crisisgroup.org/africa/southern-africa/zimbabwe/blood-and-soil-land-politics-and-conflict-prevention-zimbabwe-and-south-africa 06. 10. 2022.20.

93. Thandika Mkandawire, "Zimbabwe's Transition Overload: An Interpretation," *Journal of Contemporary African Studies*, Vol 38, no. 1 (2020): 18 – 38.

94. Thandika Mkandawire, "Zimbabwe's Transition Overload: An Interpretation," *Journal of Contemporary African Studies*, Vol 38, no. 1 (2020): 18 – 38.

95. Thandika Mkandawire, "Zimbabwe's Transition Overload: An Interpretation," *Journal of Contemporary African Studies*, Vol 38, no. 1 (2020): 18 – 38.

96. Africa All Party Parliamentary Group, "Land In Zimbabwe: Past Mistakes, Future Prospects," A Report, December 2009, https://royalafricansociety.org/wp-content/uploads/2020/01/aappg_report_land_in_zimbabwe.pdf Accessed 06. 10. 2022.

97. Africa All Party Parliamentary Group, "Land In Zimbabwe: Past Mistakes, Future Prospects," A Report, December 2009, https://royalafricansociety.org/wp-content/uploads/2020/01/aappg_report_land_in_zimbabwe.pdf Accessed 06. 10. 2022.

98. Africa All Party Parliamentary Group, "Land In Zimbabwe: Past Mistakes, Future Prospects," A Report, December 2009, https://royalafricansociety.org/wp-content/uploads/2020/01/aappg_report_land_in_zimbabwe.pdf Accessed 06. 10. 2022.

99. Peter Alexander Rupert Carrington, *Reflect On Things Past: The Memoirs Of Lord Carrington* (London: Collins, 1988), 288.

100. Peter Alexander Rupert Carrington, *Reflect On Things Past: The Memoirs Of Lord Carrington* (London: Collins, 1988), 297.

101. Peter Alexander Rupert Carrington, *Reflect On Things Past: The Memoirs Of Lord Carrington* (London: Collins, 1988), 300.

102. Joshua Nkomo, Opening Remarks At Lancaster House on Behalf of the Patriotic Fronts, London, 1979.

103. International Crisis Group, "Blood And Soil: Land, Politics, And Conflict Prevention In Zimbabwe And South Africa," *ICG Africa Report No 58*, https://www.crisisgroup.org/africa/southern-africa/zimbabwe/blood-and-soil-land-politics-and-conflict-prevention-zimbabwe-and-south-africa 06. 10. 2022.20.

104. Sam Moyo, "Three Decades Of Agrarian Reform In Zimbabwe," *Journal of Peasant Studies*, Vol. 38, No. 3 (July 2011): 493 – 531.

105. Sam Moyo, "Three Decades Of Agrarian Reform In Zimbabwe," *Journal of Peasant Studies*, Vol. 38, No. 3 (July 2011): 493 – 531.

106. Sam Moyo, "Three Decades Of Agrarian Reform In Zimbabwe," *Journal of Peasant Studies*, Vol. 38, No. 3 (July 2011): 493 – 531.

107. Sam Moyo, "Three Decades Of Agrarian Reform In Zimbabwe," *Journal of Peasant Studies*, Vol. 38, No. 3 (July 2011): 493 – 531.

108. Sam Moyo, "Three Decades Of Agrarian Reform In Zimbabwe," *Journal of Peasant Studies*, Vol. 38, No. 3 (July 2011): 493 – 531.

Address VI

109. Thandika Mkandawire, "Zimbabwe's Transition Overload: An Interpretation," *Journal of Contemporary African Studies*, Vol 38, no. 1 (2020): 18 – 38.

110. Nathan Shamuyarira, *Crisis In Rhodesia* (London: Andre Deutsch Ltd, 1965), 173.

111. Paul Moorcroft and Peter McLaughlin, *The Rhodesian War: A Military History*, (Barnsley: Pen & Sword Military, 2008), 187.

112. Paul Moorcroft and Peter McLaughlin, *The Rhodesian War: A Military History*, (Barnsley: Pen & Sword Military, 2008), 179.

113. Thandika Mkandawire, "Zimbabwe's Transition Overload: An Interpretation," *Journal of Contemporary African Studies*, Vol 38, no. 1 (2020): 18 – 38.

114. Andrew Meldrum, *Where We Have Hope: A Memoir Of Zimbabwe* (London: John Murray Publishers, 2004), 58

115. Barry R. Posen, "The Security Dilemma And Ethnic Conflict," *Survival*, Vol 35, No. 1 (Spring 1993): 27 – 47.

116. Sabelo Gatsheni-Ndlovu, *Do Zimbabweans Exist? Trajectories Of Nationalism, National Identity Formation and Crisis in a Postcolonial State* (Oxford: Peter Laing, 2009), 181.

117. Thandika Mkandawire, "Zimbabwe's Transition Overload: An Interpretation," *Journal of Contemporary African Studies*, Vol 38, no. 1 (2020): 18 – 38.

118. Max Weber, *Politics As A Vocation* (Munich: Duncker & Humblodt, 1918).

119. Max Weber, *Politics As A Vocation* (Munich: Duncker & Humblodt, 1918).

120. Paul Moorcroft and Peter McLaughlin, *The Rhodesian War: A Military History*, (Barnsley: Pen & Sword Military, 2008), 176.

121. Paul Moorcroft and Peter McLaughlin, *The Rhodesian War: A Military History*, (Barnsley: Pen & Sword Military, 2008), 176.

122. Paul Moorcroft and Peter McLaughlin, *The Rhodesian War: A Military History*, (Barnsley: Pen & Sword Military, 2008), 176.

123. Paul Moorcroft and Peter McLaughlin, *The Rhodesian War: A Military History*, (Barnsley: Pen & Sword Military, 2008), 174.

124. Paul Moorcroft and Peter McLaughlin, *The Rhodesian War: A Military History*, (Barnsley: Pen & Sword Military, 2008), 174.

125. Paul Moorcroft and Peter McLaughlin, *The Rhodesian War: A Military History*, (Barnsley: Pen & Sword Military, 2008), 178.

126. Paul Moorcroft and Peter McLaughlin, *The Rhodesian War: A Military History*, (Barnsley: Pen & Sword Military, 2008), 178.

127. Paul Moorcroft and Peter McLaughlin, *The Rhodesian War: A Military History*, (Barnsley: Pen & Sword Military, 2008), 179.

128. Paul Moorcroft and Peter McLaughlin, *The Rhodesian War: A Military History*, (Barnsley: Pen & Sword Military, 2008), 179.

129. Andrew Meldrum, *Where We Have Hope: A Memoir Of Zimbabwe* (London: John Murray Publishers, London, 2005), 47.

130. Andrew Meldrum, *Where We Have Hope: A Memoir Of Zimbabwe* (London: John Murray Publishers, London, 2005), 47.

131. Nathan Shamuyarira, *Crisis In Rhodesia* (London: Andre Deutsch Ltd, 1965), 183.

132. Nathan Shamuyarira, *Crisis In Rhodesia* (London: Andre Deutsch Ltd, 1965), 184.

133. Sabelo Gatsheni-Ndlovu, *Do Zimbabweans Exist? Trajectories Of Nationalism, National Identity Formation and Crisis in a Postcolonial State* (Oxford: Peter Laing, 2009), 114.

134. Nathan Shamuyarira, *Crisis In Rhodesia* (London: Andre Deutsch Ltd, 1965), 180.

135. Masipula Sithole, *Zimbabwe: Struggle Within The Struggle* (Harare: Rujeko Publishers, 2019), 40.

136. Masipula Sithole, *Zimbabwe: Struggle Within The Struggle* (Harare: Rujeko Publishers, 2019), 40.

137. Masipula Sithole, *Zimbabwe: Struggle Within The Struggle* (Harare: Rujeko Publishers, 2019), 46.

138. Nathan Shamuyarira, *Crisis In Rhodesia* (London: Andre Deutsch Ltd, 1965), 177.

139. Nathan Shamuyarira, *Crisis In Rhodesia* (London: Andre Deutsch Ltd, 1965), 177.

140. Masipula Sithole, *Zimbabwe: Struggle Within The Struggle* (Harare: Rujeko Publishers, 2019), 47.

141. Masipula Sithole, *Zimbabwe: Struggle Within The Struggle* (Harare: Rujeko Publishers, 2019), 49.

142. Masipula Sithole, *Zimbabwe: Struggle Within The Struggle* (Harare: Rujeko Publishers, 2019), 40.

143. Masipula Sithole, *Zimbabwe: Struggle Within The Struggle* (Harare: Rujeko Publishers, 2019), 47.

144. Masipula Sithole, *Zimbabwe: Struggle Within The Struggle* (Harare: Rujeko Publishers, 2019), 44.

145. Nathan Shamuyarira, *Crisis In Rhodesia* (London: Andre Deutsch Ltd, 1965), 185.

146. Nathan Shamuyarira, *Crisis In Rhodesia* (London: Andre Deutsch Ltd, 1965), 190.

147. Percy Zvomuya, "Unlearning The Zimbabwean Lesson." *The New Frame*, April 24, 2020 https://www.newframe.com/long-read-part-two-un-learning-the-zimbabwean-lesson/ Accessed 06. 10. 2022.

148. Peter Carrington, *Reflect on Things Past: The Memoirs of Lord Carrington*, (London: Collins, 1988), 293.

149. Paul Moorcroft and Peter McLaughlin, *The Rhodesian War: A Military History* (Barnsley: Pen & Sword Military, 2008), 166.

150. Peter Carrington, *Reflect on Things Past: The Memoirs of Lord Carrington* (London: Collins, 1988),300.

151. Andrew Meldrum, *Where We Have Hope: A Memoir Of Zimbabwe* (London: John Murray Publishers, 2005), 47.

152. Ian Smith, *Bitter Harvest: Zimbabwe And The Aftermath Of Its Independence*, (London: John Blake, 2008), 341.

Address VII:

153. Thomas Hobbes, *Leviathan* (Oxford: Oxford University Press, 1996), 14.

154. Herodotus, *The Histories* (London: Wordsworth Classics, London, 1996), 5.

155. John Locke, *The Second Treatise of Government and a Letter Concerning Toleration* (New York: Dover Thrift Publications, 2002).

156. Nigel D. White and Ademola Abass, "Countermeasures and Sanctions," in *International Law*, ed. Malcolm Gladwell (Oxford: Oxford University Press, 2018), 521 – 547.

157. Nigel D. White and Ademola Abass, "Countermeasures and Sanctions," in *International Law*, ed. Malcolm Gladwell (Oxford: Oxford University Press, 2018), 521 – 547.

158. International Law Commission, 2001 Document On Internationally Wrongful Acts By States.

159. Nigel D. White and Ademola Abass, "Countermeasures and Sanctions," in *International Law*, ed. Malcolm Gladwell (Oxford: Oxford University Press, 2018), 521 – 547.

160. Nigel D. White and Ademola Abass, "Countermeasures and Sanctions," in *International Law*, ed. Malcolm Gladwell (Oxford: Oxford University Press, 2018), 521 – 547.

161. Nigel D. White and Ademola Abass, "Countermeasures and Sanctions," in *International Law*, ed. Malcolm Gladwell (Oxford: Oxford University Press, 2018), 521 – 547.

162. Nigel D. White and Ademola Abass, "Countermeasures and Sanctions," in *International Law*, ed. Malcolm Gladwell (Oxford: Oxford University Press, 2018), 521 – 547.

163. Nigel D. White and Ademola Abass, "Countermeasures and Sanctions," in *International Law*, ed. Malcolm Gladwell (Oxford: Oxford University Press, 2018), 521 – 547.

164. Nigel D. White and Ademola Abass, "Countermeasures and Sanctions," in *International Law*, ed. Malcolm Gladwell (Oxford: Oxford University Press, 2018), 521 – 547.

165. Matthew Happold, "Economic Sanctions And International Law," in *Economic Sanctions And International Law*, eds. Matthew Happold and Paul Eden (Oxford: Hart Publishing, 2019), 1 – 12.

166. Matthew Happold, "Economic Sanctions And International Law," in *Economic Sanctions And International Law*, eds. Matthew Happold and Paul Eden (Oxford: Hart Publishing, 2019), 1 – 12.

167. Andrea Charron and Clara Portela, "The Relationship Between United Nations Sanctions And Regional Sanctions Regimes," in *Targeted Sanctions*, eds. Thomas J. Biersteker, Sue Eckert, and Marcos Tourinho (Cambridge: Cambridge University Press, 2016), 101 – 118.

168. Andrea Charron and Clara Portela, "The Relationship Between United Nations Sanctions And Regional Sanctions Regimes," in *Targeted Sanctions*, eds. Thomas J. Biersteker, Sue Eckert, and Marcos Tourinho (Cambridge: Cambridge University Press, 2016), 101 – 118.

169. Andrea Charron and Clara Portela, "The Relationship Between United Nations Sanctions And Regional Sanctions Regimes," in *Targeted Sanctions*, eds. Thomas J. Biersteker, Sue Eckert, and Marcos Tourinho (Cambridge: Cambridge University Press, 2016), 101 – 118.

170. Matthew Happold, "Economic Sanctions And International Law," in *Economic Sanctions And International Law*, eds. Matthew Happold and Paul Eden (Oxford: Hart Publishing, 2019), 1 – 12.

171. Matthew Happold, "Economic Sanctions And International Law," in *Economic Sanctions And International Law*, eds. Matthew Happold and Paul Eden (Oxford: Hart Publishing, 2019), 1 – 12.

172. Martin Loney, *Rhodesia: White Racism and Imperial Response* (Middlesex: Penguin Books Inc, 1975), 149.

173. Martin Loney, *Rhodesia: White Racism and Imperial Response* (Middlesex: Penguin Books Inc, 1975), 149.

174. Martin Loney, *Rhodesia: White Racism and Imperial Response* (Middlesex: Penguin Books Inc, 1975), 151.

175. Danny Sjursen, "The White Lobby: When The U.S. Was The Sanctions-Buster Extraordinaire," May 11, 2020, https://scheerpost.com/2020/05/11/the-white-lobby-when-the-u-s-was-the-sanctions-buster-extraordinaire/ Accessed 06. 10.2022.

176. Danny Sjursen, "The White Lobby: When The U.S. Was The Sanctions-Buster Extraordinaire," May 11, 2020, https://scheerpost.com/2020/05/11/the-white-lobby-when-the-u-s-was-the-sanctions-buster-extraordinaire/ Accessed 06. 10.2022.

177. Danny Sjursen, "The White Lobby: When The U.S. Was The Sanctions-Buster Extraordinaire," May 11, 2020, https://scheerpost.com/2020/05/11/the-white-lobby-when-the-u-s-was-the-sanctions-buster-extraordinaire/ Accessed 06. 10.2022.

178. Danny Sjursen, "The White Lobby: When The U.S. Was The Sanctions-Buster Extraordinaire," May 11, 2020, https://scheerpost.com/2020/05/11/the-white-lobby-when-the-u-s-was-the-sanctions-buster-extraordinaire/ Accessed 06. 10.2022.

179. Danny Sjursen, "The White Lobby: When The U.S. Was The Sanctions-Buster Extraordinaire," May 11, 2020, https://scheerpost.com/2020/05/11/the-white-lobby-when-the-u-s-was-the-sanctions-buster-extraordinaire/ Accessed 06. 10.2022.

180. Danny Sjursen, "The White Lobby: When The U.S. Was The Sanctions-Buster Extraordinaire," May 11, 2020, https://scheerpost.com/2020/05/11/the-white-lobby-when-the-u-s-was-the-sanctions-buster-extraordinaire/ Accessed 06. 10.2022.

181. Danny Sjursen, "The White Lobby: When The U.S. Was The Sanctions-Buster Extraordinaire," May 11, 2020, https://scheerpost.com/2020/05/11/the-white-lobby-when-the-u-s-was-the-sanctions-buster-extraordinaire/ Accessed 06. 10.2022.

182. Danny Sjursen, "The White Lobby: When The U.S. Was The Sanctions-Buster Extraordinaire," May 11, 2020, https://scheerpost.com/2020/05/11/the-white-lobby-when-the-u-s-was-the-sanctions-buster-extraordinaire/ Accessed 06. 10.2022.

183. Danny Sjursen, "The White Lobby: When The U.S. Was The Sanctions-Buster Extraordinaire," May 11, 2020, https://scheerpost.com/2020/05/11/the-white-lobby-when-the-u-s-was-the-sanctions-buster-extraordinaire/ Accessed 06. 10.2022.

184. Alois S. Mlambo, *A History Of Zimbabwe* (Cambridge: Cambridge University Press, 2014), 247.

185. Jack Lew, Treasury Secretary, Keynote Address at the Office of Terrorism and Financial Intelligence at 10 CSIS Event.

186. Samanth Subramanian, "What If The World Treated The United States As The Rogue State It Is," *The Huff Post*, October 02, 2019 https://www.huffpost.com/highline/article/sanctions/ Accessed 06.10. 2022.

187. Samanth Subramanian, "What If The World Treated The United States As The Rogue State It Is," *The Huff Post*, October 02, 2019 https://www.huffpost.com/highline/article/sanctions/ Accessed 06.10. 2022.

188. Samanth Subramanian, "What If The World Treated The United States As The Rogue State It Is," *The Huff Post*, October 02, 2019 https://www.huffpost.com/highline/article/sanctions/ Accessed 06.10. 2022.

189. Samanth Subramanian, "What If The World Treated The United States As The Rogue State It Is," *The Huff Post*, October 02, 2019 https://www.huffpost.com/highline/article/sanctions/ Accessed 06.10. 2022.

190. Samanth Subramanian, "What If The World Treated The United States As The Rogue State It Is," *The Huff Post*, October 02, 2019 https://www.huffpost.com/highline/article/sanctions/ Accessed 06.10. 2022.

191. Samanth Subramanian, "What If The World Treated The United States As The Rogue State It Is," *The Huff Post*, October 02, 2019 https://

www.huffpost.com/highline/article/sanctions/ Accessed 06.10. 2022.

192. Samanth Subramanian, "What If The World Treated The United States As The Rogue State It Is," *The Huff Post*, October 02, 2019 https://www.huffpost.com/highline/article/sanctions/ Accessed 06.10. 2022.

193. Samanth Subramanian, "What If The World Treated The United States As The Rogue State It Is," *The Huff Post*, October 02, 2019 https://www.huffpost.com/highline/article/sanctions/ Accessed 06.10. 2022.

Address VIII

194. Aeschylus, *The Oresteian Trilogy* (London: Penguin, 1984).

195. Transparency International, www.transparency.org Website Accessed: 29/11/2020.

196. James C. Scott, *Comparative Political Corruption* (New Jersey: Prentice Hall, 1972), 3.

197. Ray Fisman and Miriam A. Golden, *Corruption: What Everyone Needs To Know* (Oxford: Oxford University Press, 2017) 23.

198. Ray Fisman and Miriam A. Golden, *Corruption: What Everyone Needs To Know* (Oxford: Oxford University Press, 2017), 23.

199. Ha-Joon Chang, *Bad Samaritans: The Guilty Secrets Of Rich Nations & The Threat To Global Prosperity*, (London: Random House Books, 2008), 162.

200. James C. Scott, *Comparative Political Corruption* (New Jersey: Prentice Hall, 1972), 2.

201. Ray Fisman and Miriam A. Golden, *Corruption: What Everyone Needs To Know* (Oxford: Oxford University Press, 2017), 5.

202. Ray Fisman and Miriam A. Golden, *Corruption: What Everyone Needs To Know* (Oxford: Oxford University Press, 2017), 5.

203. Ray Fisman and Miriam A. Golden, *Corruption: What Everyone Needs To Know* (Oxford: Oxford University Press, 2017), 7.

204. Ray Fisman and Miriam A. Golden, *Corruption: What Everyone Needs To Know* (Oxford: Oxford University Press, 2017), 76.

205. Ray Fisman and Miriam A. Golden, *Corruption: What Everyone Needs To Know* (Oxford: Oxford University Press, 2017), 6.

206. Susan Rose-Ackerman and Bonnie J. Palifka, *Corruption and Government: Causes, Consequences, and Reform* (Cambridge: Cambridge University Press, 2016), 523.

207. Susan Rose-Ackerman and Bonnie J. Palifka, *Corruption and Government: Causes, Consequences, and Reform* (Cambridge: Cambridge University Press, 2016), 524.

208. Susan Rose-Ackerman and Bonnie J. Palifka, *Corruption and Government: Causes, Consequences, and Reform* (Cambridge: Cambridge University Press, 2016), 524.

209. Susan Rose-Ackerman and Bonnie J. Palifka, *Corruption and Government: Causes, Consequences, and Reform* (Cambridge: Cambridge University Press, 2016), 524.

210. Ray Fisman and Miriam A. Golden, *Corruption: What Everyone Needs To Know* (Oxford: Oxford University Press, 2017), 15.

211. Ray Fisman and Miriam A. Golden, *Corruption: What Everyone Needs To Know* (Oxford: Oxford University Press, 2017), 15.

212. Susan Rose-Ackerman and Bonnie J. Palifka, *Corruption and Government: Causes, Consequences, and Reform* (Cambridge: Cambridge University Press, 2016), 53.

213. Susan Rose-Ackerman and Bonnie J. Palifka, *Corruption and Government: Causes, Consequences, and Reform* (Cambridge: Cambridge University Press, 2016), 53.

214. Susan Susan Rose-Ackerman and Bonnie J. Palifka, *Corruption and Government: Causes, Consequences, and Reform* (Cambridge: Cambridge University Press, 2016), 53.

215. James C. Scott, *Comparative Political Corruption* (New Jersey: Prentice Hall, 1972), 11.

216. Susan Rose-Ackerman and Bonnie J. Palifka, *Corruption and Government: Causes, Consequences, and Reform* (Cambridge: Cambridge University Press, 2016), 55.

217. Yuen Yuen Ang, *China's Gilded Age: The Paradox of Economic Boom and Vast Corruption* (Cambridge: Cambridge University Press, 2020), 11.

218. Yuen Yuen Ang, *China's Gilded Age: The Paradox of Economic Boom and Vast Corruption* (Cambridge: Cambridge University Press, 2020), 12.

219. Yuen Yuen Ang, *China's Gilded Age: The Paradox of Economic Boom and Vast Corruption* (Cambridge: Cambridge University Press, 2020), 12.

220. Yuen Yuen Ang, *China's Gilded Age: The Paradox of Economic Boom and Vast Corruption* (Cambridge: Cambridge University Press, 2020), 12.

221. Yuen Yuen Ang, *China's Gilded Age: The Paradox of Economic Boom and Vast Corruption* (Cambridge: Cambridge University Press, 2020), 12 – 13.

222. Yuen Yuen Ang, *China's Gilded Age: The Paradox of Economic Boom and Vast Corruption* (Cambridge: Cambridge University Press, 2020), 14.

223. Yuen Yuen Ang, *China's Gilded Age: The Paradox of Economic Boom and Vast Corruption* (Cambridge: Cambridge University Press, 2020), 16.

224. Yuen Yuen Ang, *China's Gilded Age: The Paradox of Economic Boom and Vast Corruption* (Cambridge: Cambridge University Press, 2020), 17.

Address IX

225. Tshilidzi Marwala, *Closing The Gap: The Fourth Industrial Revolution In Africa* (Johannesburg: Pan Macmillan South Africa, 2020), 9.

226. Robert C. Allen, *The Industrial Revolution: A Very Short Introduction* (Oxford: Oxford University Press, 2017).

227. Robert C. Allen, *The Industrial Revolution: A Very Short Introduction*, (Oxford: Oxford University Press, 2017).

228. Robert C. Allen, *The Industrial Revolution: A Very Short Introduction* (Oxford: Oxford University Press, 2017).

229. Klaus Schwab, *The Fourth Industrial Revolution* (New York: Crown Publishing Group, 2017), 6.

230. Jonathan Swift, *Gulliver's Travels* (Maidenhead: Purnell Books, 1975), 140.

231. Jonathan Swift, *Gulliver's Travels* (Maidenhead: Purnell Books, 1975), 141.

232. Jonathan Swift, *Gulliver's Travels* (Maidenhead: Purnell Books, 1975), 141.

233. Jonathan Swift, *Gulliver's Travels* (Maidenhead: Purnell Books, 1975), 141.

234. Nick Bostrom, *Superintelligence: Paths, Dangers, Strategies*, (Oxford: Oxford University Press, 2017), 4.

235. Klaus Schwab, *The Fourth Industrial Revolution* (New York: Crown Publishing Group, 2017), 4.

236. Klaus Schwab, *The Fourth Industrial Revolution* (New York: Crown Publishing Group, 2017), 4.

Address X

237. Niccolò Machiavelli, *The Art Of War* (Chicago: University of Chicago Press, 2009).

238. Samuel Huntington, *The Soldier And The State: The Theory And Politics Of Civil-Military Relations* (Cambridge: Harvard University Press, 1957), 1.

239. Samuel Huntington, *The Soldier And The State: The Theory And Politics Of Civil-Military Relations* (Cambridge: Harvard University Press, 1957), 1.

240. Samuel Huntington, *The Soldier And The State: The Theory And Politics Of Civil-Military Relations* (Cambridge: Harvard University Press, 1957), 1.

241. Colonel General Valery Gerasimov, "The Value Of Science In Prediction," *The Military – Industrial Courier,* February 27, 2013 https://inmoscowsshadows.wordpress.com/2014/07/06/the-gerasimov-doctrine-and-russian-non-linear-war/ Accessed 06. 10. 2022.

242. Colonel General Valery Gerasimov, "The Value Of Science In Prediction," *The Military – Industrial Courier,* February 27, 2013 https://inmoscowsshadows.wordpress.com/2014/07/06/the-gerasimov-doctrine-and-russian-non-linear-war/ Accessed 06. 10. 2022.

243. Samuel Huntington, *The Soldier And The State: The Theory And Politics Of Civil-Military Relations* (Cambridge: Harvard University Press, 1957), 1.

244. David Chuter, *Managing And Governing The Defence Sector*, (Pretoria: ISS Publications, 2011).

245. The Mgagao Declaration, Mgagao, Tanzania, October 1975.

246. The Mgagao Declaration, Mgagao, Tanzania, October 1975.

247. Masipula Sithole, *Zimbabwe: Struggles Within The Struggle*, (Harare: Rujeko Publishers, 2019), 75.

Bibliography

Aeschylus. *The Oresteian Trilogy*. London: Penguin, 1984.

Allen, Robert C. *The Industrial Revolution: A Very Short Introduction*. Oxford: Oxford University Press, 2017.

Ang, Yuen Yuen. *China's Gilded Age: The Paradox of Economic Boom and Vast Corruption*. Cambridge: Cambridge University Press, 2020.

Beach, David. *The Shona And Their Neighbours*. Oxford: Blackwell Publishing, 1994.

Beard, Charles. *The Idea of National Interest*. New York: Macmillan Company, 1934).

Berlin, Adele, and Marc Zvi Brettler. *The Jewish Study Bible*. Oxford: Oxford University Press: 2004.

Billig, Michael. *Banal Nationalism*. London: Sage Publications, 1995.

Bostrom, Nick. *Superintelligence: Paths, Dangers, Strategies*. Oxford: Oxford University Press, 2017.

Burchill, Scott. *The National Interest In International Relations*. Basingstoke: Palgrave Macmillan, 2005.

Carrington, Peter Alexander Rupert. *Reflect On Things Past: The Memoirs Of Lord Carrington*. London: Collins, 1988.

Cesaire, Aime. *Discourse On Colonialism*. New York: Monthly Press Review, 1972.

Chang, Ha-Joon. *Bad Samaritans: The Guilty Secrets Of Rich Nations & The Threat To Global Prosperity*. London: Random House Books, 2008.

Charron, Andrea, and Clara Portela, "The Relationship Between United Nations Sanctions And Regional Sanctions Regimes." In *Targeted Sanctions,* edited by Thomas J. Biersteker, Sue Eckert, and Marcos Tourinho, 10 – 118. Cambridge: Cambridge University Press, 2016.

Chuter, David. *Managing And Governing The Defence Sector*. Pretoria: ISS Publications, 2011.

Dalley, Stephanie. *Myths From Mesopotamia*. Oxford: Oxford University Press, 1989.

Davies, Davies. *Europe: A History*, London: Random House, 1997.

Dawkins, Richard. *The God Delusion*. London: Transworld Publishers, 2006.

Engelbert, P., S. Tarango, and M. Carter. "Dismemberment and Suffocation: A Contribution to the Debate on African Boundaries." *Comparative Political Studies* Vol. 35, no. 10 (2002): 1093-1118.

Fisman, Ray, and Miriam A. Golden. *Corruption: What Everyone Needs To Know*. Oxford: Oxford University Press, 2017.

Frankel, Joseph. *National Interest*. London: Macmillan, 1970.

Gatsheni-Ndlovu, Sabelo. *Do Zimbabweans Exist? Trajectories Of Nationalism, National Identity Formation and Crisis in a Postcolonial State*. Oxford: Peter Laing, 2009.

Guibernau, Montserrat. *The Identity Of Nations*. Cambridge: Polity Press, 2007.

Hanlon, Joseph Hanlon. "Destabilisation And The Battle To Reduce Dependence." In *Zimbabwe's Prospects: Issues Of Race, Class, State, And Capital In Southern Africa*, ed. Colin Stoneman, 32 – 42. London: Macmillan Publishers, 1988.

Hanlon, Joseph et. al. *Zimbabwe Takes Back Its Land*. London: Kumarian Press, 2013.

Happold, Matthew. "Economic Sanctions And International Law." In *Economic Sanctions And International Law*, edited by Matthew Happold and Paul Eden, 1 – 12. Oxford: Hart Publishing, 2019.

Harari, Yuval Noah. *Homo Deus: A Brief History Of Tomorrow*. Vintage: London, 2016.

Herodotus. *The Histories*. London: Wordsworth Classics, London, 1996.

Hobbes, Thomas. *Leviathan*. Oxford: Oxford University Press, 1996.

Hobsbawm, Eric, and Terrence Ranger. *The Invention Of Tradition*. Cambridge: Cambridge University Press, 1983.

Huntington, Samuel. *The Soldier And The State: The Theory And Politics Of Civil-Military Relations*. Cambridge: Harvard University Press, 1957.

Lamy, Steven et al. *Introduction To Global Politics*. Oxford: Oxford University Press, 2018.

Locke, John. *The Second Treatise of Government and a Letter Concerning Toleration*. New York: Dover Thrift Publications, 2002.

Loney, Martin. *Rhodesia: White Racism and Imperial Response*. Middlesex: Penguin Books Inc, 1975.

Machiavelli, Niccolò. *The Art Of War*. Chicago: University of Chicago Press, 2009.

Marwala, Tshilidzi. *Closing The Gap: The Fourth Industrial Revolution In Africa*. Johannesburg: Pan Macmillan South Africa, 2020.

Matondi, Prosper B. *Zimbabwe's Fast Track Land Reform*. London: Zed Books, 2012.

Meldrum, Andrew. *Where We Have Hope: A Memoir Of Zimbabwe*. London: John Murray Publishers, 2004.

Mkandawire, Thandika. "Zimbabwe's Transition Overload: An Interpretation." *Journal of Contemporary African Studies*, Vol 38, no. 1 (2020): 18 – 38.

Mlambo, Alois S. Mlambo. *A History of Zimbabwe*. Cambridge: Cambridge University Press, 2014.

Moorcroft, Paul and Peter McLaughlin. *The Rhodesian War: A Military History*. Barnsley: Pen & Sword Military, 2008.

Moyo, Sam. "Three Decades Of Agrarian Reform In Zimbabwe. *Journal of Peasant Studies*, Vol. 38, No. 3 (July 2011): 493 – 531.

Murphy, Jefferson. *The Bantu Civilization Of Southern Africa*. New York: Thomas Y. Crowell Company, 1974.

O'Meara, Patrick. *Rhodesia: Racial Conflict or Co-Existence?* London: Cornell University Press.

Ozkirimili, Umut. *Theories of Nationalism: A Critical Introduction*. London: Macmillan Press, 1999.

Posen, Barry R. "The Security Dilemma And Ethnic Conflict." *Survival*, Vol 35, No. 1 (Spring 1993): 27 – 47.

Rose-Ackerman, Susan, and Bonnie J. Palifka. *Corruption and Government: Causes, Consequences, and Reform.* Cambridge: Cambridge University Press, 2016.

Rufus, Quintus Curtius. *The History Of Alexander.* London: Penguin Books, 2004.

Rupiya, Martin R. "A Political and Military Review of Zimbabwe's Involvement in the Second Congo War." In *The African Stakes of the Congo War*, edited by John F. Clark, 93 – 105. Basingstoke: Palgrave MacMillan, 2002.

Schwab, Klaus. *The Fourth Industrial Revolution.* New York: Crown Publishing Group, 2017.

Scott, James C. *Comparative Political Corruption.* New Jersey: Prentice Hall, 1972.

Seton-Watson, Hugh. *Nations and States.* London: Methuen, 1977.

Sithole, Masipula. *Zimbabwe: Struggle Within The Struggle.* Harare: Rujeko Publishers, 2019.

Shamuyarira, Nathan. *Crisis In Rhodesia.* London: Andre Deutsch, 1965.

Shelley, Bruce L. Shelley. *Church History In Plain Language.* Netherlands Antilles: Word Pub, 1995.

Smith, Anthony D. *National Identity.* Harmondsworth: Penguin, 1991.

Smith, Anthony D. *Nationalism: Theory, Ideology, History.* Cambridge: Polity Press, 2001.

Smith, Ian. *Bitter Harvest: Zimbabwe And The Aftermath Of Its Independence.* London: John Blake, 2008.

Stalin, Josef. "The Nation." In *Nationalism,* edited by John Hutchinson and Anthony Smith, 18 – 21. Oxford: Oxford University Press, 1994.

Swift, Jonathan. *Gulliver's Travels.* Maidenhead: Purnell Books, 1975.

Weber, Max. *Politics As A Vocation.* Munich: Duncker & Humblodt, 1918.

Weber, Max. *The Protestant Ethic and the Spirit of Capitalism.* London: Unwin & Hyman, 1918.

Wendt, Alexander. *A Social Theory Of International Politics*. Cambridge: Cambridge University Press, 1999.

White, Nigel D. and Ademola Abass, "Countermeasures and Sanctions." In *International Law*, edited by Malcolm Gladwell, 521 – 547. Oxford: Oxford University Press, 2018.